London's Green Belt

Aerofilms

Green Belt Settlement
An oblique air-view of London's
green belt in Hertfordshire,
showing the scatter of
residential and other
land-uses

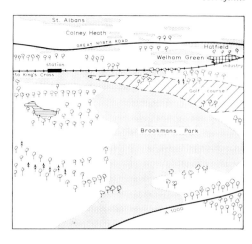

London's Green Belt

DAVID THOMAS

Reader in Geography
University College London

FABER AND FABER
London

First published in 1970
by Faber and Faber Limited
24 Russell Square London W.C.1
Printed in Great Britain by
Ebenezer Baylis and Son Limited
The Trinity Press, Worcester, and London
All rights reserved

SBN 571 09145 8

To Daphne

Contents

Tables

11

Figures in the text

13

Green fields of England! whereso'er
Across this watery waste we fare,
Your image in our hearts we bear,
Green fields of England, everywhere.

Arthur Hugh Clough (1819–1861)
Green fields of England

Preface

Arthur Hugh Clough was not one of our greatest poets. But he managed to capture, in the fragment quoted above, the intense emotion which the rural parts of this country evoke. As time has gone by, and as a swiftly increasing proportion of the total population has become urbanized, so emotional attachment to the open country-side appears to have strengthened. For some, these feelings are mani-fested quite positively in the desire to live among fields and trees, even though workplaces must remain distant in towns or cities. It is not the call of the wilderness—which is what seems to excite so many North Americans—but a call to an idealized rural calm. For others, it is sufficient that rural areas of charm should be protected from harmful development and that, where possible, they should be acces-sible to the town and city dweller so that, periodically, he too may share in a green and refreshing countryside.

Plainly, these are not universal attitudes, but they are very widely held. Their strength can be gauged from the reaction which greets proposals to build in a National Park, to drive a road through National Trust property, or to erect electricity pylons in an Area of Outstanding Natural Beauty. Proposals for green belts arouse par-ticularly violent passions. Green belts lie close to our urban-based population, they are frequently discussed in the press, their boundaries are fairly well known, and their purpose as inviolable rural surrounds to major towns and cities is widely comprehended.

Simply because feelings have been so deeply involved, this book attempts a more calm approach. Its aim is to take a cold, hard look at the green belt idea and at its implementation on the fringe of London. The book does not seek to be particularly polemical—it seeks the facts in an area of planning in which, too often, the situation on the ground has been neglected in favour of abstract dialectics, short-term expediency, or local government advantage.

London's green belt is a phenomenon capable of study from many standpoints. This work is primarily concerned with establishing the nature and geographical effects of the growth and containment of London upon the landscape of the metropolitan fringe. It sets out the steps by which the green belt came into being and attempts to show how the stricter controls over land usage, implicit in green belts, have led to modifications in the use of land over the zone surrounding London; an area already influenced by the proximity of the conurbation. The period of study is mainly the present—data for land use refer to the year 1960—but a lengthy historical introduction gives perspective to current development control, and implications for the future inevitably emerge from the discussion of the data, from the assessment of available techniques of analysis, and from the commentary upon present plans for the south-east of England.

It is hoped that the book will be timely. Dr. Wilfred Burns, chief planner at the Ministry of Housing and Local Government, supported by a staff of about forty and by three outside consultants, is currently preparing a regional plan for south-east England. New strategies for regional development have already been proposed which, in a number of fundamental respects, differ from the concepts at present in favour. Whether the new plan leans towards the traditional or towards the more modern ideas the future rôle of London's green belt, and of other green zones, will have to be considered carefully. Perhaps this is a good moment to reflect upon the development and effects of the only long-established, approved green belt which we have in this country.

Place-names abound in the text. The major places are marked on the maps relevant to each chapter, but it has been found impossible to include all names mentioned. To those unfamiliar with London and its surrounding country the Ordnance Survey Quarter Inch Map of Great Britain, Sheet 17 (South-East England) is recommended.

Finally, there are many to whom thanks and acknowledgements are owed. To Professor J. R. James and the late Mr. W. F. B. Lovett I am obliged for first suggesting, one day in 1960, that I should consider working upon London's green belt. To Professor H. C. Darby, and to his successor as head of the Geography Department at University College London, Professor W. R. Mead, I am indebted for encouragement and for the material facilities which are so necessary to any piece of research. In the Ministry of Housing and Local Government many individuals have been most helpful, but none more than the officers of the Map and Airphotograph Libraries. In local authority offices planning officers and their assistants have readily replied to my queries and given generously of their very precious time. As in the Ministry, they are far too numerous to list and I hope they will be prepared to accept my gratitude collectively. All the maps in the book have been produced in the drawing office of the Department of Geography, University College London. The final versions of the line drawings have been executed by Mrs. Mary Hayward, and the appearance of this volume owes a great deal to her skill and care. Some of the maps are original, others are derived from printed statistics or earlier works. In each instance, the source is acknowledged in the underline of the illustration. At an early stage in the work, when active field investigation was underway, valuable financial assistance was provided by two grants from the University of London Central Research Fund. Last, I should like to thank my wife, who, like the wives of so many academics, has long laboured as my private, but under-rewarded secretary. She prepared the manuscript for the press, helped check proofs, and assisted in compiling the index. I make some small amends by dedicating this book to her.

DAVID THOMAS
University College London, 1969

Part One

THE PROBLEMS OF LONDON

1 · London's Growth and its Implications

The story of the growth of London is one which has been told fully, though in different ways, by a number of authors.[1] London originated as the city of Londinium, the largest settlement of Roman Britain. Medieval London seems to have been not much larger than the Roman city, but in the seventeenth and eighteenth centuries bridge building across the Thames and the development by city merchants and wealthy landowners of spaciously planned houses and estates, particularly after the Great Fire of 1666, led first to the linking of the City of London and Westminster, and then to a more general expansion of the urban area.

The pace of growth quickened with the coming of the railways after 1836. Main line termini were located at the edge of the built-up area but to begin with, many railway companies were more concerned with long distance traffic than with providing services for local passengers. At this stage the tram and the horse-drawn omnibus had the more important effect. They enabled people to live farther from their place of work, and hence contributed to the growth of London. But gradually a network of suburban railway lines grew. At first it was the more prosperous professional workers who moved outwards to establish dwellings around many of the suburban railway stations, but later other workers also began to move out of London, assisted by the provision of cheap workmen's fares in the 1880s. The further development of the underground railway system at the end of the nineteenth century stimulated suburban dwelling still more. In the east of London the growth of the docks encouraged expansion in that direction. Along roads and railways at this period strips of development stretched into the countryside surrounding London.

[1] See, for example, S. E. Rasmussen, *London, the unique city* (London, 1937); J. A. Steers (ed.), *Field studies in the British Isles* (London, 1964), 90–105; J. T. Coppock and H. C. Prince (eds.), *Greater London* (London, 1964), 19–41, 52–166.

By the outbreak of the First World War London occupied a circle of radius six to eight miles from Charing Cross. Beyond the edge of built-up London settlements also grew rapidly: some because of their natural advantages as sites for industry but most because they served as dormitories for part of London's workforce.

Between 1918 and 1939 the area of London doubled. Over the same period its population increased by a little under one-fifth—the density of inter-war development was very low. This great expansion took place largely as a result of the increase in employment oppotunities in manufacturing and in the service industries. The growth of manufacturing plants usually occurred on the fringe of the existing urban area, and particularly in the north-west quadrant of London. Sometimes, as at Park Royal, compact estates occupied by many firms grew up; sometimes plants were disposed along main roads, like Western Avenue, the North Circular Road, and Edgware Road, or less frequently along main railway lines, as at Southall. In both types of industrial development links with the communication system were of great importance. Some of the industries, wishing to expand, had moved from more congested sites nearer the centre of London; others, freed by electricity from a coalfield site, were attracted by London's positive locational advantages. They saw benefit in London's mass market, in its substantial labour force, in contact with other manufacturers in the same or related fields, and in a location at the centre of the country's road and rail network. Generally housing developed around, and sometimes intermixed with, the manufacturing plants.

In contrast, service employment was drawn more to urban nodes. A growing population needed services of all kinds and these were provided in the central retail districts or in their suburban equivalents, but it was perhaps the increase in jobs in office administration which was most characteristic of the period. Office employment was confined largely to central London. Here it could reap the benefits of proximity to financial and governmental institutions, contact with other administrative offices, and the prestige of a reputable site and address. It was the growth of central office employment, more than any other type, which led to the purely residential suburbs of inter-war London.

It is clear that improvements in transportation played a major part in these developments. The new industries were mainly light in character and became increasingly dependent on road transport to supply raw materials and to market their products. Improved bus services and the rise in private car ownership had a strong influence upon the distance and flexibility of the journey to work. The electrification of suburban railway lines, especially to the south of the Thames, the extensions on the surface of the underground lines in north London, and the new North Circular and other roads all improved the speed of transport and hence reduced journey times or made longer journeys more acceptable.

The dwellings built during the inter-war period often provide a sharp contrast in appearance with the Victorian and other houses which preceded them. Red brick exteriors, sometimes covered with rough-cast plaster, and tile roofs replaced the yellow bricks and slates. But in other ways there was little change. Building still centred on surface or underground railway stations and ribbon development along main roads was equally popular. To some extent the gaps left in the earlier phase of development were filled at this time. The larger estates were often constructed by the rapidly expanding civil engineering firms, though local authorities also contributed to estate development, albeit to a smaller degree.[1] By 1939 London had grown to occupy a circle of radius twelve miles from Charing Cross.

Since the Second World War a tight control has been exercised over new building in and around London. This has led to a denser type of development than in the pre-war period and to a general infilling of the urban area. A great deal of redevelopment has taken place in the centre of London of war-damaged building, but there has also been a tendency to replace older commercial buildings nearing the ends of their useful lives by taller, more compact structures which make more intensive use of land. In the outer areas of London spaces left undeveloped have been used for building, and the large gardens or orchards of existing houses have also provided land for new dwellings.

Over the last 150 years London has grown from a city housing a little over one million people to a continuous urban area containing nearly eight million people. The conurbation is now the centre of a region which includes, depending upon how it is defined, twelve million or more people. While the permanent residential population of inner London reached its peak in 1901, and has since declined as a result of administrative, commercial, and industrial developments,

[1] Compare Johnson's maps in Coppock and Prince (eds.), op. cit. Figures 25 and 29.

that of outer London did not reach its maximum until 1951. The aggregate of these trends is that the conurbation as a whole achieved its peak population in 1939, since when numbers have been decreasing slowly. The counties surrounding London, however, have gained population rapidly in recent years on the receipt of overspill population from London. But they have gained population also as a result of natural increase and by migration from other parts of the country. The Census of 1961 indicates that the increase in the period 1951–61 was the highest yet, and it seems certain that this swift growth will continue.[1]

Rasmussen described London as 'the unique city'.[2] In many senses the description is justified, not least in terms of the architecture of its inner area, Rasmussen's main interest. But in respect of its current planning difficulties it shares its problems with many other cities in the developed societies of Europe and North America.[3] London's growth is sufficiently well-documented elsewhere to need no further rehearsing. Instead attention will be directed to identifying the problems of employment, population and housing, transport, and land which have stemmed from its recent explosive expansion.

Problems of employment

At the root of most of London's problems has been its command of attractive employment opportunities, and the disproportionate speed with which that employment has grown in recent years. Hall has shown that since 1861, and without doubt for centuries before that, London has been the main focus of both manufacturing and service industry employment.[4] When the Barlow Commission, surveying the period before the last World War, came to study the distribution of industrial population and the growth of employment in various parts of England and Wales it discovered that London, and its surrounding region, was absorbing an increasing share of the new industrial activity of the country.[5] Between 1923 and 1937 the com-

[1] Ibid., 34. Table I.

[2] Rasmussen, op. cit.

[3] See, for example, J. Gottmann, *Megalopolis: the urbanized north-eastern seaboard of the United States* (Cambridge Mass., 1961); P. Hall, *The world cities* (London, 1966).

[4] P. Hall, *The industries of London since 1861* (London, 1962), 10, 183–5.

[5] *Royal Commission on the distribution of industrial population, Report*, Cmd. 6153 (H.M.S.O., 1940), 164.

mission estimated that total employment in England and Wales rose by 22·3 per cent. Over the same period employment in Greater London was estimated to have risen by 36·1 per cent while in the wider area of London and the Home Counties the increase was estimated at 42·7 per cent. Later evidence suggests that the Commission over-stressed both the overall increase in employment and the London differential, but the general conclusion that the London region was gaining nearly twice its share of industrial development was substantially correct.[1]

Employment in the manufacturing and service industries expanded so swiftly in the London area because the industries with a growth potential tended to be concentrated there. Six industries contributed most to the inter-war expansion. Two were manufacturing industries —engineering and vehicle production: four were service industries— building, the distributive trades, administration, and the professional services. Together the six industries made up 41 per cent of the total employment in London and the Home Counties in 1921; in England and Wales as a whole they accounted for only 35 per cent.[2] On the other hand the declining industries like agriculture, mining and textiles were not strongly represented in the London area and so the employment gains were not offset, as they were in the depressed coalfield-industrial regions.

These facts led the Barlow Commission to recommend, among other things, that industrial growth in London and the surrounding counties should be restricted. Social, economic, and strategic considerations indicated a policy of decentralization, and this seems to have been broadly accepted after the war. The Board of Trade was given powers, through the issue or refusal of the industrial development certificate, to regulate the establishment of new industrial plants, or additions to existing plants, if more than 5,000 square feet of floor space or ten per cent of existing floor space was involved. The powers were used to direct industrial expansion away from the south-east of England and to such areas as south Wales and Tyneside. At a more local level, local planning authorities were given the power to control changes in land usage. In the London area the authorities were encouraged to limit industrial expansion and before their development plans were given final governmental approval in the

---

[1] P. Hall, *London 2000* (London, 1963), 44.
[2] Ibid., 45. See also M. J. Wise, 'The rôle of London in the industrial geography of Great Britain', *Geography*, 41 (1956), 223. Figure 1.

early 1950s modifications were introduced designed mainly to limit still further the amount of industrial land available.[1]

In practice the task was not as straightforward as it had seemed. For example, with technical advances in air transport, London Airport grew rapidly and required over 26,000 workers for its operation. The Port of London expanded to meet the needs of new export industries and the total tonnage of shipping using the port in 1958 was 20 per cent higher than the pre-war figure. The demands for office accommodation also increased enormously. Unlike manufacturing, no development certificate was required until relatively recently for buildings housing the service industries and it became difficult for the London County Council, and other authorities, to limit office construction. Commercial, industrial, insurance, and finance groups vied to acquire impressive headquarters and, in addition, accommodation was required for the increased numbers of governmental administrative staff who were needed to supervise the growing welfare services. Over the ten years up to 1958, forty-six million square feet of new office floor area were approved, almost all of it in central London, though later, the office building boom spread to the outer parts of the conurbation.[2]

Despite firm control manufacturing also continued to expand in the period after the war. Engineering, including the electrical, electronics, and television industries, and vehicle manufacture dominated this growth. The most substantial additions took place outside the London conurbation, particularly in the new towns and in existing manufacturing centres like Luton or Watford. These industries were major contributors to exports and it became more and more difficult as time passed to prevent their development. Within the conurbation most of the growth resulted from the extension or modernization of existing factories. The contrast in the growth patterns between the two most quickly expanding manufacturing industries, engineering and vehicle building, and the two most quickly expanding service industries, the distributive trades and professional services, is most marked. The former grew mainly beyond the conurbation; the latter grew mainly at the centre of the conurbation.[3]

[1] A. G. Powell, 'The recent development of Greater London', *The Advancement of Science*, 17 (1960-1), 76-7.

[2] Ibid., 77; Town and Country Planning Association, *The paper metropolis* (London, 1962), 30-2.

[3] Hall (1963), op. cit., 50-3. Maps 2A, B, C, D.

Two recent reports upon south-east England have thrown light on the present employment situation in London and its surrounding region.[1] They reveal that most of the changes already identified for the 1950s are still under way. The increase in employment over the period 1955–62 in south-east England was 10·1 per cent, a higher growth rate than in any other region, and well above the national average increase of 6·8 per cent.[2] In the conurbation itself the expansion in employment was more moderate at 6·6 per cent. But despite lack of space for development and the restraints imposed by both national and local government, particularly over manufacturing industry, the attractions of the central area for office employment, and the continued extensions of manufacturing plant adjacent to the North Circular and Great West Roads, in the Lea and in the Wandle valleys, nevertheless maintained the growth of employment within London very close to the national average. Over the last few years the number of workers in the manufacturing industries in the conurbation has declined, but marked growth in the service industries has more than compensated for this, and the total number of jobs available has continued to increase.

Beyond the London conurbation growth over the period 1955–62 was much more rapid. In the zone immediately outside the built-up area including the green belt, the new towns, and a number of other large centres detached from the conurbation, employment rose by 24·7 per cent. While the new towns provided the bulk of the new employment in the zone, the contribution of such towns as Watford, St. Albans, Romford, and Hornchurch to the increase should not be underestimated. Over a six year period in the 1950s they had all increased their employment by 15 per cent or more.[3] So swift, in fact, has been the expansion in workplaces in this area that one of the major problems faced by the manufacturing and service industries in recent years is shortage of labour.

In the outer part of the Metropolitan Region (as currently defined for official statistical purposes) stretching beyond the inner zone and up to forty-five miles from central London, the increase in employment between 1955 and 1962 was 16·7 per cent. The growth seems

[1] Ministry of Housing and Local Government, *The south east study 1961–1981* (H.M.S.O., 1964), 13–19, 35–40; South East Economic Planning Council, *A strategy for the South East* (H.M.S.O., 1967), 4–5, 22–8.
[2] These statistics are based upon Ministry of Labour returns and are open to some error. See discussion *infra* p. 161–2.
[3] Powell, op. cit., 84.

to have been mainly in centres to the north and west of London, such as Chelmsford, Dunstable, Luton, and Reading. These are towns which draw their labour from the fringe of London's catchment area and which are well-placed to serve both the London market and the remainder of the country. In the parts of south-east England outside the Metropolitan Region employment grew at a much lower rate.

The rapid growth in employment in London and its surrounding region has been the cause of great pressures upon land. Offices and manufacturing plants have needed space for development and have, in purely economic terms, proved formidable competitors in the scramble for developable land. But the greatest pressure has been exerted indirectly. Employment growth has encouraged population growth by attracting into London and its region people from other parts of the country and from abroad, all of whom have needed living space. Until 1964 the migration flows into the south-east were substantial, but since then the influx of migrants has fallen away sharply.

Problems of population and housing

With the taking of the Census of 1961 a set of population statistics was produced which was directly comparable with the 1951 figures. Set side by side these figures reveal in detail the population trends of the post-war period in the London area.

Between 1951 and 1961 the total population of England and Wales increased by 5·3 per cent. This increase was far from evenly distributed throughout the country and it is clear from Figures 1 and 2 that the London area shared fully in this lack of uniformity. But there was consistency within the diversity. With the exception of its periphery, most of the districts and boroughs of the built-up area of London lost population. Losses were greatest in the central area, in the east, and in the Lea Valley, where they exceeded 5 per cent and, in a number of instances, 10 per cent. It was only towards the fringe of the conurbation that administrative areas made modest gains in population, a feature more noticeable in the south-east of London than elsewhere. Overall the population of the conurbation in 1961 was 2·3 per cent below that in 1951, an absolute decrease of 176,000 persons, but allowing for a high natural increase, the total outmigration over the period must have involved over half a million people.

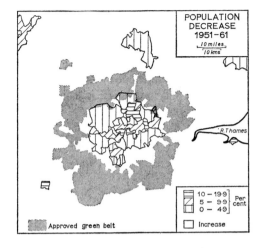

1.
Population decrease in the
London area, 1951–61
(Source: *Census 1951*;
Census 1961)

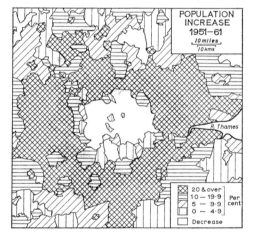

2.
Population increase in the
London area, 1951–61
(Source: *Census 1951*;
Census 1961)

Outside the boundary of the conurbation, within the green belt
and in the area beyond, population increases were substantial. The
growth of population is impressive not only because the percentage
increases are so high, but because, as these areas are among the most
densely peopled parts of England and Wales, the absolute increases
are also very large when compared with other parts of the country.
Few administrative areas in the green belt, for example, gained
population by less than 20 per cent over the period 1951–61, and
many increased their numbers by more than 40 per cent. Much of

the growth in population in the area beyond the conurbation may be interpreted as overspill from built-up London. For example, nearly half the 36 per cent increase in Hertfordshire's population between 1951 and 1961 is contributed by the county's four new towns, and to this must be added the unplanned overspill for which no precise statistics can be adduced. But although important, it would be an error to think of the population increases only in terms of London's overspill. Most major towns have expanded their industrial and administrative employment and so have, in addition, generated their own population growth. This has been supplied both by migration from London and elsewhere, and by natural increase.

Further guidance on population trends in the London area springs from recent revisions in national and regional population projections. *The south east study 1961–1981* based its estimates of population increase in south-east England upon an assumed increase for England and Wales of seven million people (six million by natural increase and one million from net immigration) and upon assumptions which implied large inflows to the south-east of people from elsewhere in Britain and from abroad. Current official projections produced in 1966[1] have taken into account a large reduction in estimated inward migration to the country and also the much-reduced net flow into south-east England from the remainder of Britain. It is now suggested that between 1964 and 1981 the total population gain in the South East Standard Region will be 2·14 millions and that roughly four-fifths of this will be contributed by natural increase. Since the conurbation itself is unlikely to be able to accommodate more than a tiny proportion of the total increase it is clear that this population will inevitably exert pressure upon presently undeveloped land in the surrounding region.

The growth of population in the London area has caused a great demand for houses. In 1951 the Census showed that there was an excess of households over dwellings in the London conurbation of about 350,000. The redevelopment of slum property, war damaged areas, and other older buildings has helped to reduce this gap by over half, but, since such redevelopment, even in high flats, cannot accommodate all who originally lived in those areas, let alone keep pace with natural and migration gains, population has overspilled into the green belt and the outer parts of the Metropolitan Region where most of the housing deficit has been, and will have to be,

---

[1] Cited in South East Economic Planning Council, op. cit., 72–6.

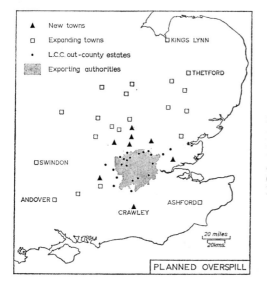

3.
**Planned overspill
from London, 1963**
(Source: Ministry of
Housing and Local
Government. *The south
east study 1961–1981*
(H.M.S.O., 1964);
London County Council)

made up. Between 1964 and 1981 about one million people are likely
to be involved in overspill from London.[1]

The movement outwards from the conurbation to dwellings outside its bounds has been the result both of private, unorganized
overspill, and of planned dispersion schemes. The forces which lie
behind private overspill are broadly similar to those which operated
in the past, and which led to the creation of suburban London. The
volume of movement has been great. Powell estimated that between
1952 and 1958 180,000 people moved privately into and beyond the
green belt and completely filled the land allocated for residential
purposes up to 1971.[2] The pattern of development has remained
essentially the same, with dormitory settlement clustering around
railway stations, though, of course, the form of the settlements has
been guided by planning control.

Planned overspill schemes accounted for over 175,000 people
between 1952 and 1958.[3] London County Council housing estates
or 'quasi-satellites' took 45,000 of these. The bulk, 120,000 people,
went to the eight new towns. The remaining 10,000 people were
housed in town expansion schemes. Unlike the private developments

[1] South East Economic Planning Council, op. cit., 75.
[2] Powell, op. cit., 80.
[3] Ibid. 79.

every effort has been made in the new and expanded towns to match the growth of housing and employment in an effort to prevent excessive journeying to work. Few of the London County Council estates, however, have industrial sectors—they are essentially dormitory suburbs and large proportions of their populations travel into London daily. The local authorities exporting population in planned schemes, together with the various kinds of reception settlements, are shown in Figure 3, as they were at the end of 1963.

Though at the moment a high proportion of the development outside the conurbation is under planned schemes, which include the provision of employment, most of the existing settlement outside London is haphazardly planned at best. The journey to work pattern is consequently very complicated, and large numbers travel to work in central London. This presents a further problem which will be treated in the following section.

Problems of transport

There are two major problems of transportation in London. First there is the problem of the journey to work; second, the problem of traffic congestion. The two are closely linked and in large part stem from the same causes.

Every day about a million and a quarter people travel into central London to work. At the moment the number of commuters into this area seems to be falling slightly. A peak was reached in 1962 and the present figure is about 5 per cent below this, though it is too soon to say if this is a trend which will continue.[1] But not only are the numbers large, the average length of journey is increasing.[2] By 1951, though nearly half the workers in the central area lived within five miles of their workplaces, about 10 per cent travelled from outside the conurbation making journeys morning and evening in excess of twelve to fifteen miles.[3] Places as distant as Southend and Sevenoaks contributed over 10 per cent of their resident workforce to central London, while many other extra-metropolitan urban and rural areas, for example, Berkhamsted, Bishop's Stortford, Egham, and Gravesend, lost over 5 per cent of their resident workers daily to the

[1] South East Economic Planning Council, op. cit., 98.
[2] R. Lawton, 'The journey to work in England and Wales: forty years of change', *Tijdschrift voor Economische en Sociale Geographie*, 54 (1963), 61-9.
[3] Town and Country Planning Association, op. cit., 23.

central area. Though there are many factors which have led to these circumstances the most important are clearly the growth of the urban area itself, the outward movement of population from the central areas of the conurbation unaccompanied by a commensurate outward movement of employment, and the marked tendency towards the centralisation of business administration.

While the growth of office employment has been the major generator of the new and longer work journeys into central London, it has been by no means the only cause of commuting in the London area. Manufacturing industry has expanded inside the conurbation and also outside, and in many ways has encouraged more complex, though shorter distance, travel patterns. Industrial growth has been more dispersed than that in office buildings and has led far more frequently to 'cross movements' to work, which contrast with the centrewards movement characteristic in the service industries. It has been observed that the importance of the central area as a destination of work journeys originating outside London tends to increase with distance outwards from the conurbation.[1] That is, in the zone immediately adjacent to the conurbation a sizeable proportion of all journeys to work in London are short distance trips to parts of London outside the central area. Journeys originating at greater distance from London tend, obviously, to be longer, but also more often to terminate in central London. For example, 37 per cent of the Hornchurch to Greater London conurbation work journeys in 1951 were to the central area, but 69 per cent of the work journeys from Brighton were so directed, almost all of them by rail. There is little concrete evidence, but it seems reasonable to suppose that a far higher proportion of the cross-trips are undertaken by private transport.

Far more is known about the types of transport used for work journeys into the central area of London. The London Transport Executive estimated that in 1960 of all passengers entering central London between 7 a.m. and 10 a.m. 91 per cent were carried by public transport. Of total passengers 35 per cent travelled by surface train, 39 per cent by underground train, and 17 per cent by bus. Only 7 per cent travelled into the central area by car. Over the seven years up to 1960 some interesting changes in the pattern of travel had been underway. Overall, the numbers travelling into the central area in the three-hour period increased by 10 per cent; but while those

[1] Coppock and Prince (eds.), op. cit., 269-70.

35

travelling by public transport grew by 6 per cent, those journeying by car increased by 74 per cent. Not only did the number of passengers increase, but an increasing proportion of those passengers arrived at the peak hours between 8.30 a.m. and 9.30 a.m.[1] The stringent parking regulations of recent years may have curbed, to some extent, the rate of increase in car traffic, but even though car commuters are still relatively few, the dislocation they cause is out of all proportion to their numbers. The average number of passengers per car is only 1·5 and they each use seven times as much road space as the bus passenger.[2] When this traffic to work is added to the commercial and other traffic using the same road and rail network, it is easy to see how congestion results, particularly upon the roads.

It is not difficult to over-emphasize present road congestion. Although the volume of movement has been increasing rapidly through the century, and very sharply over the last two decades, traffic has by no means ground to a halt. Without the aid of major road-works, except in a very few places, the traffic carrying capacity of existing streets has been expanded to meet the increased demands upon road-space. Traffic-light control at intersections, parking restrictions, the widespread adoption of one-way street systems, have all contributed to traffic flow and prevented a dramatic decline in traffic speeds. Despite the great increase in its volume the average speed of central London traffic in normal working hours had by 1960 not fallen below ten miles an hour.[3] But clearly, the superficial reorganization of road use cannot postpone indefinitely street paralysis. Major road reconstructions, like the inner motorway box currently being so hotly debated, seem inevitable. Such developments precipitate the displacement of other land uses as the space taken by the communication system expands.[4]

Problems of land

The problems of land and land allocation are in many ways the sum of the employment, population, housing, and transport problems described above. London and its surrounding region has the most rapidly expanding workforce in England and Wales. Its population

[1] Town and Country Planning Association, op. cit., 22.
[2] R. J. Smeed, *The traffic problem in towns* (Manchester, 1961), 21–3.
[3] Ibid., 9.
[4] G. L. Drake and W. F. Hoey, 'The characteristics of travel in Greater London', *Journal of the Town Planning Institute*, 50 (1964), 445.

is thicker on the ground than in any other part of the country and, with the exception of the central parts of the conurbation, it is increasing at a rate well above the national average. The housing deficit is large within London and this, together with other social forces, has led to a substantial population overspill across the boundary of the conurbation and into the towns and countryside beyond. The increasing divorce of dwelling and workplace, with employment increasing rapidly in the central areas, and population increasing beyond the limits of built-up London, has encouraged and lengthened journeying to work. Commuter traffic and other transport necessary in the economically booming centre of London has caused traffic congestion, the relief of which will create pressure upon space elsewhere. These are problems which, when added together, produce an acute demand for land, and an intense competition between different uses of land. Land values rise and speculation in land tends to develop.

None of these problems is new, and none of the causative factors is a purely post-war phenomenon. Land-use competition has long been a characteristic of London and its fringes, and remedies of the problems it creates have been forwarded on many occasions over many centuries. The problems are not only of the nature and scale of land-use development, they are also very much concerned with the distribution of that development. Hence ideas of land-use control have emerged, based upon the assumption that by organising and planning land-usage a landscape might emerge more pleasant, and more efficient in satisfying the needs of the greatest number, than one produced by chance, or by economic pressures alone.

Land-use planning, particularly planning within a regional framework, is a goal towards which many of the schemes for allocating land among the various uses have gradually been moving through this century. For London and the London region these culminated in the wartime advisory plans which provided a remedy for the problems of the conurbation and a strategy for regional development.[1] However much they misjudged population and industrial trends the tactics which the advisory plans advocated have, with some recent modification, been broadly accepted as a basis for planning the London region; the techniques by which they proposed to achieve their ends have also been widely adopted, though not

---

[1] J. H. Forshaw and P. Abercrombie, *County of London plan* (London, 1953); P. Abercrombie, *Greater London plan 1944* (H.M.S.O., 1945).

37

sufficiently widely to have solved London's problems. Among the main aims of the advisory plans was the prevention of the further spread of continuously built-up London; the means of achieving this was by designating a broad, inviolable green belt.

The green belt was not envisaged as an isolated remedy. It was one of a series of measures the broad purpose of which was to control population and industrial redeployment within the London region and to assist in the creation of a pleasant setting in which 'the good life' could be lived to the full. Nevertheless, the green belt has had marked effects upon the landscape. It has contained a conurbation, it has given a cleaner edge to town and country, and it has, by excluding or modifying many economic and other activities, influenced the landscape of the country fringe of London. This, in itself, is worthy of study, and it is to the origins, nature and effects of green belt control that the remainder of this work is devoted.

Part Two

THE DEVELOPMENT OF A REMEDY

2 · Planning the Urban Region

Green belts are a product of the need and desire to plan urban regions. They are an important means of controlling the development of the town or city and its hinterland, and can only be fully understood when viewed against the wider background of the evolution of ideas on city or planning regions. The following chapter sketches the progress towards regional planning in England and Wales, and focuses particularly upon the successive attempts to introduce regional control in the area centred upon London.

Nineteenth-century precedents of regional planning

The notion of the planned urban region is one which grew slowly in England and Wales. Through the nineteenth century proposals for planned towns were made by a number of individuals—mainly philanthropic industrialists who took an enlightened view of the conditions in which their employees ought to live. They were plainly dissatisfied with the standards of housing, health, and amenity within the cities which developed piecemeal and so rapidly during the industrial revolution. They saw a solution in organized communities in which the level of housing design was higher than anything previously thought worthwhile for industrial workers, in which public hygiene was consciously accepted as a factor in town development, and in which some attempt was made to improve the overall appearance of settlements.

Robert Owen is an obvious example of such an industrialist in the early part of the century. As well as providing education and training for his workers and their families, and improving working conditions in his factory at New Lanark, in the Clyde valley, Owen planned to create new communities in 'villages of co-operation'; model settlements of 1,200 persons each, which would provide a

41

healthy and pleasing environment for industrial workers.[1] His New Lanark experiment was an undoubted success, both socially and economically, but his model village proposals foundered largely because of the political and religious undertones of his philosophy, which was widely held to be a subversive social doctrine.[2] Owen's plan, however, became well known and later authors, such as J. M. Morgan and J. S. Buckingham, adopted substantially the same schemes when they attempted solutions to the problems of industrial squalor and overcrowding.[3] Their proposals, like Owen's, were never put into effect. In the 1840s, it seems, private investors found far more attractive outlets for their capital in manufacturing plants and in railway construction. Only where progressive, and sometimes eccentric, industrialists were themselves prepared to invest capital in model settlements was there any practical advance at this time.

Small beginnings were made at Bessbrook, County Armagh, in 1846 and at Bromborough, Cheshire, in 1853, but the largest, and certainly the best known planned industrial town of the mid-nineteenth century was the work of Titus Salt in Yorkshire. Saltaire, begun in 1851, was completed according to the founder's plan over a period of twenty years. It included not only Salt's textile mill and, by the standards of the time, a liberally planned residential area, but also public buildings, churches, schools, a park, a hospital, and an efficient drainage system.[4] Saltaire became a widely acknowledged model, but despite the personal prestige which it brought to Salt— a baronetcy was conferred upon him in 1869—it was a model which was not immediately copied. The next major attempt at planned industrial settlement, that of George Cadbury at Bournville, Birmingham, did not begin until 1879 and developed rather slowly, and it was not until 1888 that W. H. Lever began building his model village at Port Sunlight, Cheshire, as part of a scheme to expand his soap business.[5]

The plans produced through most of the nineteenth century were

[1] R. Owen, *A new view of society* (London, 1813–14), *passim*.

[2] W. Ashworth, *The genesis of modern British town planning* (London, 1954), 120–1.

[3] J. M. Morgan, *Letters to a clergyman on institutions for ameliorating the condition of the people* (London, 1846), 113–19; J. S. Buckingham, *National evils and practical remedies* (London, 1849), 183–233.

[4] R. Balgarnie, *Sir Titus Salt, Baronet: his life and its lessons* (London, 1877), 112–50; A. Holroyd, *Saltaire and its founder* (Saltaire, 1871), 6–12.

[5] Bournville Village Trust, *Sixty years of planning* (Bournville, 1942), 8–10; W. L. George, *Labour and housing at Port Sunlight* (London, 1909), 6–8.

for towns or villages only. Little detailed attention was given to the surrounding countryside, and in this sense, the schemes have small regional content. The plans are relevant to this discussion because in a number of ways they contributed to later concepts of the planned urban region. For example, the planning of an urban region is merely a physical extension of the idea of planning a town; a result of the realization that a town and its hinterland are interconnected both economically and socially. The important and decisive step, it may be argued, is the adoption of town planning. Again, the layout of model industrial towns, particularly in the later part of the nineteenth century, evolved along lines which were to lead to some of the main ideas propagated by the garden city movement. Compare, for example, the arrangement of the mid-century residential area of Saltaire, which apart from wider streets is hardly different in plan from other industrial housing of the time, with the arrangement of Port Sunlight, where, by the end of the century, back gardens had been introduced and where effective use was made of centrally placed ornamental open spaces.[1] Finally, certain elements of a broader strategy do appear in some of the plans. Particularly interesting in this context are the schemes of Owen and of Buckingham, in which each settlement was to have a maximum population; 1,200 in Owen's villages, 10,000 in Buckingham's towns. Natural increases in population were to be met not be extending the area of the town, but by building similar settlements at some distance, and separated from the parent town by agricultural land.

It was in the work of Ebenezer Howard that the first co-ordinated attempt was made to visualise the development of a city region. In 1898 Howard published *Tomorrow: a peaceful path to real reform*, and four years later re-issued the book with slight revisions under the now better known title *Garden cities of tomorrow*.[2] The central ideas of the book were quite simple. In order to reap the benefits of both town and country life and avoid the disadvantages of each it was proposed that cities of about 30,000 population should be built with an open plan, and set within an agricultural reservation. Features of the garden city design were the public buildings at the town centre, surrounded by a large park, the houses with gardens beyond the park which occupied only a little over one-third of the area of the

[1] L. Keeble, *Town planning at the crossroads* (London, 1961), 13–14. Compare Figures 1 and 2.
[2] E. Howard (ed. F. J. Osborn), *Garden cities of tomorrow* (London, 1946).

settlement, and finally the industry, segregated from the housing, and forming the outer ring of the town adjacent to the agricultural belt. The financial arrangements were based upon the community ownership of all land. Profits from increases in land values as a result of development were first to be used to pay interest on borrowed capital, the remainder would contribute to the further development of the town and its services. The city was conceived as a complete social unit in which the growth of population and industry was to be as carefully planned as the layout. When the city had grown to full size future development was to be steered to new garden cities beyond the agricultural zone, which would remain inviolable.

Many of the ideas which Howard propounded were not new. For example, he leant heavily, with full acknowledgement, upon the work of Buckingham for his notions of town arrangement; his town centre seems to owe much to developments like that at Port Sunlight; his agricultural belt was clearly inspired by the Adelaide parklands. Even the term 'garden city' was not new.[1] To be fair, Howard never claimed that the details of his plan were unprecedented. Indeed, he explained at some length the origins of his work, which he described as 'a unique combination of proposals'.[2] Plainly, the importance of Howard's work lies not in its originality, but in its comprehensiveness as a model for a growing city region.

The links between Howard's work and the rapidly expanding London of the day are closer than may at first appear. Howard was born in the City of London and later returned to work as a shorthand writer in parliament and in the law courts. It is clear that it was the congestion of London, as much as of any other city, which caused him to write *Garden cities of tomorrow*, and he devoted the whole of the last chapter to its problems. But it remained for others in later years to suggest that the logic of his garden city principles he applied to the growing city. Howard felt that the first priority was to establish a successful garden city elsewhere as a working model. It was little more than chance, after inspecting sites in many parts of the country, that the first garden city, planned by Raymond Unwin and Barry Parker, was begun in 1903 at Letchworth, thirty-seven miles from central London.[3] When Henrietta Barnett and her supporters

[1] Ibid., 26; Ashworth, op. cit., 141.
[2] Howard, op. cit., 118-27.
[3] C. B. Purdom, *The garden city* (London, 1913), 27-31; *The Letchworth achievement* (London, 1963), 9-30.

commissioned Raymond Unwin to draw up plans for the layout of the 240 acre Hampstead Garden Suburb, a further link between Howard's ideas and London was made.[1]

But perhaps it was the indirect association of Howard's book with a set of circumstances in London which had the greatest effect in following years. Cheaper housing in London, like that in many other cities in the country, while in general solidly built as a result of housing by-laws, was monotonously designed with little thought for variety of street scene or of access to urban services. Dissatisfaction with these conditions led to an atmosphere more receptive than ever before of schemes which promised more attractive town developments. The creation of the London County Council in 1889, with an administrative area covering most of the built-up metropolis, allowed for the first time the possibility that plans covering the whole of London and its fringes could be considered.

By the beginning of the twentieth century in London, therefore, there was a small public sympathetic to a certain amount of planning, an elected authority with administrative support was in existence to oversee and stimulate projects, and a body of ideas was beginning to be compiled. Progress in practical regional planning awaited the legislation which would give a statutory basis for action, and the further development of notions of regional organization.

The birth of regional planning

The halting steps toward regional planning in the first quarter of this century were a mixture of parliamentary, local authority and purely private initiative. The first parliamentary encouragement of planning came in 1909, with the passing of the Housing, Town Planning, etc., Act;[2] a measure introduced by John Burns, president of the Local Government Board, whose early years in public service had been with the London County Council.[3] Support for the Act was prompted by the insanitary conditions of many towns, but its

---

[1] Dame H. Barnett, *The story of the growth of Hampstead Garden Suburb, 1907–28* (1928), 5–8; W. A. Eden, 'Hampstead Garden Suburb, 1907–59', *Journal of the Royal Institute of British Architects*, 3rd Series, 64 (1956–7), 489–95.

[2] 9 Edw. VII, *c*.44. For the detailed background and commentary to the Act see Ashworth, op. cit., 167–90; D. Heap, *An outline of planning law* (4th edn., London, 1963), 5.

[3] Sir G. Gibbon and R. W. Bell, *History of the London County Council, 1889–1939* (London, 1939), 527.

inspiration was undoubtedly derived from the obvious success of garden suburbs, villages, and towns; models which, largely due to the enthusiasm of Unwin and Parker for the new and more humane provision of space, were rapidly becoming associated with the idea of low density suburban development.[1]

The terms of the Act were modest. Its aim was to secure adequate health standards in suburbs which were about to be built by the introduction of by-laws more rigorous than those allowed under the Public Health Act of 1875. If it wished—there was no compulsion—a local authority could propose a 'scheme' or plan for the development of an area within or around a town, and seek the approval of the Local Government Board. Provision was made for the payment of compensation to anyone whose property was adversely affected by the scheme, and the Act also allowed the local authority to recover a limited amount of betterment where property increased in value. Land already developed, or unlikely to be developed, could be included in a scheme only in exceptional circumstances.

Though limited in scope, the Act was warmly welcomed by those interested in planning.[2] While a relatively small number of local authorities drew up plans under the Act, the few which were approved became widely known. One of the most famous was the Ruislip–Northwood scheme, covering an area of about 6,500 acres twelve miles north of the centre of London, and approved in 1914. The central part of the area, about 1,300 acres in extent, was owned by King's College, Cambridge, which was eager to develop its land as a garden suburb. The extension of the scheme by the local authority made possible the rather exceptional scale of the plan. Provision was made for public buildings, commercial areas, industrial land, open spaces, and for a reservoir, but well over two-thirds of the area was to be taken up by residential development at a housing density ranging between four and twelve to the acre.[3]

Though not many schemes were forthcoming under the 1909 Act it was a time of great excitement and action in planning circles. The

[1] R. Unwin, *Nothing gained by overcrowding* (London, 1912); B. Parker, 'Economy in estate development', *Journal of the Town Planning Institute*, 14 (1927–8), 177–86.

[2] Editorial, 'Town planning in the rut of routine', *Town Planning Review*, 4 (1913–14), 1–2.

[3] F. J. McCullock *et al.*, *Land-use in an urban environment* (Liverpool, 1961), 157, Figure 5; W. Thompson, 'The Ruislip-Northwood and Ruislip Manor joint town planning scheme', *Town Planning Review*, 4 (1913–14), 133–44.

garden city supporters were extremely active propogandists and considerable numbers of books appeared explaining and promoting Howard's ideas.[1] In reply, a number of authors attacked the garden city concept, largely on the grounds of its inclination towards low density development.[2] The Act further stimulated planning activity; a quickening of interest in which London received more than its share of attention.

In the first few years of the century there had been attempts to discuss in a regional context the implications of the growth of London's urban area. Notable among these were the proposals of such men as Lord Meath, chairman of the Parks and Open Spaces Committee of the London County Council, and William Bull, a Member of Parliament, which dealt with the creation and retention of public open space on London's fringe.[3] The Act of 1909 brought hope that these schemes could eventually be given effect, and in the Town Planning Conference in London in the following year far more comprehensive thinking was directed at London's problems.

G. L. Pepler was particularly concerned with traffic congestion in central London.[4] He suggested that a parkway should be built encircling London at a radius of about ten miles from Charing Cross. The parkway would act both as a ring-road, by which fast traffic could avoid London, and also as the basis of a zone of garden suburb or parkland development. The solution offered by Arthur Crow to the same problem was perhaps more fundamental.[5] Congestion in London, he argued, could be alleviated by constructing new and modified traffic arteries in the city centre, by greatly improved means of communication from city centre to suburb, and by the gradual building of ten 'cities of health' to accommodate London's growing and already overcrowded population. Each city (Barnet, Bromley, Croydon, Dartford, Epping, Epsom, Romford, Uxbridge, Waltham and Watford were suggested) was to be fourteen miles from Charing

[1] For example, R. Unwin, *Town planning in practice* (London, 1911); J. S. Nettleford, *Practical town planning* (London, 1914).

[2] For example, A. T. Edwards, 'A criticism of the garden city movement', *Town Planning Review*, 4 (1913-14), 150-7; A further criticism of the garden city movement, ibid., 312-8.

[3] W. J. Bull, 'A green girdle round London', *The Sphere*, 5 (1901), 128-9; Lord Meath, 'The green girdle round London', *The Sphere*, 6 (1901), 64.

[4] G. L. Pepler, 'Greater London', in Royal Institute of British Architects, *Town planning conference—Transactions* (London, 1911), 611-27.

[5] A. Crow, 'Town planning in relation to old and congested areas, with special reference to London, ibid., 407-33.

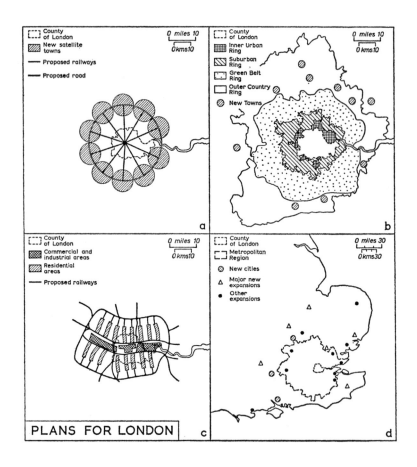

4. Plans for London and the London region

   a. Arthur Crow's ten cities of health, 1910 (Source: Royal Institute of British Architects; *Town planning conference—Transactions* (London, 1911).)

   b. Patrick Abercrombie's advisory plan, 1944 (Source: P. Abercrombie, *Greater London plan 1944* (H.M.S.O., 1945).)

   c. The M.A.R.S. group plan, 1942 (Source: F. J. McCullock et al., *Land use in an urban environment* (Liverpool, 1961).)

   d. South east study proposals, 1964 (Source: Ministry of Housing and Local Government, *The south east study 1961–1981* (H.M.S.O., 1964).)

Cross and linked with central London by an improved road and new rail system. It was envisaged that the cities themselves would be joined by 'The Great Ring Avenue'—500 feet wide and eighty-eight miles long (Fig. 4a). Each new city had a prescribed size (about 25,000 acres and 500,000 people) and would be separated from London and adjacent new cities by areas of land devoted to non-urban uses. It was an imaginative, though costly, proposal which seems to have owed a great deal to Ebenezer Howard.

Further stimulus to regional planning was given by the activities of The London Society. In 1914 the Society launched a scheme to prepare a development plan for Greater London.[1] It hoped to combine the work and ideas of a large number of people who had relevant special knowledge, following the example of the Paris plan of 1893. A team of planners and architects worked through most of the war period and in 1919 the plan was published.[2] For its time, it was a thorough and detailed proposal. Its main concern was with the routes for new roads, and with the reservation of public open space in the area outside built-up London of the day. Attention was given not only to the flow of traffic in and out of London but also to new road routes circumventing the metropolis. The open space proposals seem to rest upon the combination of large, sometimes landscaped, public parks (for example, the Royal Stanmore Public Park), with narrow elongated strips of open space, often along streams, which as far as possible linked the larger parks (for example, the Roding Waterside Reservation). The detail of the work may be judged from the fact that the sixteen sheets of the map were published on the scale of three inches to one mile.

Meanwhile, the influence of Patrick Geddes was making itself felt. Geddes was a biologist who took a far wider view of the scope of town planning than most of his contemporaries. The whole of the urban environment and the town setting was his concern. A town was a phenomenon which could only be understood fully when set against a survey of its present conditions and its past evolution.[3]

---

[1] The Earl of Plymouth, 'The London Society and its scheme for a development plan of Greater London of the future', *Journal of the London Society*, 5 (1914), 1–5.

[2] The London Society, *Development plan of Greater London* (London, 1919); see also Sir Aston Webb, 'The London Society's map, with its proposals for the improvement of London', *Geographical Journal*, 51 (1918), 273–93.

[3] P. Geddes, *City development: a study of parks, gardens and culture institutes* (Edinburgh, 1904), 221–2.

Hence Geddes' insistence on the 'city survey', the outline of which is itself indicative of the breadth of his approach.[1] By his writings, by exhibitions, by lecturing and by discussions Geddes influenced not so much the established architectural planners of his day, but a number of younger planners, such as Pepler, Unwin, and Abercrombie, who were to become the proponents of comprehensive regional development at a later date.[2] Judged by the Geddes standard the Act of 1909 was an inadequate statutory basis of town planning, and it soon became obvious to others that a revision of the official procedure was necessary if the day-to-day processes of local authority planning were to improve.[3]

The Housing, Town Planning, etc., Act of 1919[4] was an attempt to meet a number of the criticisms and it made some small, though no sweeping, changes. In some circumstances the preparation of a planning scheme became obligatory, depending upon the status and population of the local authority area. The consent of the Local Government Board was no longer necessary before beginning to prepare a scheme, but the Board could compel a local authority to draw up a scheme if satisfied that the circumstances warranted one. The first hint of regional planning appeared in a section of the Act which allowed two or more authorities to act together in making a planning scheme by appointing a joint committee. A joint committee could prepare a plan dealing with the whole area administered by constituent authorities, but the committee's function was advisory with no executive rights, unless the planning powers of all the local authorities were delegated to the joint committee. The importance of allowing joint action is clear. County borough and county district councils, which were the planning authorities and of which there were over 1,400 in England and Wales, were not large enough for anything but small scale and short term planning. The effective units of planning could now be enlarged if adjacent local authorities so wished. By the Ministry of Health Act[5] of the same year the newly founded Health Ministry succeeded the Local Government Board as the department responsible for land planning.

[1] P. Geddes (ed. J. Tyrwhitt), *Cities in evolution* (London, 1949), 131-2.

[2] Ibid., see introduction by J. Tyrwhitt, xi-xiii; McCullock *et al.*, op. cit., 158-60.

[3] For example, Nettleford, op. cit., 179-83.

[4] 9 and 10 Geo. V, c. 35. See also Ashworth, op. cit., 199-200; Heap, op. cit., 5-6.

[5] 9 and 10 Geo. V, c. 21.

Following the Housing, Town Planning, etc., Act of 1919 many reports of surveys and regional plans were issued for the area around London. Here development was imminent and borough and district councils began to see a threat not only to their open landscape, but also to their own authority, as London grew. The grouping together of local authorities, usually within the same county, produced new planning regions which rarely had any geographical unity. Sometimes all the districts within a county combined to produce a plan. The Hertfordshire regional plan in 1927 prepared by W. R. Davidge is a good example of a county report.[1] The plan covers the areas of the thirty-six separate planning authorities of Hertfordshire. As do most of the other plans, it recommends routes for new roads, it zones certain areas for agricultural, industrial, and urban development, and it designates proposed open spaces, including a mid-county and Middlesex boundary green belt.

It was not until the Local Government Act of 1929[2] that county councils generally could take an active part in the preparation of planning schemes. The London County Council, however, had held the anomalous position since 1909 of being the only county which was the primary planning authority for its area. But there was limited scope for the use of these powers, since they applied to new developments only, and there was little undeveloped land within the County of London. It was largely as a result of pressure from the London County Council that further legislation in 1932[3] enabled planning schemes to be applied to all land, irrespective of whether it was likely to be developed or redeveloped.[4]

Like the Act of 1909, that of 1919 stimulated private as well as local authority planning proposals. Garden city supporters had already suggested that new town building and decentralisation schemes should be adopted as national policy[5] and a government committee, the Unhealthy Areas Committee of the newly created Ministry of Health, in 1920 and 1921 proposed a solution to London's overcrowding which involved the preparation of a regional plan

[1] W. R. Davidge, *The Hertfordshire regional planning report, 1927* (London, 1927). A list of regional plans produced at this period is contained in G. L. Pepler, 'Twenty-one years of town planning in England and Wales', *Journal of the Town Planning Institute*, 17 (1930–31), 67.

[2] 19 and 20 Geo. V, c. 17. See also Heap, op. cit., 7.

[3] Town and Country Planning Act, 1932; 22 and 23 Geo. V, c.48. See also Heap, op. cit., 7–9.

[4] Gibbon and Bell, op. cit., 529–31.

[5] F. J. Osborn, *New towns after the war* (2nd edn., London, 1942), 7.

followed by the state-assisted construction of self-contained garden cities.[1] In 1921 Purdom edited a volume in which the regional element of the garden city idea was developed.[2] The building of the second garden city at Welwyn had begun in the previous year and the town was considered a model for future overspill or satellite settlements. Purdom, therefore, proposed that twenty-one garden cities should be located within thirty miles of the centre of London and indicated possible sites for these in a plan.[3] But by far the most revealing section of the book is that composed of chapters by Raymond Unwin and Theodore Chambers.[4] Unwin argues the case for restraining the growth of a town once the optimum economic and social size has been reached, while Chambers outlines the way in which an agricultural belt should mould city development.

By the late 1920s there were signs that in parliament, in the counties, boroughs, and districts, and also among private planners, a broader view of town and country planning was beginning to prevail. Though the wider ideas were confined largely to those involved professionally in planning or administration, and probably to a small minority among these, it was a sufficiently vigorous minority to ensure that regional planning progressed in its concepts, in its scale, and in its detail over the period to the outbreak of the Second World War.

London's first official regional plan

In 1926, a number of bodies presented a memorandum to the Ministry of Health advocating the preparation of a statutory plan for Greater London. Later in the year a conference was called by the Minister which led in 1927 to the creation of an advisory panel, the Greater London Regional Planning Committee. The committee was composed of representatives of the local authorities within a radius of about twenty-five miles of central London (Fig. 5). There were 138 authorities in all, and they controlled an area of 1,846 square miles.[5]

The committee first met in November, 1927. By December, 1929, it had issued its *First report*, from which can be judged its enthusiasm

---

[1] Ashworth, op. cit., 201, 215; P. Abercrombie, *Greater London plan 1944* (H.M.S.O., 1945), 1.

[2] C. B. Purdom (ed.), *Town theory and practice* (London, 1921).

[3] Ibid., facing 32.

[4] Ibid., 80–117.

[5] Gibbon and Bell, op. cit., 540–1.

LONDON'S REGIONS

Greater London Conurbation

•Cambridge

Bedford

Colchester•

Oxford

Basingstoke•

Maidstone

•Southampton

•Brighton

0 miles 30

0 kms. 30

— — — Administrative County of London
———— Greater London Regional Planning Committee
------- Greater London Plan 1944
———— Ministry of Housing and Local Government Metropolitan Region
············ Second Standing Conference on London Regional Planning
—·—·—· South East Study

5. Various London regions: some boundaries of areas adopted for planning London and its region (Source: Greater London Regional Planning Committee, *Second report* (London, 1933); P. Abercrombie, *Greater London plan 1944* (H.M.S.O., 1945); *The Advancement of Science*, 17 (1960); Standing Conference on London Regional Planning, *Constitution and membership* (London, 1964); Ministry of Housing and Local Government, *The south east study 1961– 1981* (H.M.S.O., 1964).)

and progress over the two years since its creation.[1] It set up sub-committees to consider decentralization, open spaces (including the possibility of a permanent agricultural belt around London), and traffic, and also an advisory technical committee. But perhaps the most important of its early steps was the appointment of Raymond Unwin as technical adviser. Unwin quickly made his mark upon the work of the committee and, in fact, a substantial part of the *First report* is composed of three memoranda by him upon open spaces, urban development and sporadic building, and the additional powers required by the committee before it could become an effective regional planning authority.[2] This early formulation of Unwin's ideas, as they applied to the London region, was an important stage in the development of a regional plan.

The lack of open space and of playing fields had, for some time, been recognized as a serious problem. But when it was realized that haphazard urban growth, which in practice was out of the control of local authorities, was endangering large areas of land suitable for recreation, then the need for action became clear. The Greater London Regional Planning Committee therefore recommended that a regional planning authority should be established with powers to

[1] Greater London Regional Planning Committee, *First report* (London, 1929), 1-7.
[2] Ibid., 8-39.

prepare a regional master plan to which the schemes of all local authorities should conform.[1] The regional authority never came into being, but Unwin's recommendations were accepted in principle by most members authorities. Unwin produced further evidence and proposals in two interim reports on open spaces and decentralization which were published in 1931.[2] Then in 1933, in the *Second report* of the Greater London Regional Planning Committee, he embodied the earlier work in a comprehensive review of the region.[3]

The Unwin memorandum of 1933 was more than a commentary upon the problems of Greater London. It provided the basis of a general development scheme or plan which in scale and comprehension had few precedents. First, Unwin dealt with the functions and organization of the regional authority. It was obvious that the committee which he advised was in no position to undertake regional planning and he wished to see any agreed plan effectively implemented. Then population growth and movement was examined and the likely housing requirements estimated. It became clear that both the distribution and character of new residential developments would need to be controlled, and because of the important industrial and commercial rôles which London played, special attention would have to be given to these aspects. Transport, particularly the flow of road traffic, received adequate notice, as did the related problem of the incompatability between certain land uses, for example, land for main through routes and land for dwellings. The problems of providing sufficient open spaces and playing fields were treated at length once more, but here firmer proposals than ever before were advanced as solutions.

The outline of the regional plan appears in two maps.[4] The one shows the main new and improved road proposals. It includes not only details of new and widened roads to relieve traffic overloading on existing, heavily-used routes, but also proposals for the extensive introduction of parkways (some for pleasure use only) linked with the prohibition of frontage building on many roads not suited to parkway treatment. The second map is designed to show the general lines of proposed building development. Upon the framework of the

[1] Ibid., 6-7.
[2] Greater London Regional Planning Committee, *Interim report on open spaces* (London, 1931); *Interim report on decentralization* (London, 1931).
[3] Greater London Regional Planning Committee, *Second report* (London, 1933), 12-85.
[4] Ibid., facing 32, 72.

older and more recent building the map indicates a large number of substantial town expansions beyond the outer limits of the conurbation, with a more limited number of new satellite developments. Unwin recognized that to relieve London's congestion, many economic activities and many people would have to be decanted from the central area into the surrounding countryside and that, if properly planned, this could be to the benefit both of the central area and of the activities and population which moved away from the centre. To assist the rational distribution of the new developments, to provide adequate recreation land for London and its detached suburbs, and to segregate new and old settlements from the conurbation, an intricate green girdle of open spaces was proposed.

The central and most strongly argued idea underlying Unwin's plan was that the planning of the city could not be independent of the planning of the city region as a whole. Unless planning activities within the conurbation and outside were inspired by common purposes and co-ordinated towards compatible ends, then, he stressed, they might easily become mutually obstructive. Hence the need for a strengthening of the power of the Greater London Regional Planning Committee, arguments for which were marshalled in the *Second report* as they had been in the first document.

Unwin's hopes for more unified planning of the London region received an immediate check. The financial stringencies of 1931 had substantially reduced the income of the regional committee and early in 1933 it ceased to exist in its original form. A new regional committee for the same area was set up later in the year. It was to co-ordinate planning schemes in the region, make suggestions for development within the region, and exercise powers delegated to it by any local authority in the region. No executive power was transferred to the committee and, though it was able to give helpful advice to some of the smaller authorities, its scope and usefulness as a regional planning committee were severely restricted.[1] It did not set up a technical sub-committee, as the first regional committee had done, but did appoint as technical adviser in succession to Unwin, Major R. Hardy-Syms. A report was issued by Hardy-Syms early in 1934 in which it seems clear that he supported the basic tenets of the Unwin regional plan,[2] but the committee was leading a precarious

1 Gibbon and Bell, op. cit., 542-3.
2 W. L. Hare, 'The green belt—its relation to London's growth', *Journal of the Royal Institute of British Architects*, 3rd Series, 44 (1936-7), 680-3.

life and although it did not finally disband until September, 1936, it was able to make no further progress.

The Minister of Health then took an initiative and constituted a Standing Conference on London Regional Planning which held its first meeting in October, 1937. Again it was composed of representatives of the local authorities in the region, though it had a very limited income and restricted terms of reference. It was given no powers to originate planning recommendations but could consider only such questions as might be referred to it by the Minister or by local authorities. The change from a 'committee' to a 'conference' was held by some to be significant of a further weakening in the power of the regional group to plan the city region.[1]

The effective body of the conference was a technical committee composed of the chief technical officers of the constituent authorities, and it was to this committee that questions and proposals were referred from time to time. But it was not until shortly before the outbreak of war in 1939 that the Conference was able to persuade the Minister of Health to approve an investigation into the ways and means of preparing a master plan for the London region, and into the possibility of establishing an agricultural belt around London. Before the technical committee could begin work the preparations for war prevented any long-term planning activities.[2]

The failure of the various regional bodies to make any general progress with Unwin's proposals was disappointing, but understandable. There is a natural reluctance among local authorities to yield powers to other groups, particularly when those groups are not responsible directly to the electorate. At this time, when there was a dearth of experience in joint action, the suspicion which often exists between neighbouring authorities must also have inhibited co-operation. It was only on Unwin's public open space proposal, perhaps the most tangible and emotive of all his suggested developments, that any progress was made in the period before 1939.

The Abercrombie plan

Arguments in favour of regional organization and administration had never attracted much public attention in Britain. Town planners had gradually moved towards regionalism largely because the

[1] Gibbon and Bell, op. cit., 543.
[2] Abercrombie, op. cit., 2.

practical problems presented in many areas of the country needed solutions on a scale larger than that of the existing local planning authority areas. Geographers and other scholars had found regionalism a convenient descriptive and analytical device, and a few workers, such as G. D. H. Cole, C. B. Fawcett and W. A. Robson,[1] had applied these notions to the planning and administration of England and Wales. But with the outbreak of war regional organization became a necessity and was quickly accepted. Civil Defence regions were hastily drawn up. Scotland and Wales became regions with capitals at Edinburgh and Cardiff, while England was subdivided into ten regions, each with its own capital. Many government departments adopted these regions when dispersing their activities from Whitehall and so, though the Civil Defence regions were far from ideal geographical units, they grew to have some administrative importance.[2] The interest in regionalism and its general approval encouraged geographers, particularly, to devise an improved regional framework for the country, but despite the notable contributions and E. G. R. Taylor and E. W. Gilbert[3] the Civil Defence regions, which with small post-war modifications became the Standard Regions, persisted until 1965.

It was in this atmosphere sympathetic to regional study, though in a period of great wartime difficulty, that Patrick Abercrombie began his work on the London region. In 1941 the Minister of Works and Buildings asked the London County Council to prepare a plan for the development of its area. Abercrombie, acting as consultant, and J. H. Forshaw, the Council's architect, jointly produced the report.[4] In 1942 responsibility for planning passed from the Minister of Health to the Minister of Works and Planning and in that year he asked the Standing Conference on London Regional Planning if they would agree to his appointing an expert to prepare a plan and report for the Greater London region. They agreed, and Abercrombie, though he had not completed his work on the County of London, was commissioned to produce the plan on the understanding that

[1] G. D. H. Cole, *The future of local government* (London, 1921); C. B. Fawcett, *The provinces of England* (London, 1919); W. A. Robson, *The development of local government* (London, 1931).

[2] R. E. Dickenson, *City region and regionalism* (London, 1946), 279, 291–3.

[3] E. W. Gilbert, 'Practical regionalism in England and Wales', *Geographical Journal*, 94 (1939), 29–44; 'Discussion on the geographical aspects of regional planning', ibid., 99 (1942), 61–80.

[4] J. H. Forshaw and P. Abercrombie, *County of London plan* (London, 1943).

he should co-operate fully with the technical committee of the Standing Conference. The *Greater London plan 1944* was published in 1945.[1] It covered the areas of 143 local authorities and dealt with 2,599 square miles of land outside the Administrative County of London (Fig. 5). In its areal coverage, in its scope and in its detail it far exceeded any earlier plan for London, including that of Unwin, with which, in general outline, it bore some similarities.

Three government committees of enquiry reported in the early 1940s and had an influence upon Abercrombie's work—the Barlow Commission on the distribution of industrial population, the Scott Committee on land utilization in rural areas, and the Uthwatt Committee on compensation and betterment.[2] All had insisted on the regional treatment of planning, but the Barlow Commission, of which Abercrombie himself was a member, more than the other two committees, produced data and arguments which had an important bearing upon the way the London region should be planned. The Commission had been set up to examine the whole question of industrial distribution against the background of the great differences in unemployment rates which existed in the 1930s between the comparatively prosperous south-eastern part of England, where most of the recent industrial development had taken place, and the north and west of the country, where the depressed industries were concentrated. The Committee concluded that there should be a reasonable balance of industrial development throughout the country, that the industry in each part of the country should be appropriately diversified, that consequently the drift of industry and industrial population to the south-east of England needed to be controlled, that congested urban areas, like London, should be redeveloped where necessary, that this should be accompanied by the dispersal of industry and workers, and that where dispersal took place, consideration should be given to such developments as garden cities, satellite towns, trading estates, or to the development of existing small towns and regional centres. The recommendations of the Commission were criticized by many as being too mild, and six of the thirteen members, including Abercrombie, signed minority reports urging stronger actions, but

[1] Abercrombie, op. cit.

[2] *Royal Commission on the distribution of industrial population, Report*, Cmd. 6153 (H.M.S.O., 1940); Ministry of Works and Planning, *Committee on land utilization in rural areas, Report*, Cmd. 6378 (H.M.S.O., 1942); Ministry of Works and Planning, *Expert Committee on compensation and betterment, Report*, Cmd. 6386 (H.M.S.O., 1942).

the general arguments of the Barlow Report were accepted by Abercrombie and incorporated in the *Greater London plan 1944*.

The Abercrombie plan for the London region was based upon five assumptions, the first three of which were derived directly from the Barlow Report.[1] First, it was assumed that, except in special instances, no new industry was to be admitted to the Greater London region. Secondly, it was assumed that both industry and workers would be moved from the congested central areas of the County of London and from some areas immediately outside the county boundary into the less densely populated zones towards the fringe of the region. Abercrombie's estimate of the total numbers of people to be dispersed in this way was in excess of one million. The third assumption was that as a result of the Barlow recommendations and in accord with what were thought to be national trends, the overall population of the region would not increase, but would decrease slightly. The planning problem was therefore one of determining the optimum redistribution of people and workplaces. The fourth assumption was that the Port of London would continue to be one of the world's great ports and fifth, that new powers for the control of planning and land values would become available.

The structure of the plan was a simple one. The region was conceived as being composed of four concentric zones (Fig. 4b). The first, the Inner Urban Ring, covered the most overcrowded central part of London, much of which had been severely damaged by bombing. In order to rebuild to adequate standards and create acceptable population densities (75–100 persons per acre) a substantial movement of population and industry out of this area was proposed. The second, or Suburban Ring covered the remainder of built-up London. It was, in a sense, a static zone; it was neither to receive population and industry nor, in general, did it need thinning, though a certain amount of adjustment within the area seemed to be required to achieve a maximum net residential density of fifty person per acre. The third zone was the Green Belt Ring, and followed the recommendations of the Scott and Uthwatt Committees. It stretched up to ten miles beyond the outer edge of London and was intended to include as much open land as possible. Some quite large towns already lay within the zone but the future expansion of these and the creation of new settlements would be strictly limited, and the further growth of London prevented. Finally, the Outer Country Ring

[1] Abercrombie, op. cit., 5.

extended to the boundary of the regional plan. It contained distinct communities set in an agricultural background, and though this general character was to be preserved it would be the chief reception area for overspill population and industry from central London.

Into this straightforward framework the details of the plan fitted. A revised communication system was proposed which, in addition to new and enlarged air terminals and rail links, contained ten new radial and five new ring roads to take express and distance traffic. Eight new towns (ten possible sites are shown on the Master Plan—see Fig. 4b) together with other satellite and town expansions were suggested which would absorb over three-quarters of a million of the overspill population. Great emphasis was laid upon the provision and location of community facilities and open space. Attention was given to the problems of suburban sprawl, to the control of urban densities, and to the redistribution of industrial employment. But it is, perhaps, the green belt and new town proposals which at the time, and since, have attracted most attention. It is paradoxical that neither was greatly emphasized in the plan and that neither was introduced with any justification or strong arguments for their necessity. Abercrombie seems to accept it as axiomatic that his proposals, which were firmly in the garden city movement traditions and which had been so intensively canvassed by others, had become sufficiently widely accepted to need no further support when applied to the London region.

Late in 1944 Abercrombie submitted his plan to the Standing Conference on London Regional Planning for transmission to the new Minister of Town and Country Planning, who had become responsible for planning in the previous year. In 1945 the Minister created a new Advisory Committee for London Regional Planning and asked it to review the plan. When it reported back to the Minister in 1946 the Committee agreed with Abercrombie in most respects, the only major point of divergence being on the methods of accommodating overspill population. The Minister accepted the plan in principle though he expressed reservations about a number of projects for development.[1]

The London regional plan was a sensible, thorough and workmanlike approach to London's problems and was accorded general support. The alternative plans available for London at the period were never seriously considered. The Abercrombie plan was com-

[1] D. L. Foley, *Controlling London's growth* (Berkeley, 1963), 31–2.

missioned by the authorities responsible for planning London and its region, and so had an initial advantage, but in addition it was far more comprehensive and also more realistic than any of the likely competitors.[1] Three of the alternative plans are worth mention. The London Regional Reconstruction Committee of the Royal Institute of British Architects, with the help of some outside experts, produced a plan for London which adopted an approach nearer than any other to that of Abercrombie, though it was much more limited in its proposals. The plan was concerned to conserve the character of London as it had been in pre-war days by improving existing transport lines and by creating self contained communities within London, using transport routes and open spaces as barriers between adjacent communities. An increase in the amount of open space, the segregation of industrial and residential areas, and the integration of all modes of transport were proposed. Essentially the plan advocated a tidying of London rather than a fundamental reorganization. The Royal Academy's Planning Committee, whose chairman was Sir Edwin Lutyens, also produced plans for London in the early 1940s. These were principally concerned with the nature of architectural developments along proposed main roads and were limited in their regional application. Finally, there was the plan of the Modern Architectural Research Society, the most original of the three alternatives, but one which required sweeping changes to be made in the form and organization of London. It proposed an east-west commercial and industrial spine running along the Thames with residential areas in strips of development north and south of the core (Fig. 4c). The elements in the plan were integrated by a new communication network and allowed for future growth by lengthening the commercial-industrial core and by introducing additional residential strips running from it. Though ingenious, the plan's disregard for the existing form of London and the expenditure which the necessary reorganization would incur, meant that few planners, and even fewer political leaders, were able to give it serious consideration.[2]

[1] E. C. Kent and F. J. Samuely, 'Physical planning, a method of comparative analysis on London plans', *Architects Journal*, 100 (1944), 99–114.

[2] A. Korn and F. J. Samuely, 'A master plan for London, based on research carried out by the planning committee of the M.A.R.S. group', *Architectural Review*, 91 (1942), 143–50; Foley, op. cit., 24–5, 46–8.

Post-war planning in the London region

Planning in the mid 1940s was undertaken very much in the shadow of the Barlow, Scott and Uthwatt reports. The principal planning Act remained that of 1932 but planning authorities were aware that new and radical legislation was forthcoming, and this, with the encouragement received from the new Ministry of Town and Country Planning, enabled them to begin preparing planning schemes which were much more flexible and far ranging than any hitherto possible. But legislation in the spirit of Barlow, Scott and Uthwatt was not long delayed.

In 1946 the New Towns Act was passed.[1] The Bill was hurriedly drafted on the basis of the interim reports of a committee set up to enquire into the feasibility of new towns, and before its final report was published. The speed of enactment demonstrated the government's determination to tackle the problems presented by the congested urban areas. Planned decentralization was accepted as the main policy and this was given effect by appointing independent Development Corporations which were to be responsible for the building of new towns on sites selected by the Minister. It was the intention that new towns should develop as self-contained and balanced communities, and that they should not be merely dormitory suburbs of the existing urban areas. Over the period 1946–9 eight new towns were designated on the fringe of the London conurbation (Basildon, Bracknell, Crawley, Harlow, Hatfield, Hemel Hempstead, Stevenage, Welwyn Garden City). Although the number of new towns coincided exactly with Abercrombie's proposal and although the towns lie in the same zone, between twenty and thirty miles from Charing Cross, only two of the designated sites were among those suggested in the *Greater London plan 1944*.[2]

Then in 1947 the Town and Country Planning Act was passed.[3] The Act repealed all previous planning legislation, though it incorporated some provisions of earlier enactments, and set up a comprehensive and obligatory planning code. Direct planning powers were removed from the district councils and placed in the hands of county and county borough councils. Although the new planning depart-

[1] 9–10 Geo. VI, c. 68. See also Heap, op. cit., 190–207.
[2] J. T. Coppock and H. C. Prince (eds.), *Greater London* (London, 1964), 314. Figure 69.
[3] 10 and 11 Geo. VI, c. 51. See also Heap, op. cit., 11–13.

ments were hardly regional authorities, the reduction in number from over 1,400 to 147 planning units was a step in that direction. Under the general guidance of the Minister of Town and Country Planning local planning authorities were required to prepare development plans for their areas showing how they considered land ought to be used, submit them to the Minister for approval, and undertake quinquennial reviews of the plans. Local planning authorities were given wide powers to control land use. Before building, engineering, or mining could occur, before new outdoor advertising space could be used, or before a material change in the use of land could be made, other than to agriculture or forestry, the approval of the local planning authority was necessary. In only a few instances was planning permission not required, for example, when the development was made by, or on behalf of, the Crown, or where certain types of development were undertaken by the local planning authorities themselves. It was possible for powers to be delegated to district councils within the county but practice has varied widely from place to place. The most debated part of the Act was that which dealt with the financial aspect of development control, provisions which had been derived from proposals of the Uthwatt committee. A betterment charge was to be levied by a new body, the Central Land Board, on any kind of development which increased the existing value of a piece of land, and compensation was to be paid, initially from a fund of £300 million, for loss of development value resulting from planning decisions.

The Act of 1947 was modified by a series of Town and Country Planning Acts in the 1950s. The compensation and betterment provisions particularly underwent drastic change, but with this exception, the outline of the 1947 Act still forms the basis of town planning legislation in England and Wales. The 1947 Act and those amending it have now been repealed and their provisions collected into one enactment, the Town and Country Planning Act of 1962.[1]

Since 1947, therefore, there has been an adequate statutory framework within which to implement plans for the London region. But while there has been a unified plan for the region, there has never been a single planning authority to administer or oversee it as Abercrombie advocated.[2] The position in 1947, when there were six counties and three county boroughs within the limits of the

---

[1] 10 and 11 Eliz. II c. 38.
[2] Abercrombie, op. cit., 183–4.

Abercrombie region, was better than before the Town and Country Planning Act was passed, when there were 143, but the problem of the co-ordination of development plans within the region remained. It was with this problem in mind that the Minister of Town and Country Planning set up the London Planning Administration Committee to advise on the appropriate machinery for securing concerted action in the implementation of a regional plan for London as a whole.[1]

The Committee did not report until February, 1949, having been delayed by internal disagreements. The majority report recommended the immediate establishment of a regional advisory committee with an independent chairman to be appointed by the Minister, and in due course the investigation by a local government commission of the organization of local authority administration in the London region. The minority report, signed by three of the nine members of the Committee, contained stronger recommendations. The authors pointed to the ineffectual record of the pre-war advisory committees and suggested that yet another such committee would prove equally feeble. They were firmly committed to a joint planning committee which would exercise planning powers throughout the region until such time as local government reform could be brought about. No immediate action was taken on the majority recommendation and that of the minority group never seems to have been seriously entertained, although powers existed under the 1947 Act for the formation of joint planning boards by merging the areas of adjacent planning authorities.

In the absence of formal regional planning there were two methods of co-ordinating development plans for the London region. The first was by informal consultation among the local planning authorities, and the second was by the Ministry co-ordinating plans through its research departments, in its development plan reviews, and in the rulings given through the appeal machinery when a developer formally objected to a local authority planning decision. The first of these methods of co-operation evolved slowly. From 1948 onwards, local authorities prepared their development plans more or less independently and it was not until these began to be presented to the Ministry in the middle 1950s that it was realized that, when viewed together, the plans contained some substantial departures

[1] Ministry of Town and Country Planning, *London planning administration committee, Report* (H.M.S.O., 1949), 3.

from the Abercrombie proposals. For example, to meet the growing population pressures the plans provided for a population 7 per cent larger than that envisaged. Fresh information on the growth of population and office employment caused even greater concern, and on the initiative of the Surrey County Council a preparatory meeting of officers of counties and county boroughs in the London region was held in April, 1960. The officers recommended a permanent co-ordinating body to review the problems of the region and in December, 1962 the Standing Conference on London Regional Planning was established (Fig. (5.[1] Although its name is identical with that of an earlier body, which had a similar function and membership, there seems to have been no direct link between the two Standing Conferences.

The second means of co-ordination was through the planning Ministry. Widely diverging proposals were adjusted in the Ministry when local authority development plans were under study before finally being approved, but perhaps the greatest contribution towards regional co-ordination came from the London regional office of the Ministry. The office was based in central London and dealt with an area corresponding closely with the Abercrombie study area. From the middle 1940s until 1951 the regional offices acted as intermediaries between the Ministry and the local authorities. During the 1950s the regional offices gradually disappeared but, because of its special problems, the planning Ministry (now the Ministry of Housing and Local Government) continued to assume a general responsibility for the London region through the regional office, which acquired an increasingly important research function. With the passing of time the regional area of study became larger than that of Abercrombie, but since 1960 the boundary of the Metropolitan Region seems to have become fixed (Fig. 5).[2]

If the actions of the local authorities and of the planning Ministry may be thought of as jointly satisfying one recommendation of the majority in the London Planning Administration Committee, then the appointment of the Royal Commission on Local Government in Greater London (Herbert Commission) in 1957 surely contributed to the satisfaction of their second recommendation. The Commis-

[1] Standing Conference on London Regional Planning, Paper L.R.P. 4 (1962); *Constitution and membership* (London, 1964).
[2] A. G. Powell, 'The recent development of Greater London', *Advancement of Science*, 17 (1960), 82.

sion's review area was limited to little more than the conurbation and so the possibility of a true regional authority hardly arose. But the Commission did strongly urge in its report that a unified authority, the Greater London Council, covering the whole of built-up London inside the green belt, should be set up to take responsibility for a number of local government functions, including planning.[1] These, and other of the recommendations of the Herbert Commission, were put into effect in 1965.

The final stage in the development of a regional plan for the London area began with the production by the Ministry of Housing and Local Government of *The south east study 1961–1981* in 1964.[2] Early in the previous year when it was nearing completion a White Paper had made clear the thinking behind the study.[3] It was based on the premise that to organize jobs, land, transport and housing in and around London implied the existence of a regional plan, and that if that regional plan was to be effective, particularly when dealing with London overspill, it should cover sufficient ground to enable new and expanded towns to be sited far enough away from London to divert some of the pressure from the capital. When the study area was defined, therefore, it included three of the existing Standard Regions, the Eastern, the London and South Eastern, and the Southern, together with that part of Dorset which fell within the South Western Standard Region (Fig. 5). In all, the study area covered more than a quarter of England and Wales.

As the title implies, the study was not in itself a detailed plan, but in addition to providing factual background material for the planning of the region, it made concrete proposals for the solution of its major problems.[4] Population increase in the south-east in the period 1961–81 was estimated at about three and a half millions. London's overspill was likely to amount to about one million over the same period. Though normal planning processes could accommodate much of this population, a second generation of new and expanded towns was needed; settlements to be planned on a much larger scale than hitherto so that they could act as counter-magnets to London. The Southampton–Portsmouth area, the Bletchley area, and the

[1] *Royal Commission on local government in Greater London, 1957–60, Report,* Cmnd. 1164 (H.M.S.O., 1960), 254–5.
[2] Ministry of Housing and Local Government, *The south east study 1961–1981* (H.M.S.O., 1964).
[3] *London—Employment: housing: land,* Cmnd. 1952 (H.M.S.O., 1963), 2.
[4] Ministry of Housing and Local Government, op. cit., 98–101.

Newbury area were suggested as likely sites for large cities, new towns were proposed at Ashford (Kent) and Stansted, and large town expansion schemes were advocated for Ipswich, Northampton, Peterborough and Swindon (Fig. 4d). The transport of people and goods would need attention to allow for increased population. Substantial improvements in London's suburban rail and road services were suggested and it also seemed necessary to improve links between Southampton and the Midlands. Finally, the importance of the green belt was affirmed but it was argued that a certain amount of green belt land might be needed for building.

The publication of the study of south-east England was followed by similar studies of other areas.[1] A number of these had been underway for some time and they were quickly adapted, where necessary, to comply with the new economic planning regions defined early in 1965. Meanwhile professional planners and others had continued to attempt to improve the arrangement of city or planning regions to make them more suitable for land-use control,[2] and this interest was gradually communicated through the press to an increasingly aware general public.[3] As time passed it became clear that a review of the conclusions of *The south east study 1961–1981* was being undertaken by the government. When the review was eventually published early in 1966, however, it was produced not by the government, but was pieced together from ministerial statements, circulars, and official letters by the Standing Conference on London Regional Planning.[4]

The boundary of the South East region had already been modified in 1965, upon the adoption of economic planning regions. Dorset had been excluded completely and had been placed in the South West region, while the Soke of Peterborough, originally in the former North Midland Standard Region, was included within the South East. Later the revised South East region was divided into two, the administrative counties of Cambridge, Isle of Ely, Huntingdon, Norfolk, Soke of Peterborough, East Suffolk, and West Suffolk forming the new region of East Anglia. By adding Oxfordshire the Standing Conference was able to make its own area coincide with that of the

---

[1] For example, Department of Economic Affairs, *The West Midlands, a regional study* (H.M.S.O., 1965); *The North West, a regional study* (H.M.S.O., 1965).

[2] For example, D. Senior (ed.), *The regional city* (London, 1966), *passim.*

[3] *The Guardian*, (January 30, 1967).

[4] Standing Conference on London Regional Planning, Paper L.R.P. 600 (1966).

smaller South East region (Fig. 6). In mid 1966 it adopted a new title, 'Standing Conference on London and South East Regional Planning'.[1]

The review itself revealed no dramatic changes in policy, though there were a number of shifts of emphasis. For example, the estimates of overall population growth in the region remained substantially unchanged; it was the significance, location and nature of the growth that seemed to have undergone a transformation. The estimate of a population increase for the South East of three and a half million between 1961 and 1981, as a result of revised national

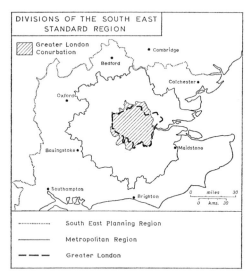

6.
Major divisions of the present South East Standard Region (Source: South East Economic Planning Council, *A strategy for the South East* (H.M.S.O., 1967).)

population projections, now represented a much lower proportion of national growth than envisaged in the original study. Indeed, the implication of the figures seemed to be that the rate of population increase in the South East might be no higher than in the rest of the country. There had also been a change of view on the location of the urban development to accommodate the increases in population. Far more of the new developments would be in those parts of the region distant from London, rather than immediately beyond the green belt as earlier suggested, and counties such as Berkshire,

[1] It is possible that further changes will take place in the boundary of the South East region, and certainly in the boundaries of the local government areas within it, following the publication of the Redcliffe-Maud report—See *Royal Commission on local government in England, Report*, Cmnd. 4040 (H.M.S.O., 1969).

Hampshire, and East Sussex were proposed for the major increases in growth targets. This re-allocation of growth, as a result of the review, was much more consistent with the provisions for new development made by the counties in their own development plans, and also may have been an attempt to combat the trends, which were only becoming known early in 1966, of changes in employment in the inter-censal period 1951-61. Contrary to the widely held belief, based upon Ministry of Labour statistics, the Census showed that employment in Greater London had been growing at a very modest rate, by only 3·8 per cent over ten years; the rapid growth had been on the fringes of London, in counties such as Buckingham, Essex, and Hertford, all of which experienced increases in employment of more than 20 per cent over the same ten year period.[1] Finally, comparing the proposals emerging from the review with the original study, it seemed that the government proposed a marked reduction in the scale of 'forced' developments—new cities, new towns and formal town expansions. It was mainly the medium sized developments close to London which were not to be pursued, such as the expansions by 30,000 persons each of Chelmsford, Colchester, Hastings, Maidstone, the Medway towns, Reading, and Southend. Of the larger schemes, only the new city in north Buckinghamshire had been agreed in principle at the date of the review.

A further shift of emphasis is represented by *A strategy for the South East*, produced in 1967 by the South East Economic Planning Council.[2] Economic planning councils are advisory bodies set up in each region by the Secretary of State for Economic Affairs to make recommendations to the government upon economic and physical planning. In this instance the Council was both swift and radical. It was the first to produce a long term physical plan for its area; a plan which was remarkable because in a number of respects it suggested major departures from earlier thinking.

Instead of the series of scattered overspill centres, large and small, proposed in *The south east study 1961-1981* the Council envisaged a pattern of development based upon sectors following the main radial routes out of London. Substantial growth corridors, sometimes up to twenty miles wide, led urban and industrial development towards

---

[1] Standing Conference on London and South East Regional Planning, Paper L.R.P., 721 (1966).
[2] South East Economic Planning Council, *A strategy for the South East* (H.M.S.O., 1967).

the major expansion areas of Ashford—East Kent, Ipswich—
Colchester, Northampton—Milton Keynes, and Southampton—
Portsmouth. Minor corridors stretched in the direction of Brighton,
Hitchin, and Southend (Fig. 7). The existing green belt, it was
suggested, should be retained and the physical extention of London
restricted. Green 'buffers' were recommended between the growth
sectors and also between individual urban agglomerations within the

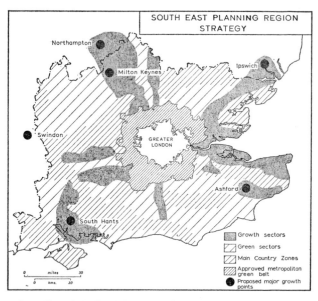

7. **The main outline of the South East Planning Region strategy** (Source: South
East Economic Planning Council, *A strategy for the South East* (H.M.S.,
1967).)

sectors, and a number of largely rural areas were proposed as Main
Country Zones. In choosing a corridor plan the Council clearly
indicated its feeling that a different strategy was required. It was a
change of emphasis designed to bring the development of the
London region very much closer to that planned for Copenhagen,
Hamburg, Paris, Stockholm, and Washington, than to the model
outlined by Abercrombie and his predecessors.[1]

On the whole local authorities in the London region have given

[1] P. Hall, 'Planning for urban growth: metropolitan area plans and their
implications for south-east England', *Regional Studies*, 1 (1967), 101–34.

the new strategy a hostile reception. At the time of writing no firm official decision had been made. The only reaction came in March, 1968 when the Minister of Housing and Local Government announced that Ashford would not be designated a new town as its location close to the Channel Tunnel was considered contrary to the policy of spreading the benefits of the tunnel throughout the country.[1]

Over a period of more than a century ideas about city or planning regions, and specifically about the London region, have developed considerably. The above chapter has tried to chronicle the history of regional planning, a task which other authors, notably Peter Self,[2] have attempted from different standpoints. It is clear that *The south east study 1961–1981*, together with its subsequent revisions, and *A strategy for the South East* are but the latest stages in a long development, and that they now pave the way for an integrated physical plan for an extended London region. Alongside this evolution of concepts, as the foregoing discussion has from time to time hinted, has been a concomitant development in ideas about green belts, in ideas about urban recreation and amenity land, and of techniques of controlling the growth of towns and cities. The following chapter deals in detail with the growth of these ideas and shows how they are related to the developing notions of the planned city region.

---

[1] *The Guardian* (March 27, 1968).

[2] P. Self, 'Regional planning in Britain', *Urban Studies*, 1 (1964), 55–70; 'Regional planning in Britain: analysis and evaluation', *Regional Studies*, 1 (1967), 3–10.

3 · The Green Belt as a means of Land-Use Control

Green belts have a long, though intermittent, history. Towns and cities with inviolable rural hinterlands were described in the Old Testament and in the works of the classical writers. Later authors, such as Sir Thomas More, Robert Owen and J. S. Buckingham contributed to the idea that town and country should be functionally related but physically distinct.[1]

London's green belt is not of such antiquity. It is true that a proclamation of Elizabeth in 1580 established a *cordon sanitaire* three miles wide around the City of London in an attempt to limit the effects of plague and other contagious diseases. Within that area all new buildings were prohibited, except upon sites where, within living memory, there had previously been a building. In the city no sub-division of dwellings was allowed.[2] But neither the proclamation, nor the similar measures which followed it over the next half-century, proved effective. The Crown was always short of money and the granting of dispensations provided welcome revenue.[3] A further attempt to contain London was made by the Commonwealth parliament in 1657, but it was not until the end of the nineteenth century that fresh plans for a green belt around London began to emerge. The remainder of this chapter is devoted to tracing the confused development of the philosophy of green belts from that time until the present, a period in which the nature and aims of green belt proposals have varied greatly.

---

[1] F. J. Osborn, *Green belt cities* (London, 1946), 167–80; J. W. Reps, 'The green belt concept', *Town and Country Planning*, 28 (1960), 246–50; *supra* p. 41–2.

[2] 'Ye olde English green belt', *Journal of the Town Planning Institute*, 42 (1955–6), 68–9.

[3] S. E. Rasmussen, *London: the unique city* (London, 1937), 67–75.

Early green belt ideas: 1890–1927

Towards the end of the last century the feeling strengthened that, because London was growing so rapidly, there was a need to conserve pleasant open spaces for recreation and for visual amenity before they became built over. The idea received stimulus from two sources. First, the success of schemes for constructing parkways or preserving green girdles in and around cities in other European countries and, more particularly, in the United States was becoming well known.[1] The second stimulus came from Ebenezer Howard and his followers in the garden city movement, whose arguments became more developed and also more vociferous as time passed. Howard's dissatisfaction with the existing urban forms, which had evolved with the industrial expansion of the preceding century, led him to suggest that garden cities should be constructed which would be not only cities with gardens, but cities within gardens, that is, with attractive rural surrounds.[2] Howard was quite clear about what functions his rural or country belt would perform.[3] First, he saw the belt of country as a means of preventing the inordinate growth of a town beyond the point where its facilities and services became overloaded. Secondly, he intended the rural belt as an agricultural reservation which would ensure the bulk of the town's food supply. Thirdly, the rural belt was visualized as a place for recreation and a place in which reserves of recreational land could be retained to satisfy future demands. Lastly, he saw the rural belt as an attractive setting within which the town could develop and which would maintain, close at hand, the 'fresh delights of the countryside—field, hedgerow, and woodland'.[4]

The first set of modern proposals for a green belt around London seems to owe more to the first stimulus than the second. During a visit to the United States, Lord Meath was favourably impressed by the broad boulevards of Chicago, Boston and other cities. On his return in 1890 he suggested to the Parks and Open Spaces Committee of the London County Council, of which he was first chairman, that suburban parks and open spaces should be linked by 'broad sylvan

---

[1] See, for example, A. Faludi, 'Der Wiener Wald und Wiesengürtel und der Ursprung der "green belt" idee', *Raumforschung und Raumordnung*, 25 (1967), 193–206.

[2] E. Howard (ed. F. J. Osborn), *Garden cities of tomorrow* (London, 1946), 17.

[3] Ibid., 55–65, 140–2.

[4] Ibid., 142.

73

avenues and approaches'.[1] Eleven years later William Bull, M.P.,
published proposals for a green girdle around London again modelled
on American examples. His plan was to join existing open spaces by
a park belt, half-a-mile wide, running a little beyond what was then
the outer edge of built-up London (Fig. 8). He envisaged 'a circle
of green sward and trees which would remain permanently inviolate'.
The estimated cost of the scheme was £12 million.[2] There is no evidence

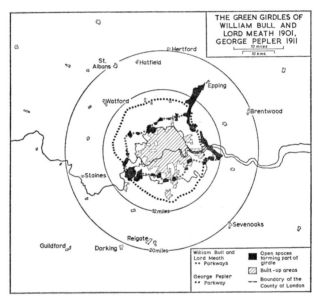

8. **The green girdles of William Bull, Lord Meath and George Pepler, 1901–11**
(Source: *The Sphere*, 5–6 (1901); *Garden Cities and Town Planning*, 1 (1911).)

that Bull was aware of Lord Meath's earlier suggestion. Bull submitted his plan to the Parks and Open Spaces Committee of the
London County Council, but there seems to have been little
enthusiasm for it.[3] Within a few weeks Lord Meath published his
own plan for a green girdle round London, again motivated by the
need to provide amenity. It was substantially the same as that of

[1] Lord Meath, 'The green girdle round London', *The Sphere*, 6 (1901), 64. The
article was reprinted, with some omissions, in *The Garden City*, n.s. 1 (1906–7),
59–60.

[2] W. J. Bull, 'A green girdle round London', *The Sphere*, 5 (1901), 128–9.

[3] London County Council Minutes, Parks and Open Spaces Committee
(June 28, July 8, July 26, 1901).

Bull (the girdles are shown coincident in Fig. 8), except that the parkways linking open spaces were more involved in plan, and not of standard width. He hoped that the London County Council and neighbouring authorities would combine to acquire the land and so furnish London with 'one continuous chain of verdure'.[1]

The green girdle schemes of Lord Meath and Bull were based entirely on the need to preserve amenity and recreational land. They were intended not to regulate London's growth but to introduce a green ring into that development. Rather different was the intention of the London County Council when in 1891 it required Lord Meath's committee to consider 'the desirability of the Council drawing the attention of parliament, by petition or otherwise, to the need of statutory control and direction as to the extention of building in the suburbs of the county of London and in the adjacent parts of the neighbouring counties'.[2] The aim, like that of the Elizabethan and later sixteenth- and seventeenth-century green belt proclamations, was to safeguard the health of the growing metropolis.

Yet another aspect of the early green girdle schemes is exemplified in the plan of George Pepler, published in 1911. He concentrated upon the ring-road idea in an attempt to improve communications around London. The proposal was that a strip of land should be bought one-quarter of a mile wide and further from the centre of London than the earlier green girdles (Fig. 8). The belt was again conceived as linking existing open spaces. In the centre of the belt

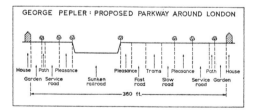

9.
The central section of George Pepler's proposed parkway round London, 1911 (Source: *Garden Cities and Town Planning*, 1 (1911).)

there was to be a system of roads, railways and tramways, interspersed with grass and trees (Fig. 9), while the remaining open land was to be developed either as garden suburb, which would assist in recovering the cost of purchase, or as parkland. The estimated cost

[1] Lord Meath, op. cit.
[2] London County Council Minutes (July 28, 1891); Sir G. Gibbon and R. W. Bell, *History of the London County Council, 1889–1939* (London, 1939), 503.

was about £4·8 million.[1] The plan was very similar to one which had been advanced a year earlier by Niven.[2]

It was only the suggestion of Arthur Crow which came close to the ideas of Ebenezer Howard at this early stage in the development of ideas about green belts. His ten 'cities of health', which were to take London's overspill population, were separated from each other, and from London, by land restricted to non-urban uses. This section of his plan, however, was in outline form and it has hardly enough detail to be considered as a specific green belt proposal.[3] No action was taken on any of the plans put forward. The difficulties and costs were thought insurmountable and the youthful London County Council had fully committed its resources to more immediate problems wholly within its own territory.

The outbreak of war in 1914 for a time put an end to green belt schemes, but gradually fresh plans began to appear as the need for planning control over the London region became more urgent. The first of these was contained in the plan of the London Society published in 1919. The open space proposals of the plan included a circular parkland design in which narrow strips of open space linked larger existing and proposed public parks. The aim of the plan seems to have been the same as those of Lord Meath and Bull, though the girdle was not as formally circular, not as wide, and generally much further from the centre of London.[4]

During the 1920s concern was again felt about the growth of London. In 1924 the London County Council carried a resolution asking its Town Planning Committee 'to consider and report whether or not the preservation of a green belt or unbuilt-on zone or zones within the boundaries of or adjacent to Greater London is desirable and practicable and, if so, what steps can be taken to effect this'. Apart from containing the first recorded use of the term *green belt* to describe an inviolable rural zone around London, neither the resolution nor the subsequent reports to the Committee are helpful

[1] G. L. Pepler, 'Greater London', in Royal Institute of British Architects, *Town planning conference—Transactions* (London, 1911), 611–27; 'A belt of green round London', *Garden Cities and Town Planning*, n.s. 1 (1911), 39–43, 64–8.
[2] D. B. Niven, 'A zone scheme for London', *Architectural Review*, 27 (1910), 55–9.
[3] A. Crow, 'Town planning in relation to old and congested areas, with special reference to London', in Royal Institute of British Architects, op. cit., facing 410.
[4] The London Society, *Development plan of Greater London* (London, 1919); W. L. Hare, 'The green belt—its relation to London's growth', *Journal of the Royal Institute of British Architects*, 3rd Series, 44 (1936–7), 682.

in giving an idea of what was intended. It was assumed by the Committee that a width of half a mile was reasonable for the belt under consideration, but no further plans were made as the difficulties of controlling land outside the Council's territory were thought too great.[1]

In other counties around London a certain amount of progress was being made, on paper if not in practice. Unlike London, there were in these other counties substantial amounts of undeveloped land for which joint planning schemes could be drawn up under existing legislation. The schemes frequently contained parkland and green belt proposals—the Hertfordshire plan by Davidge published in 1927 has already been cited, as an example.[2] The open spaces were often intended both to provide amenity and recreation land, and also to limit London's growth. But although these regional plans, and especially those for the area around London, were carefully drawn and sometimes quite detailed, their implementation was as difficult and as costly as the schemes discussed by the London County Council.

Unwin's green girdle: its formulation and implementation

In November, 1926, Neville Chamberlain, who was then Minister of Health and responsible for planning, asked the London County Council to make a survey in Greater London of the need for playing fields and open spaces, and of the suitable land available. He had observed the rate at which vacant land within, and immediately outside, the county of London was being appropriated for building and felt that it would be unwise to delay any remedial action longer than was necessary.[3] In the following year, when he was addressing the first meeting of the Greater London Regional Planning Committee, Chamberlain developed the same theme. Among other things, he asked the Committee to consider how far and in what direction it might be possible to direct London's growth, what might be the advantages of trying to concentrate development in particular spots by establishing planned new towns, or satellite towns, and also whether London should be provided with an agricultural belt so that

[1] Mrs. Hugh Dalton, 'The green belt around London', *Journal of the London Society*, 255 (1939), 70.
[2] *Supra* p. 51.
[3] Dalton, op. cit., 70.

a dividing line could be established between Greater London and the fresh developments that might take place at a greater distance.[1]

The report of the London County Council's investigation into the need for playing fields and open spaces was published in March, 1929. When in December of that year Unwin's technical memorandum was published in the Greater London Regional Planning Committee report it was clear that he was as much influenced by the County Council's report as he was by the statements of the Minister to the Committee.[2] By whatever standard Unwin judged the supply of recreation land it always fell far short of the need. For example, within the London County Council study area (equivalent broadly to the area of the conurbation of the day) the existing recreation land was estimated at fifty square miles. To satisfy the standard of the London County Council an additional twenty-nine square miles was required, to satisfy the standard of the National Playing Fields Association an additional forty square miles was required, and to meet the standard Unwin himself was proposing for the Greater London region, an extra sixty-five square miles of recreation land was needed. This conclusion led Unwin to recommend strongly to his Committee that land should be acquired for recreation purposes as a matter of urgency. He suggested that in the inner areas priority should be given to the purchase of playing fields, while most of the general and more extensive open space needs could be met in the outer areas of the region.

In his interim report on open spaces published in 1931 Unwin produced further alarming evidence.[3] As the result of a survey undertaken in the summer of 1930 it emerged that nearly 8·5 square miles of land suitable for open space purposes had been lost to building since the London County Council report was prepared. All parts of London were deficient in open space and again he urged the need to reserve land. In the course of the survey plots of land, in general lying about ten miles from Charing Cross, had been noted as being suitable and available for acquisition. Of these he proposed that areas amounting to thirty-one square miles should be purchased to form a chain of open spaces and playing fields around London. The report was received and approved by the Committee.

[1] Greater London Regional Planning Committee, *First report* (London, 1929), 8.

[2] Ibid., 8–26.

[3] Greater London Regional Planning Committee, *Interim report on open spaces* (London, 1931).

In the *Second report*, published in 1933, Unwin codified his proposals, and outlined in some detail his scheme for a green girdle.[1] The girdle was not to be what Howard and Chamberlain had envisaged. He suggested not an agricultural belt, but a park belt which would compensate for the deficiency of playing fields and pleasant open land nearer the centre of London: in effect it was an extension of the ideas of Lord Meath and Bull. The belt was not continuous, though he attempted to make it as nearly so as possible,

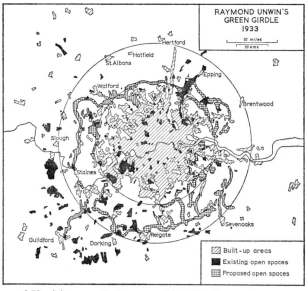

10. **Raymond Unwin's green girdle proposed in 1933** (Source: Greater London Regional Planning Committee, *Second report* (London, 1933).)

and it was wider than any suggested earlier—there are sometimes as many as six miles between the inner sections, drawn close to the edge of London, and the outer sections (Fig. 10). It was Unwin's hope that the green girdle would provide 'a break in the outward sporadic spreading of London' and that attention would be paid to the way in which satellite and other extra-metropolitan settlement developed. He impressed upon the Regional Committee the importance of planning the area beyond the girdle not as a limitless field of potential building land in which there were occasional stretches of open space,

[1] Greater London Regional Planning Committee, *Second report* (London, 1933), 78-83.

but as an area where settlement was distributed on a background of open land reserved temporarily or permanently from building.

Recently Mandelker has interpreted Unwin's proposal as being the origin of the crawling green belt concept,[1] but he is surely mistaken. The crawling green belt, such as that around Edinburgh and other Scottish cities, is gradually moved outwards as pressure upon building land increases within the town or city. Its function is not to prevent the expansion of the continuous urban area, but to reduce ribbon and scattered development over a limited zone in the surrounding countryside. Unwin's parkland girdle, however, was certainly meant to be permanent. His suggested restrictions, temporary or otherwise, upon the development of open land referred to the whole of the London region, and are akin to present ideas of development control. Though his green girdle may have departed from the garden city model, Unwin was firmly committed to the notion that satellite developments should be restrained from further growth once their planned size had been reached.[2]

On a number of occasions the London County Council had considered proposals for green belt schemes, but had been forced to reject them because of the difficulties of implementing the plans. Three things conspired to change these decisions. First, the rate at which building was proceeding was obvious and many surveys had revealed the loss of recreation land. The force of Unwin's arguments therefore became clear and his solution appeared increasingly attractive as time passed. Secondly, in February, 1934, a deputation representing the Regional Planning Committee met the Minister of Health. He welcomed Unwin's scheme but saw no way in a period of financial difficulty of making government funds available for the reservation of recreation land. Thirdly, in the following month the Labour Party gained control of the London County Council and, largely through the enthusiasm of Herbert Morrison and Richard Coppock, who was chairman of the Parks Committee, adopted more direct methods to prevent the loss of recreation land. In 1935 the London County Council green belt scheme was launched.[3]

The objects of the scheme were set out in the recommendations made to the London County Council by its Parks and Town Planning

[1] D. R. Mandelker, *Green belts and urban growth* (Madison, 1962), 29–30, 35, 153.

[2] R. Unwin, 'The town and the best size for good social life', in C. B. Purdom (ed.), *Town theory and practice* (London, 1921), 80–102.

[3] Dalton, op. cit., 72.

committees. It was intended 'to provide a reserve supply of public open spaces and of recreational areas and to establish a green belt or girdle of open space lands, not necessarily continuous, but as readily accessible from the completely urbanized area of London as practicable'.[1] To achieve this the London County Council offered to make grants to the county councils of Buckingham, Essex, Hertford, Kent, Middlesex, and Surrey, and to the county boroughs councils of Croydon, East Ham, and West Ham, to enable them to acquire open space and farm land, and secure it against harmful development. The Council agreed to pay up to half the cost of an approved acquisition and was prepared to spend as much as £2 million over three years. The costs of laying-out and maintaining the 'sterilized' land was to be borne by the authorities in whose territory the land lay. In the preamble to the recommendations, administration of the scheme by a joint committee of the authorities represented on the Greater London Regional Planning Committee was rejected on the ground 'that practical difficulties and delay were likely to arise from any attempt to use existing powers through a joint committee . . . and that further legislation would be inevitable'. The insistence by the London County Council upon direct contact between itself and the other county authorities in the scheme foreshadowed the Council's withdrawal from the Regional Committee in 1936, and had the effect of removing control of the green belt scheme from the committee in which it had originated.

The response to the London County Council's offer was immediate. Within fourteen months the purchase of 28·5 square miles had been provisionally approved and grants totalling £713,000 promised. The most comprehensive proposals came from Buckinghamshire (4·3 square miles), Essex (11·1 square miles), and Middlesex (6·9 square miles) and comprised areas of land, partly linking existing open spaces, stretching in a discontinuous zone around north London from Egham in the west to Rainham in the east.[2] Though not all the land acquired was open to the public a major contribution was made in a very short time to satisfying the need which had been outlined a few years earlier by Unwin. The Parks Committee of the London County Council was able to say with some justification that 'the green belt is already beginning to take definite shape'.[3]

[1] Dalton, op. cit., 73–4; Hare, op. cit., 680–5.
[2] London County Council, *Green belt around London* (London, 1961), 5–6.
[3] Ibid., 5.

By 1936 it was becoming clear that there might be difficulty in ensuring the permanent preservation of some of the lands forming the belt. Despite earlier hopes that new legislation would be unnecessary the London County Council was forced to introduce a Bill into parliament to safeguard the acquired land and to make certain that it was legally preserved. Under the Bill neither the sale nor the development of green belt land was to be premitted without the

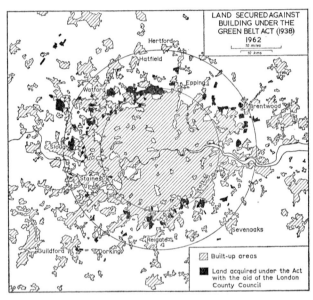

11. **Land bought under the Green Belt Act (1938) with the aid of the London County Council, 1962** (Source: London County Council)

consent of the Minister responsible for planning and of the contributing county councils. In due course the Bill became the Green Belt (London and Home Counties) Act, 1938.[1]

Much of the land now held under the scheme was acquired by 1944, when about forty square miles had been safeguarded, but occasionally land is still bought. Between the end of March, 1956, and the end of March, 1961, nearly two square miles were added to the protected land and at present over forty-four square miles are preserved (Fig. 11). The land lies broadly in the zone where Unwin proposed his green girdle. Apart from open spaces and playing fields

[1] 1 and 2 Geo. VI, c. 93.

it includes farmland, woodland, downs, stretches of water, and also large country houses with surrounding grounds used privately or as institutions. Of all this land 27 per cent is open space with full public access, 14 per cent more will eventually be open to the public, while 59 per cent is devoted to other uses, mainly agricultural.[1] From the outset it was intended that much of the agricultural land should remain in that use to maintain the rural character of the land on London's fringe. In addition to the land shown in Figure 11, considerable areas have been purchased under the 1938 Act by local authorities without financial assistance from the London County Council. With this land a total of over fifty-six square miles is now reserved against building.

Abercrombie's green belt

When, in the early 1940s, Abercrombie began formulating his ideas about a green belt for London there were a number of models upon which he could base his own conception. He was familiar with the work of Ebenezer Howard and the proposals which had followed from it for an all purpose green belt of some width around London. The belt would serve as a means of preventing the growth of London, as an agricultural reserve, as a zone where recreational activity could take place, and as an area in which amenity could be preserved and fostered. He was equally conversant with the schemes proposed by the London Society; parkland and recreational plans which had been developed by Raymond Unwin and brought into effect by the London County Council.

There seem to have been two factors which made Abercrombie incline more towards the Howard all-purpose green belt, than the alternatives. First, paradoxically, there was the effect of Unwin's own writing, and particularly the passages where he had posed alternative solutions to London's outward spread. Given the choice of conceiving the outer parts of the London region as universal building land with a few patches of open space, or as a continuous green background embedded at suitable places with building development, Unwin had argued strongly for the latter. When considering his strategy for the Green Belt and Outer Country Rings Abercrombie accepted Unwin's conclusion without reservation.[2] This implied a

[1] London County Council, op. cit., 7.
[2] P. Abercrombie, *Greater London plan 1944* (H.M.S.O., 1945), 11.

certain depth to the green belt in order to produce a broad agricultural and recreational background.

But it was probably the second influence which was the more telling. In 1942 the Scott Committee on land utilization in rural areas had reported and, in what must be one of the most influential footnotes in the history of planning, had defined what it envisaged a green belt should be.[1] A green belt, where no building or constructional development was to be allowed, would be used by a planning authority when a town had reached a maximum or optimum size. It would not be merely an artificially preserved or sterilized ring of commons, woods and fields around a town to offset its smoke and dirt. That concept represented an exclusively townsman's point of view. Sterility must be avoided. Consequently a green belt was conceived as a tract of ordinary country, of varying width, round a town where the normal occupations of farming and forestry could be continued so that, as elsewhere in rural areas, the farmer was the normal custodian of the land. But a green belt had a second role. Because of its proximity to a large town it would normally include golf courses and other recreational land for the townsman's use. The farmer, on his part, would recognize that certain types of farming, such as sheep rearing, were unsuited to such an area. Nevertheless, in essence, a green belt would remain an ordinary tract of countryside.

The green belt which appears in the *Greater London plan 1944* occupies a zone up to ten miles wide (Fig. 12). Its aims, following the Howard and Scott Committee precepts, were to restrict urban growth (London's overspill population and industry was to leapfrog to new sites in the Outer Country Ring) while actively encouraging agriculture, fostering recreational possibilities, and enhancing the natural beauty of the area. Much of the land in the belt was privately owned and used for farming, but a substantial proportion of the land which had been bought under the Green Belt Act of 1938 was included within it. The control needed to achieve the aims of the green belt was not to be brought about by the purchase of land as under the 1938 Act, which was quite impractical on the scale of Abercrombie's proposal, but by controlling the actions of owners and leaseholders. The Uthwatt Committee on compensation and betterment had already suggested a method for controlling land use, and Abercrombie hoped that this, or a similar method, would allow his

[1] Ministry of Works and Planning, *Committee on land utilization in rural areas, Report*, Cmd. 6378 (H.M.S.O., 1942), 71.

green belt plan to be given effect. It was not Abercrombie's intention that his green belt proposals should replace the London County Council scheme. Indeed, he hoped that land would continue to be acquired where suitable for playing fields and where it consisted of specially beautiful pieces of natural or artificial landscape.[1]

Beyond the metropolitan green belt in the Outer Country Ring Abercrombie recommended local green belts around the smaller

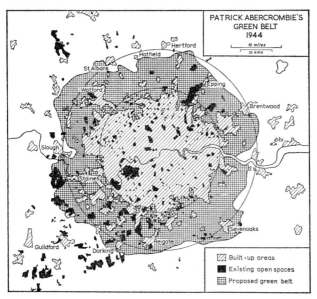

12. **Patrick Abercrombie's green belt, proposed in 1944** (Source: P. Abercrombie, *Greater London plan 1944* (H.M.S.O. 1945).)

towns. He is not absolutely clear on this point, but it seems that he intended the local belts to contain a higher proportion of parkland and recreation space than the wider metropolitan green belt.[2] Though they are comparatively small, usually about half a mile wide, the Master Plan reveals that, because of the frequency and gerneralized form of the local green belts, they cover a lot of ground. The Letchworth belt, however, is no more extensive than that originally proposed by Unwin and Parker.[3]

In 1946 Abercrombie's plan for the Greater London region,

[1] Abercrombie, op. cit., 8.
[2] Ibid., 108.
[3] Compare Howard, op. cit., 105.

together with its green belt proposals, was accepted in principle by the Ministry of Town and Country Planning; the first formal government recognition of the need for a continuous green belt around London. The decision was confirmed in the following year by a Ministry memorandum and in the same year the Town and Country Planning Act was passed, which enabled, *inter alia*, Abercrombie's green belt ideas to be implemented by introducing development control. County and county borough authorities no longer needed to buy land to prevent building, they were empowered to refuse permission for development. Any compensation payments which resulted from such decisions were met not locally, but by the central government. Local planning authorities' actions were thus not inhibited by the possible strain upon local funds.

Three years later, in 1950, the Ministry prepared a green belt map based upon that of Abercrombie, for the guidance of local planning authorities. When submitting their development plans for the approval of the Minister, county planning departments in the London area included this green belt, though small alterations were often made to the boundaries. Between 1954 and 1958 the development plans for the counties around London were approved, and the green belt which they contained, with further minor changes, became part of statutory documents (Fig. 13). The differences between the Abercrombie and the development plan green belts are a result of the modifications to boundaries at the Ministry and in the county planning departments (Fig. 14).

One effect of the powers now held by planning authorities is that there is no longer such a need to protect farmland under the Green Belt Act of 1938. Land is now usually acquired only where it is, or will soom become, open space, and at a speed very much less than during the early years of the scheme's operation. The designation of the green belt has also assisted in steadying the costs of acquiring such land, for any value it might have had for building development has now, in most instances, been removed. In 1961 the London County Council was able to comment that the costs of purchasing land under the Green Belt Act was generally less than in pre-war days.[1] In a number of recent examples it appears that stretches of woodland have been bought because it was found that the cost was little more than the high compensation payable to preserve the trees for amenity.

[1] London County Council, op. cit., 16.

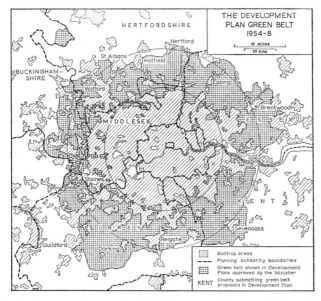

13. **The development plan green belt, finally approved between 1954 and 1958**
(Source: Ministry of Housing and Local Government)

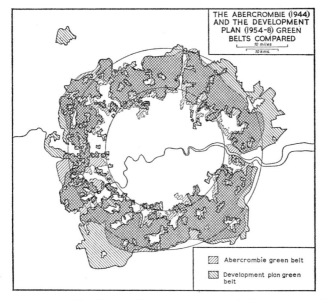

14. **A comparison of the Abercrombie green belt proposal with the green belt
as shown in development plans approved between 1954 and 1958** (Source:
as in Figs. 12 and 13)

Changes in green belt ideas: 1955 onwards

Throughout England and Wales in the 1950s local authorities were preparing and beginning to implement their development plans. Those in the London region and those in and near many other large towns and cities had advisory plans upon which to base their strategies. Others had to begin their planning with little background material and with little experience. A few cities, Birmingham, Leeds, and Sheffield are perhaps the best examples, had, even before the 1939–45 war, bought tracts of land beyond their peripheries or had arrived at agreements with owners in order to reserve areas from building development.[1] Following the 1947 Town and Country Planning Act some local authorities outside the London region again attempted to restrict urban development, now with the aid of the new planning controls. But there was little uniformity between different areas and this began to cause concern.

In a statement in the House of Commons in April, 1955, Duncan Sandys, then Minister of Housing and Local Government, attempted to set the matter right. He was pleased with the way local planning authorities in the Home Counties had provided a broad green belt, and affirmed that no further urban expansion would be allowed in the belt except for some limited 'rounding-off' of existing small towns and villages. He regretted that to that time no formal green belts had been proposed elsewhere. Consequently he invited all planning authorities to consider their own policies and to make proposals for clearly defined green belts where they though appropriate.

The statement was followed in August by the now well-known circular on green belts, which defined, more clearly than any previous document, the official attitude to their purpose and nature.[2] A green belt was recommended under three circumstances. It could be used to check the growth of a large built-up area, it could prevent the merging of two neighbouring towns, or it could assist in preserving the special character of a town. If possible, the green belt was to be of sufficient width to ensure that a substantial rural zone would be preserved. Except in very special circumstances no new buildings, or

[1] Ministry of Housing and Local Government, *The green belts* (H.M.S.O., 1962), 4.
[2] Ministry of Housing and Local Government, *Green belts* (H.M.S.O., 1955), Circular No. 42/55.

changes in the use of existing buildings, were to be allowed other than for agriculture, sport, cemeteries, institutions standing in extensive grounds, or other uses appropriate to a rural area (the list of desirable land uses is very close to one produced over twenty years earlier by Raymond Unwin).[1] Apart from a small amount of 'infilling' and 'rounding-off', towns and villages within the belt should not be allowed to grow. Even inside the urban areas every effort was required to prevent further building for industrial and commercial purposes, since this would lead to a greater demand for labour, which in turn would create pressure for additional housing land in the green belt. Local planning authorities contemplating the creation of green belts, after consulting any neighbouring authorities affected, were asked to submit to the Minister a sketch plan indicating the approximate boundaries. After discussions with the Ministry any agreed sketch submission would be accepted in principle, and eventually, after further consideration, might be approved as a formal amendment to the development plan. This procedure might be lengthy and while it was underway county authorities were empowered to treat any area provisionally agreed as if it were approved green belt.

This first official definition of a green belt seemed to focus attention away from the character and viability of the belt itself, and onto its effect upon the town or city. The Minister's attitude was immediately critized as being that of a townsman who saw the green belt as a means of solving urban problems, with little regard for those of the countryside.[2] There may well have been some substance in this view, for some of the main functions of green belts as outlined by the Scott committee and by Abercrombie were omitted. There was no mention in the Ministry circular of amenity and no proposal to encourage agriculture, except by restricting urban growth. That this was not an oversight was confirmed later by a senior officer of the Ministry who, in an address to a national conference sponsored by the Council for the Preservation of Rural England, said, 'May I say at once that the designation of the green belt is not a measure for the protection of the countryside'.[3]

The Ministry of Housing and Local Government's view of green

[1] Greater London Regional Planning Committee (1933), op. cit., 82-3.
[2] For example, B. J. Collins, 'A talk on green belts', *Town Planning Review*, 28 (1957), 219.
[3] J. R. James, 'Dispersal of the urban population'. Unpublished paper read at Scarborough, 1959.

belts was clearly more limited than that of its predecessor in immediately post-war years, but the contrast with the Abercrombie notion
may be offset in two ways. First, since Abercrombie's plan was
published many statutory powers had become available for protecting
countryside, preserving amenity, and retaining space for recreation.
National Parks and Areas of Outstanding Natural Beauty could be
designated by the National Parks Commission, nature reserves and
Sites of Special Scientific Interest might be proposed by the Nature
Conservancy, and Areas of Great Landscape, Scientific or Historic
Value could be outlined by local planning authorities. Any of these
could occur (and most now do) within green belts. In effect, land
within a green belt of special amenity or other value could be clearly
identified as such and specifically protected.[1] Secondly, as time has
passed and green belts have become more widely accepted, greater
attention has been paid in planning decisions to amenity, and to the
balance between land uses, though agriculture has never since held
the important place it did in Abercrombie's scheme.

A second circular in September, 1957, described how a formal
proposal for the alteration of a development plan to include a green
belt was to be made.[2] It dealt with the mapping of green belt boundaries, the way in which existing settlements in the green belt should
be treated, the notation to be used on maps in the county plan, and
finally with the written statements which should accompany development plan amendments. In this last section the possible reasons for
establishing a green belt are repeated unchanged from the 1955
circular, but there is an additional note inviting local authorities to
include a reference in their written statements to the special attention
which they would give to visual amenity when they considered
proposals for developments in the green belt, or developments which
might be conspicuous from it. There is also advice on the handling
of rural areas outside green belts. It is stressed that stricter control
on urban fringes and in areas of landscape value should not lead to
permission being given elsewhere for development which might be
inappropriate or detrimental to the countryside.

In the light of these two circulars many local planning authorities
outside the London region eagerly submitted green belt proposals.

[1] D. Thomas, 'Statutory preservation of the countryside in England and Wales',
Zeitschrift für Wirtschaftsgeographie, 6 (1962), 34–8.
[2] Ministry of Housing and Local Government, *Green belts* (H.M.S.O., 1957),
Circular No. 50/57.

Although the circulars were not specifically directed at the planning authorities in the London area, neither were they excluded. They took advantage of the new instructions to propose substantial extensions of the green belts shown in their development plans. These gradually began to move through the various stages of approval. A revised version of the Buckinghamshire extension was accepted by the Minister of Housing and Local Government in 1960, when he indicated that he would eventually approve the green belt in the agreed form as part of the county development plan. No other extension of the London green belt has since achieved this status, though small additions to the approved green belt were made when the development plans for the Ascot and Chesham Town Map areas were agreed by the Minister. An extension of the green belt into East Sussex to the south and east of Crawley was accepted provisionally but, following a public enquiry, has since been rejected.

The result of these submissions was that the green belt came to occupy a substantial area of the Home Counties outside the London conurbation. The effective green belt grew well beyond the zone,

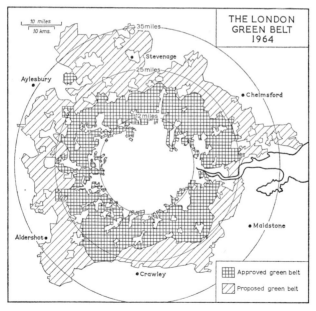

15. **London's green belt, 1964** (Source: Ministry of Housing and Local Government)

from between twelve and twenty miles from the centre of London, in which most of the earlier proposed green belt schemes were located. In Figure 15, showing the position early in 1964, the combined approved and provisional belt is in some places, to the north of London for example, over thirty miles wide. In all, it covered nearly 2,000 square miles. The distinction drawn by Abercrombie between the metropolitan and the local green belts had by this stage ceased to exist, though a number of local planning authorities in the London area clung to the terminology, possibly in the hope that to maintain the distinction might help to disguise their true motives for extending their green belts. Local authorities around London by no means accepted readily the Duncan Sandys criteria for green belt definition and were often more concerned with preserving their open agricultural land and retaining intact their county territories than they were with the problems of London's growth as such. Hertfordshire seems to have been franker than most when in a policy document published in 1957 this difference in aim was admitted.[1] While the Abercrombie plan, and Londoners generally, saw the green belt as a means of maintaining recreation space and rural scenery within reach of the population of the conurbation, Hertfordshire saw it as a defence against the spread of suburbia on inter-war lines. 'Between London and Hertfordshire, therefore, there is a common purpose in the means, if not in the object!'

Successive Ministers of Housing and Local Government from Duncan Sandys onwards had affirmed their intention to maintain green belt policy and to ensure that belts were not nibbled away at their edges by urban development. These statements always applied to the fully approved inner green belt around London, and also, though with less force because their boundaries had not been finally settled, to the provisional green belts around provincial cities. There seem, however, to have been certain reservations about the provisional extensions to the London green belt. In an address to a meeting of the Town Planning Institute as early as the spring of 1960 the deputy chief technical planner to the Ministry of Housing and Local Government had emphasized that a green belt 'was never intended as a defensive measure against the reasonable peripheral expansion of the urban areas'. He continued, 'The green belt is an excellent instrument of policy for providing the town dweller with

[1] Hertfordshire County Council, *Report on the administrative problems of the green belt* (Hertford, 1957), 4.

readier access to the open country, for giving sharper edge between town and field, for preventing unlimited sprawl and for stopping the coalescence of neighbouring towns but its value must not be debased by being mis-applied. It cannot stop growth in the city region. It can only shape it.' An analysis of development plans had revealed that the rate of local dispersal has been underestimated. This was particularly severe in London and the Midlands which had attracted more population and industry from other regions than was foreseen.[1] These views were given wide press publicity[2] and caused some unfounded concern about the future of green belts. But, more important, they gave the first hint from official quarters that in drawing the boundaries for their proposed extensions to the approved green belt, local authorities in the London area were providing insufficient room for future expansion.

The White Paper of February, 1963, dealt with the problems of employment, housing and land in and around London. In this, and in statements he made in the House of Commons, the Minister of Housing and Local Government made it clear that not all the existing green belt should be regarded as sacrosanct. Allowing for the homes that could be built within the conurbation, in new and in expanded towns over a ten-year period, there still remained the need to find land around London for about 200,000 houses. Many of these would have to be built on land designated as green belt. The government believed that the green belt should remain a permanent feature of the planning policy of London and intended to retain, without great change, the approved belt, and eventually to add to it. But not all the 2,000 square miles of approved and provisional green belt was essential to the purposes of the belt, nor had it all high amenity value. 'Nibbling' into the belt could not be allowed. Instead the Minister proposed to ask local authorities to consider, in the light of the needs set out in the White Paper, what green belt areas might be suitable for housing. Any proposals put forward would be the subject of a public local inquiry. Hertfordshire and Essex were thought particularly suited to such building because spare railway capacity existed in these counties to carry commuters into London.[3] Almost immediately a stretch of approved green belt in the Lea

---

[1] J. R. James, 'The next review of development plans'. Unpublished paper read at Newcastle upon Tyne, 1960.
[2] *The Times* (May 27, 1960); *The Guardian* (May 27, 1960).
[3] *London—Employment: housing: land*, Cmnd. 1952 (H.M.S.O., 1963), 12-13.

valley, occupied largely by disused greenhouses, was proposed as the first residential area, though final approval was not given to development on the 400 acre site until mid 1966.[1]

In practice, as a study of the Ministry of Housing and Local Government's annual series *Selected Planning Appeals* will verify, there had already been a movement away from the rigid attitude to green belts adopted in the 1955 circular, with greater attention being paid particularly to amenity. On paper, however, the White Paper marks a sharp change of view, especially when read alongside a popular booklet on green belts issued only a few months previously.[2] The booklet repeats verbatim the three reasons for the establishment of a belt given in the 1955 circular, and clearly subscribes to the view that London's green belt has one primary purpose—to check the growth of Greater London. The White Paper, on the other hand, proposes to build not upon 'the fine countryside which forms an important part of the green belt', but upon land 'of little amenity value' which is not 'essential to the purpose of the green belt'. If the purpose of the green belt were to check London's growth, that purpose could not be achieved by allowing building, whether on unattractive country or not. Implicit in the White Paper is that the purpose had changed, and changed to embrace in principle as well as in practice the amenity and recreational aims of Howard, Unwin and Abercrombie.[3]

The White Paper of 1963 had hinted that the proposed extentions to London's approved green belt could not be firmly settled at that date. The White Paper of a year later, which accompanied *The south east study 1961–1981*, stated unequivocally that, in view of the search being made by local authorities for land within the green belt suitable for housing, the Minister did not intend to approve the extensions in their existing form (that is, as shown in Fig. 15).[4] But *The south east study 1961–1981* was far from negative in respect of the green belt; indeed, in a chapter devoted solely to London's green belt it undertakes a more searching analysis of its purpose and nature than any other previous Ministry pronouncement.[5]

[1] *The Guardian* (July 20, 1966).
[2] Ministry of Housing and Local Government (1962), op. cit.
[3] D. Thomas, 'Green belt attitudes', *Town and Country Planning*, 31 (1963), 386–90.
[4] *South East England*, Cmnd. 2308 (H.M.S.O., 1964), 6.
[5] Ministry of Housing and Local Government, *The south east study 1961–1981* (H.M.S.O., 1964), 88–95.

The study considers the likely demands upon land for housing in he green belt against the background of total demand in the South East Region. It accepts that some of the demands in the ring immediately surrounding London could not reasonably be shifted elsewhere and that land would have to be found, even within the approved green belt where changes would be very small in relation to the whole. The study rejects two suggested new approaches, one in which it was advocated that the inner edge of the green belt should be pushed back half a mile or so from the edge of the conurbation all the way round, and the other, in which a radical reorganization of the belt was proposed, from its present constricting girdle form into a star-shaped design with green wedges being carried into the built-up area and development taking place in corridors between the green areas. The first was inadequate because it lacked selectivity, the second because it had come too late. The study held that the approach through the local authorities was the only realistic one and suggested that a good deal of the necessary increase in population could be accommodated by redevelopment within green belt towns at densities higher than previously, by high density development on areas created by modest adjustment of town map areas, and by the further 'infilling' and 'rounding-off' of villages. Additional building land could be found in areas of low amenity value.

In the areas beyond the approved green belt the study suggests a further change of strategy. While there were strong arguments for strengthening and extending the green belt, such additions should allow for foreseeable future developments. Green belt boundaries would not have to be drawn too closely around towns, and some margin of unallocated land should be left to meet long term needs. The two main aims in the extensions of London's green belt should be first, to maintain the separate identity and the physical separation of country towns, and secondly, to prevent building on fine landscape. Such was the rigidity of the green belt system that in areas at some distance from London positive and immediate reasons should exist before bringing land under strict control.

One sentence summarizes the fresh attitude of *The south east study 1961–1981* to green belts. 'All land in the green belt should have a positive purpose; whether it be its quality as farmland, its mineral resources, its special scenic value, its suitability for public open space or playing fields for Londoners, or for those land uses generated by the main built-up area, which cannot suitably be located within it—such as reservoirs and institutions needing large areas of open land around them.'

There is no advance on these green belt ideas in *A strategy for the South East*.[1] Great importance is clearly attached to the retention of the approved green belt, and it appears in its existing form in the Master Plan (Fig. 7). The need for better access to amenity and recreation areas is stressed and a plea is made for better public information about the facilities available, so that interference with agriculture may be minimized. But beyond the approved green belt radical changes are proposed. The present extentions to the London green belt are rejected on the grounds that, in the past, full use has not been made of land protected from development by its green belt status. In any case, the extentions are quite inconsistent with the growth-corridor plan. Instead green sectors are suggested. These are intended to separate growth zones by providing largely non-urban interstices between the star-like growth corridors, which would be based 'on green belt principles'. In other rural areas country zones would protect the rural economy and its characteristics, safeguard high value agricultural land, confine development to rural activities, and resist the incursion of urban development. But though the new countryside policy is regarded as the keystone of the strategy, it is very difficult to establish precisely the differences between the green sectors and country zones on the one hand, and between the green sectors and the approved green belt on the other.

In concept and in physical expression London's green belt has undergone many changes over the last seventy or eighty years. In the future it seems certain that it will undergo further changes in the light of new ideas and changing circumstances. At the moment yet another study of south-east England is underway in which an attempt is being made to take forward the work already done by the South East Economic Planning Council and the Standing Conference on London and South East Regional Planning.[2] This will doubtless bring to light fresh material and generate new proposals. But there has been sufficient stability in recent years for the effects of the green belt to have become detectable in the countryside. It is these effects which are studied in detail in Part III of this work.

[1] South East Economic Planning Council, *A strategy for the South East* (H.M.S.O., 1967).
[2] *The Guardian* (May 3, 1968).

4 · Other Controls Over Land Within the Green Belt

A green belt is not the only method by which open country-side may be protected from undesirable development. Two further means are available which assist the implementation of public policy on the use of land. First, there exist a number of statutory controls upon land use, and changes in land use, which are quite distinct from green belt protection though, like green belts, the powers are often exercised by local planning authorities through their normal develop-ment control procedures. They constitute not a single, unified body of land-use restraints, but a varied armoury of protective devices. Secondly, publicly owned land can act as a buffer against unwanted urban and industrial expansion. Here, obviously, the effectiveness of the buffer depends both upon the disposition of the public land in relation to the threat upon open countryside, and also upon the willingness of the public body owning the land to co-operate with the planning ministry and with the local authority. Different public bodies may well have conflicting aims in respect of particular pieces of land. While these two additional means of controlling land use have an effect throughout the country, they are especially important within the green belt because they can be used to support and supple-ment green belt powers.

In studying the influence of London's green belt upon the country-side of the conurbation's fringe a distinction has to be drawn between the effectiveness of the green belt and that of other methods of control. This is a difficult task. The boundaries of the green belt were often drawn to coincide with those of the other areas, and through the effects upon physical development can sometimes be distinguished, the effects upon the visual attractiveness of the countryside are hard to differentiate. The other land-use controls and land ownership usually act more positively than green belt procedures in preserving attractive countryside. To some degree this is because the areas of

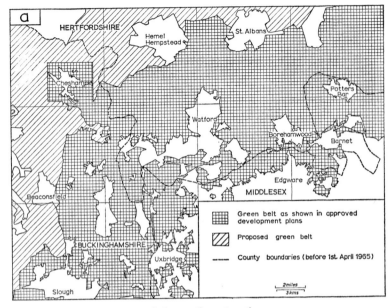

16a. London's approved green belt—north-west section
(Source: Ministry of Housing and Local Government)

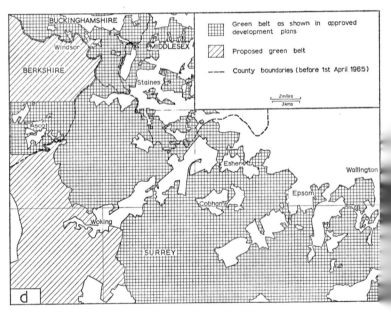

16d. London's approved green belt—south-west section
(Source: Ministry of Housing and Local Government)

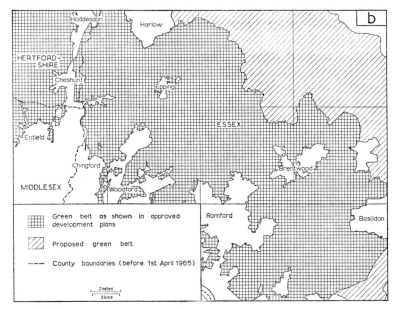

16b. London's approved green belt—north-east section
(Source: Ministry of Housing and Local Government)

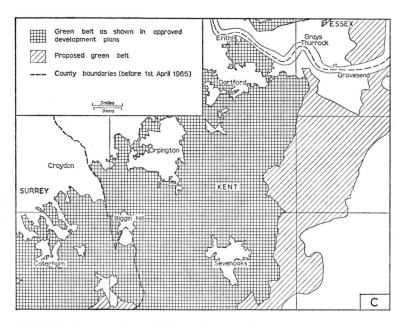

16c. London's approved green belt—south-east section
(Source: Ministry of Housing and Local Government)

land involved are smaller in extent, and are sometimes overseen by statutory bodies which are concerned specifically with amenity, recreation, research in the natural sciences, or timber production, but it is also because the purposes of the additional land-use controls and of the publicly owned land are often more clearly defined.

In order to estimate their potential, as well as actual, effectiveness in modifying the evolution of the green belt landscape it is necessary to study each of these groups of controls in turn. The area of study is defined in Figure 16a–d. It includes most of the green belt at present shown in approved development plans together with small sections of the outer parts of the London conurbation, more substantial portions of the extentions to the approved green belt, as they have been proposed by local authorities, and fragments of land beyond the outer limit of the proposed green belt. It stretches from Chesham in the north-west to the outskirts of Chelmsford in the north-east; from beyond Sevenoaks in the south-east almost to Aldershot in the south-west.

The figure is reproduced in quarters, each containing the area covered by ten 1 : 25,000 Ordnance Survey sheets. The 1 : 25,000 sheet boundaries, that is, the ten kilometre National Grid lines, have been inserted in this and subsequent maps in this chapter in order to assist the establishment of location. The area covered by the approved belt is also carried over to following maps. County boundaries are shown as they were up to April 1, 1965, the date from which the new administrative framework for the London conurbation came into effect. The designation and all but the most recent management of the green belt has been the responsibility of counties as they were, rather than as they are now, and it is therefore more realistic at the moment to view the green belt against the background of the old county boundaries.

One thing is very clear from Figure 16: that in one sense at least, the term 'green belt' is misleading. Far from being a girdle uniform in width and composition, the green belt has extremely involved boundaries, and also contains within it not only a wide range of rural uses of land, but also semi-urban and urban uses. It includes major industrial centres, such as Slough and Watford, dormitory settlements such as Caterham and Potters Bar, London County Council housing estates, such as Borehamwood and Romford, and it is fringed and indented by new towns, such as Basildon and Hatfield. It is not surprising that a senior officer of the Ministry of Housing and Local Government has described the green belt plus its proposed extensions as being more like a blanket full of moth-holes than a belt.

Land-use controls in the approved green belt

In comparison with the 846 square miles covered by the approved green belt most of the areas affected by each of the other land-use controls are modest. But when taken together the land to which they refer occupies a high proportion of the green belt. Of the land shown as approved green belt in the area adopted for study (Fig. 16) 30·1 per cent is taken up by these other land-use controls. That is, of the whole approved green belt, including those parts which do not fall within the study area, it may be estimated that a little over 250 square miles is subject not only to green belt restraints, but also to additional, statutory, landscape-preservation devices. There is some variation in the amount of this additional protection between the four quarters of the green belt (Fig. 17a–d). While 51·8 per cent of the approved green belt in the south-eastern part of the study area (c) is subject to these controls, 28·3 per cent of the north-western part (a), 22·8 per cent of the south-western part (d), and only 19·9 per cent of the north-eastern part (b) are given extra protection.

These figures, though reliable enough estimates of the extent of green belt land covered by the additional controls, by no means tell the whole story. Indeed, in two ways they may tend to mislead. First, as is clear from Figure 17, the areas subject to the controls overlap in many places. It is not uncommon for small tracts of land to be designated under two or three different statutory devices, and occasionally areas are protected by four. For example, the south-east corner of Great Wood, Northaw, a few miles to the north-east of Potters Bar, apart from being approved green belt, is protected under the Green Belt Act of 1938, it is an Area of Great Landscape Value, it is a Site of Special Scientific Interest and the trees are protected under a local authority Tree Preservation Order. Similarly parts of Ranmore Common, north-west of Dorking, lie within an Area of Outstanding Natural Beauty, are scheduled as being of Great Landscape Value, are of Special Scientific Interest and have their woodland cover protected. Secondly, it would be misleading to suppose from the figures quoted above that all the protective controls have similar effects. Not only is each designed to undertake a specific rôle, but those which are implemented by local authorities may also

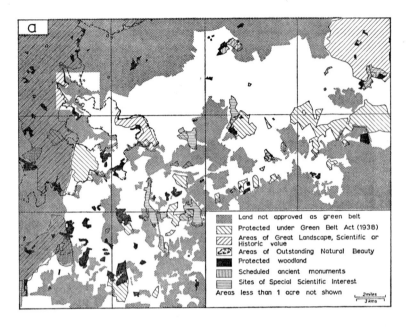

17a. Land–use controls in the green belt to the north-west of London
(Source: Ministry of Housing and Local Government)

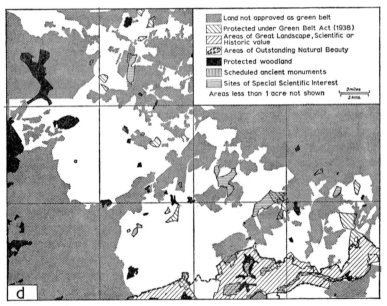

17d. Land–use controls in the green belt to the south-west of London
(Source: Ministry of Housing and Local Government)

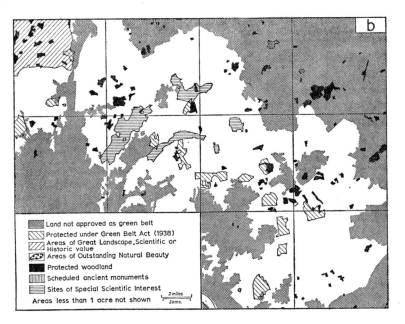

17b. Land–use controls in the green belt to the north-east of London
  (Source: Ministry of Housing and Local Government)

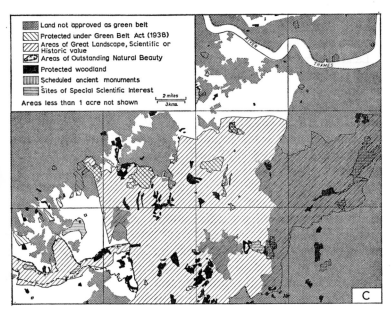

17c. Land–use controls in the green belt to the south-east of London
  (Source: Ministry of Housing and Local Government)

be applied with varying stringency, according to the attitude of the county or county borough council. It is plain that each land-use control must be examined separately to establish the mechanism by which it operates and also the precise nature of the protection which it gives to the land it covers.

The first of the methods of controlling land is one about which a good deal has already been written.[1] The Green Belt Act of 1938 confirmed a scheme already being operated by the London County Council, under which unbuilt-upon lands could be acquired, or become subject to an agreement between the local authority and the owner, so that they might be permanently protected against urban and industrial development. The Act forbade the sale or appropriation of any such land without the consent of the Minister and the contributing authorities, and also prohibited building, except where an equal area of suitable adjacent land, which could thereby substitute as green belt, could be provided in exhange. The Act also enforced any covenant entered into by private owners. Some of the land shown as protected under the Green Belt Act in Figure 17 is therefore owned outright by the local authorities in whose area it falls; some of it remains in private hands, though owners have agreed, mostly in return for a payment but occasionally without, to abide by the provisions of the Act. A little over a quarter of the land is laid out as open space with public access.

Land secured by the Green Belt Act gives protection to a large number of areas on the immediate fringe of London. Most of it lies within the approved green belt (Fig. 17). The single most extensive tract is that lying to the north of the conurbation in an east-west zone between Barnet and Potters Bar. It is composed of a number of separate purchases made before the Second World War by the Middlesex and Hertfordshire County Councils, with the assistance of the London County Council. It includes Enfield Chase, an area of nearly four square miles acquired from the Duchy of Lancaster, Dyrham, Wrotham and High Canons parks, also amounting to nearly four square miles, together with a number of smaller, but contiguous, areas. The securing of these areas played an important part immediately before and immediately after the war in preventing the merging of Barnet, Borehamwood, Enfield and Potters Bar. Apart from a small golf course, the land was, and has remained, largely agricultural, despite the pressures exerted by the Great

[1] *Supra* pp. 80–3.

104

North Road and two railway lines carrying heavy commuter traffic into London. Other large areas safeguarded under the Green Belt Act are found in Buckinghamshire, around Amersham where the Shardeloes and other estates provided two compact areas of farmland exceeding three square miles in extent, in Essex, where a number of substantial areas, composed of a mixture of agricultural and recreational land, are disposed in a semi-circular belt between Romford and Brentwood, in Kent, where the High Elms Estate provides one and a half square miles of public open space and farmland on the fringe of Orpington, and in Surrey, where the Banstead Woods and Downs occupy over a square mile.[1]

The second land-use control operates where Areas of Great Landscape, Scientific or Historic Value have been designated (the areas are sometimes referred to as 'V-land', following the notation used in development plan land-use maps). Local authorities were empowered to outline such areas in their development plans by regulations issued in 1948 under the Town and Country Planning Act of the previous year. The Minister of Town and Country Planning became aware that many local authorities were intending to propose substantial areas and so in 1951 he circulated some general recommendations on the definition of Areas of Great Landscape and other value.[2] As landscape value was so much a matter of opinion, and as the designation of such areas was bound to carry a restrictive connotation in respect of development, it seemed evident that the public were likely to take a highly critical interest in the size of the areas outlined and also in the nature of possible restrictions. The Minister therefore advised planning authorities to include as Areas of Great Landscape Value in their development plans only those tracts which seemed likely to command general acceptance among those interested, to explain in the written statement accompanying development plans what specific developments were likely to be rejected by them in each area, and to indicate what special attention should be given to the design and external appearance of those buildings which might be allowed. Where areas which possessed special value crossed the boundary between authorities, consultation was required to evolve a common policy of control. Sharp differences should not arise in the

---

[1] London County Council, *Green belt around London* (London, 1961), 18–34.
[2] Ministry of Town and Country Planning, *Reproduction of survey and development plan maps* (H.M.S.O., 1951), Circular No. 92, 2.

treatment of an area, the Minister stressed, merely because it fell within the jurisdiction of more than one authority.

These admonitions by the Minister seem to have had very little effect. When the development plans of the local authorities in England and Wales were submitted it was found that great areas of the country were covered.[1] But not only were Areas of Great Landscape and other value more widely distributed than any of the other special land-use controls, they were also the most widely misunderstood. They have consequently often been the subject of formal public enquiry, and even more often, of informal public debate. It has not escaped notice that the boundaries of the designated areas frequently coincide with administrative boundaries—it would be remarkable if so many tracts of special quality land actually terminated at the county line. Neither has it escaped the notice of developers that the nature of the restrictions upon building vary from one area to another. This is not altogether the fault of the local planning authorities concerned with development control. Though there is a general presumption in these areas against developments which harm attractive landscape or features of scientific or historic interest, the severity with which control should be applied has never been clearly defined.

As in the country generally, substantial areas of London's approved green belt were outlined as of great value. The grounds for designation, again as in the country generally, were based largely upon the landscape value of the countryside, in this instance particularly of the wooded areas and of the Chalk downlands. Only Middlesex, a largely built-over county, proposed no areas of value. As Figure 17 shows, in Buckinghamshire there are considerable Areas of Great Landscape Value on the back-slope of the Chiltern Hills, and in the woodland area south of Beaconsfield, but only small parts of these areas lie within the approved green belt. In Hertfordshire, the lower vale of Chess has been outlined and also the large area of Broxbourne Woods, stretching between Hatfield and Hoddesdon. Though small parts of northern and eastern Essex are designated, there is no Area of Great Landscape Value within the Essex approved green belt. In Kent, on the other hand, the notation has been very liberally used in the development plan, and almost all the green belt south of Dartford is covered. The North Downs clearly form the core of this area, but as well as occupying the crest and most of the back-slope to the north,

---

[1] D. Thomas, 'Statutory preservation of the countryside in England and Wales', *Zeitschrift für Wirtschaftsgeographie*, 6 (1962), 34–8. Figure 4.

it overlaps southwards over the Darent valley to cover the Greensand ridge south of Sevenoaks. In Surrey, where these physical features are continued westwards, it is only a limited zone along the crest of the Downs which has been outlined as an area of Great Landscape Value. No better example could be found of the inconsistencies which arise when national land-use policies are implemented by local authorities without co-ordination from above, or without extensive consultation and agreement with neighbouring authorities on matters of policy.

Areas of Outstanding Natural Beauty are designed to perform a rôle very similar to that of Areas of Great Landscape Value. However, in their origin, in their methods of designation, and, to some extent, in the way in which they are controlled, they differ, and consequently the effects which they have upon the landscape are not precisely the same.

Areas of Outstanding Natural Beauty are a product of the National Parks movement which culminated in the National Parks and Access to the Countryside Act of 1949.[1] The National Parks Commission, set up under the Act but recently replaced by the Countryside Commission, performed two main functions. First it was charged with the duty of encouraging or improving facilities for open-air recreation and study in National Parks. Secondly, it had the more general duty of guardian of the whole countryside, but with particular responsibility in National Parks and Areas of Outstanding Natural Beauty, which it designated. National Parks in England and Wales lie in the remoter, in the more sparsely populated, and, with one exception, in the higher parts of the country.[2] They nowhere overlap green belts, though around the Peak District National Park, the green belts of the cities of Huddersfield, Sheffield, Stoke-on-Trent, and Manchester abut the Park.[3] It is not necessary to pursue their administration and characteristics further. Areas of Outstanding Natural Beauty do occur within green belts, two of them overlapping London's approved green belt, and they therefore require further examination.

Areas of Outstanding Natural Beauty form the subject matter of

[1] 12, 13 and 14 Geo. VI, c. 97. See also H. M. Abrahams (ed.), *Britain's National Parks* (London, 1959); *National Parks and access to the countryside* (H.M.S.O., 1950).

[2] H. C. Darby, 'British National Parks', *The Advancement of Science*, 20 (1963–4), 307–18; 'National Parks in England and Wales', in H. Jarrett (ed.), *Comparisons in resource management* (Baltimore, 1961), 8–34.

[3] Thomas, op. cit., compare Figures 2 and 3.

Sections 87 and 88 of the 1949 Act. They are areas which, for some reason, failed to qualify as National Parks, but in which the National Parks Commission felt that special attention should be given to the preservation of attractive countryside. They were delimited in much the same way as the Parks, through consultation with the local authorities, and, like the Parks, their designation had to be confirmed by the Minister responsible for planning. In a sense they are lower order National Parks. But unlike the Parks, which are administered through a local park committee with one-third of its membership nominated by the planning Minister on the advice of the National Parks Commission, Areas of Outstanding Natural Beauty have no special arrangements for their administration. They are controlled by the county planning departments through the normal planning machinery. Planning authorities are obliged, in consultation with the Commission, to concentrate upon preserving landscape beauty, but they are not given the same wide powers for promoting facilities for enjoyment and study as the park planning committees.

The work of delimitation began in 1955 and, to the present, over a dozen areas have been approved by the Minister. Most of them contain far less unenclosed land than the Parks. Because there is less scope for recreational and amenity developments, and because financial support is less readily forthcoming, Areas of Outstanding Natural Beauty have had less dramatic effects than National Parks. They provide a measure of protection against unsightly development, but ultimately their impact on the landscape depends upon the interest and activity of the administering local authority. In one way they have operated more consistently than the Areas of Great Landscape Value. In preparing or altering the part of its development plan covering an Area of Outstanding Natural Beauty a county was obliged to consult the National Parks Commission. This has lead to a much greater uniformity of policy between areas controlled by different local authorities.

Parts of two Areas of Outstanding Natural Beauty occur within the study area (Fig. 17). In the north-west the relatively recently confirmed Chilterns area, covering 309 square miles in all, occupies considerable areas in the counties of Buckingham and Hertford. It stretches well into the approved green belt and assists in the containment of towns such as Chesham, Chorleywood, and Little Chalfont. Like the Buckinghamshire Area of Great Landscape Value it protects the back-slope of the Chiltern Hills, but its extension south-

108

wards and eastwards into the approved green belt,where it is tightly drawn around some of the rapidly expanding urban areas, seems to indicate that prevention of town growth on the vulnerable fringe of the Chilterns proper was also a factor in its design.[1] The second Area of Outstanding Natural Beauty lies to the south of London and covers 160 square miles of the Surrey Downs. The parts that lie within the study area are virtually co-incident with the county Area of Great Landscape Value. As Figure 17c shows, the Area of Outstanding Natural Beauty does not extend eastwards of the county boundary to cover the Kent Downs. Though an area, presumably much more limited in extent than the county's Area of Great Landscape Value, has been under consideration for some time, it has not yet been formally designated, let alone approved. With the exception of the area in the Chorleywood district, all Areas of Outstanding Natural Beauty on the periphery of London confirm and support the landscape conservation areas already outlined by county planning authorities.

It is possible for woodland to be more particularly protected than any other form of land-use. Trees can be preserved by two principal methods. The first is by the direct action of the local planning authority which, in the interests of amenity, may issue a Tree Preservation Order in respect of a woodland or of a single tree. When confirmed by the Minister responsible for planning, the order has the effect of preventing the felling or trimming of trees except with the consent of the planning authority. The order may also provide for the replanting of trees after felling. In some instances compensation may be payable by the local planning authority for losses caused by their refusal to allow felling and trimming to take place. The second method is by the Forestry Commission entering into a Forestry Dedication Covenant with the owner of woodland. In return for financial assistance the landowner undertakes to use the land only for the growing of timber, and in a way approved by the Forestry Commission. The covenant is generally binding upon future owners of the land, though it is possible under certain circumstances to withdraw from the agreement.

Though most of the areas of protected woodland within the approved green belt are smaller than the other conservation areas already discussed, their number compensates for their size. In Figure

[1] See also J. T. Coppock, 'The Chilterns as an Area of Outstanding Natural Beauty', *Journal of the Town Planning Institute*, 45 (1958-9), 137-41.

17 both types of protected woodland have been depicted by the same shading: the methods of designation are different, but the effects of the two systems in preserving woodland are broadly similar. To the north-west of London the major concentration of protected woodland is in an area around Chalfont St. Peter and Gerrards Cross. Here extensive tracts of Black Park and Chalfont Park are subject to control, while hardly smaller areas of Newland and Pollards parks are also conserved. To the north and east of London the Broxbourne Woods area is well-covered, while further concentrations of protected woodland are associated with Warlies Park, on the fringe of Epping Forest, and with Weald and Thorndon parks near Brentwood. South of London it is mainly the woodland of the Chalk and Greensand ridges which has attracted conservation measures. The only major exceptions lie in Windsor Great Park and upon the sandy land west of Bagshot, which are in large part devoted to woodland and which have been given protection.

It is clear that there are two main factors which have determined the present distribution of woodland in London's green belt. The first is physiographic. Areas which, because of the nature of their bedrock or soil, or because of their altitude or steepness, have proved unattractive to agriculture, and which have not subsequently been developed for urban or industrial purposes, are often occupied by woodland. Secondly, woodland was employed in the past as an integral part of landscape gardening,[1] and it is notable that so many of the areas of protected woodland are associated with landscaped grounds. As a result of its origins the distribution of woodland in the green belt is such that it supports green belt purposes only fortuitously, as on the fringes of Chalfont St. Peter or Orpington. Its major rôle in the green belt is scenic. It enhances areas of natural beauty and very often screens otherwise unsightly developments.

A minor land-use control which operates over very limited areas of the approved green belt is exercised by the Ministry of Works. This Ministry has powers to 'list' those monuments of archaelogical or historical interest which it deems necessary to preserve. No developments or alterations may take place in respect of scheduled ancient monuments without reference to the Ministry. To some extent there is an overlap of powers with the local authorities, which also may protect areas of great historic value. But the Ministry of

[1] J. T. Coppock and H. C. Prince (eds.), *Greater London* (London, 1964), 333–57.

LAND-USE CONTROLS IN THE APPROVED GREEN BELT

Works has possessed and used its authority over a much longer period, and hence has had the greater influence in controlling landscape development.

Small areas scheduled as ancient monuments exist in most parts of the green belt, both within towns and in the open countryside. They limit change over their restricted areas, but only one scheduled monument seems to have had a marked influence upon urban growth. The expansion of St. Albans westwards has been limited and moulded by the existence of the protected Roman remains of Verulamium, parts of which are also public open space.

Finally, there is a land-use control which conserves land of scientific interest. The Nature Conservancy is an official body created in March, 1949. The Royal Charter by which it was incorporated made clear its functions. It was to provide scientific advice on the conservation and control of the natural flora and fauna of Great Britain, it was to establish and manage nature reserves, which might include physical features of scientific interest, and lastly, it was to promote research upon nature conservation. When the National Parks and Access to the Countryside Act was passed later in the year the Nature Conservancy received further powers. Among these was the responsibility of notifying local planning authorities of areas which, because of their flora, fauna, geology, or geomorphology, were of particular interest. No major nature reserves occur within the approved green belt but designated Sites of Special Scientific Interest abound. Sites of Special Scientific Interest (sometimes known as 'Section 23 areas', after the relevant part of the 1949 Act) are given protection because local planning authorities must consult the Conservancy before allowing any development. They are areas which, had their claims been slightly stronger, might have become nature reserves, and from time to time some do.

As in the previous land-use control there is some overlap, at least in theory, between the areas designated by the Nature Conservancy and the areas outlined by local authorities as of great scientific value. In practice local planning authorities rarely seem to have proposed scientific conservation areas, and this is certainly true of London's green belt, judging by the lack of coincidence between Sites of Special Scientific Interest and Areas of Great Landscape, Scientific or Historic Value. Scientific interest, as defined by the Nature Conservancy, seems in London's green belt to be centred upon areas of woodland, and upon stretches of water together with the surrounding land. In the north-western portion of the approved green belt, for example, substantial parts of Burnham Beeches, Copse and Park Woods, near Northwood, Bricket Wood, and Great Wood, Northaw are now Sites of Special Scientific Interest, while areas in which features associated with water have attracted scientific attention are found at Water End, near Brookman's Park, at Elstree Reservoir, and in the gravel-worked parts of the Colne valley between Rickmansworth and Uxbridge (Fig. 17). Similar associations exist in the other sections of the green belt. In the north-east, Epping Forest and the woods between Epping and North Weald Bassett have been designated, together with two large portions of the Roding valley. To the south of the Thames it is mainly the woodland of the Downs which has been the subject of Nature Conservancy action, but sizeable areas have also been outlined on Ashted and Esher commons, and in the marshy areas of Staines Moor and the Wey valley, near Woking.

In November, 1967, the Countryside Bill was introduced into parliament. It contained three main provisions. First, it outlined the intention to set up a new Countryside Commission, with wide powers, to replace the National Parks Commission. Secondly, it suggested that new powers should be given to local authorities to acquire land and carry out works for the creation of such things as country parks, picnic places, and camping sites. And thirdly, it proposed that the law affecting footpaths, bridleways, and access to the countryside should be generally liberalized. Now that the Bill has become law, it is likely that the amount of recreation land in the green belt will eventually be greatly increased, and that the existing amenity land will be much more widely and rationally used.

All the land-use controls discussed so far in this chapter assist in achieving green belt aims as they are now broadly accepted, particularly in maintaining the greenness of the urban fringe land. They have all prevented urban and industrial expansion over the scattered areas to which they apply, but more important, they have added greatly to the visual amenity of the green belt and helped to preserve within it many features of historic and scientific interest. These are ends which the green belt itself is singularly ill-equipped to achieve unaided.

Land ownership in the approved green belt

Land ownership often acts rather more negatively than the controls already described as a factor modifying land usage within the green belt. Urban expansion depends upon the acquisition of sites on the fringes of towns and cities by private individuals or by large-scale developers. The land most readily available will be that which is privately owned, though in a number of instances, it is true, such as at Hatfield and Watford, the owners of large private estates have tenaciously resisted building. Publicly owned land, on the other hand, can frequently serve as a barrier against urban growth and, particularly where the owner is a local authority or a government department, may be used as an instrument of public policy.

Some of the land publicly owned in London's approved green belt is shown in Figure 18. The map, in a number of ways, underestimates the amount of such land. It does not show the large areas held by local authorities other than under the Green Belt Act of 1938. The Hertfordshire County Council, for example, owns a very extensive tract of land east and south of St. Albans, and upon which schools, an agricultural college, and five mental hospitals together with their related grounds and farmland are located.[1] The map does not show the land held by London University and its various schools and institutions, for example, the Royal Veterinary College farm and field station lying between Potters Bar and Brookman's Park, which plays such an important rôle in maintaining a strip of open county between the two settlements.[2] Neither does the map show other similar categories of public land upon which information is difficult or impossible to collect. Nevertheless the land shown in public ownership in Figure 18 amounts to 12·9 per cent of the approved green belt. That is, in the whole of the approved green belt, including those parts outside the study area, it may be estimated that very nearly 105 square miles of the 846 square miles are owned by public bodies as defined in the map key. Like the land-use controls there is some variation in the amount of this land between the four quarters of the green belt. While 19·9 per cent of the north-western part of the green belt is publicly owned (a), the figure for the south-west is 18·6 per cent (d), for the north-east 9·5 per cent (b), and for the south-east only 4·0 per cent (c). On the whole, the publicly owned land which it

[1] See Coppock and Prince (eds.), op. cit., Figure 68.
[2] Ibid. Figure 68.

H   113

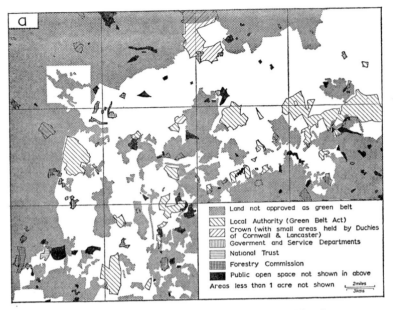

18a. Publicly owned land in the green belt to the north-west of London
(Source: Ministry of Housing and Local Government; London County
Council)

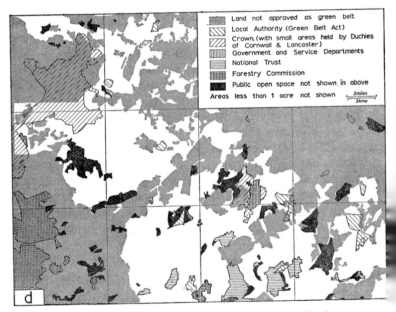

18d. Publicly owned land in the green belt to the south-west of London
(Source: Ministry of Housing and Local Government; London County
Council)

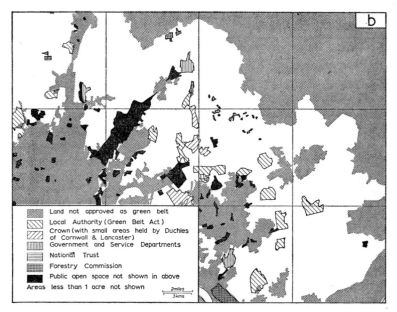

18b. Publicly owned land in the green belt to the north-east of London
(Source: Ministry of Housing and Local Government; London County
Council)

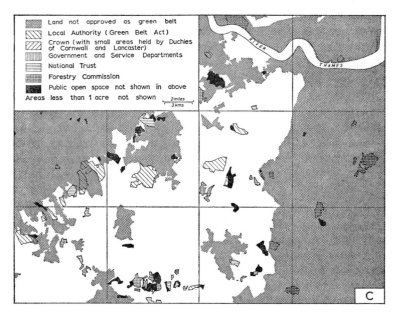

18c. Publicly owned land in the green belt to the south-east of London
(Source: Ministry of Housing and Local Government; London County
Council)

is possible to identify covers less ground in the green belt than the land-use controls, though as has been stressed, the areas shown in the figure probably greatly under-represent public holding.

The first category of public land, that secured under the Green Belt Act of 1938, has already been discussed. Not all of it is strictly publicly owned, as some is still in private hands though subject to covenants entered into with local authorities. In effect it is all controlled in accordance with public policy as defined in the Act, and constitutes an important instrument of land-use control within the green belt, both because of the firmness with which development is resisted and because of its extensive distribution.

The second category of land is that held by the Crown, to which, for the sake of simplifying the map, has been added small areas held by the Duchies of Cornwall and Lancaster. Unlike land subject to the Green Belt Act there is no firm presumption that Crown land will remain undeveloped, or that it must necessarily comply with national land-use policy, particularly as Crown land is exempt from normal planning control. But it is notable that almost all the Crown land lying within the green belt is completely rural in character, and that in a number of instances the existence of Crown land has either prevented the merging of adjacent towns or has given a clean edge to urban development which has impinged upon it. For example, Crown land forms an effective barrier between St. Albans and Hemel Hempstead, it limits the westward expansion of Collier Row, north Romford, and it maintains open land south of Esher. The largest single area of Crown land near London lies at Windsor. Much of this is outside the approved green belt, but sections of it support the green belt in limiting Ascot's growth on the north and west.

The effects of land belonging to government and service departments upon the green belt are rather more difficult to assess. The uses to which the land is put are extremely varied, many of them being activities which have overspilled from London, either seeking more extensive or better sites, or seeking safer locations during the last war. Few of the areas occupied are very large, but a number of them are most noticeable because they involve uses of land which are obviously inconsistent with a green and pleasant green belt. For example, the British Broadcasting Corporation has a large transmitting station at Brookman's Park, the Building Research Station is sited at Garston, north Watford, the Royal Air Force has a barracks at Uxbridge, there are army barracks at Caterham and Mill

116

Hill, and there is a government owned aerodrome at Hornchurch. Again, the largest area of all, the military training grounds around Camberley and Aldershot, lie outside the approved green belt, but within the present proposed extentions to it. A further problem is that most of these areas are outside the control and influence of the local authority planning departments which are, in the first instance, responsible for green belt planning decisions. In many ways the land belonging to government and service departments has detracted from, rather than supported, the effectiveness of the green belt.

The land owned by the National Trust is altogether different in character. With the exception of an area north of Burnham, all the National Trust property within the green belt is south of the Thames, most of it associated either with the Chalk or with the Greensand ridges of the North Downs and beyond. Some of the land is wooded, some includes, or is closely associated with, landscaped estates, while some is rough open space. The greatest concentration is upon the downland north of Dorking, almost all of which is open to the public and serves as public recreation land. Clearly National Trust land, both because it offers stiff resistance to development and because it contributes to the amenity and recreational diversity of the green belt, is a great asset on London's fringe.

Land owned outright by the Forestry Commission is not abundant in the London area. Some of that lying within the green belt is wooded Crown land which has been handed to the Commission for its care and continued use as woodland. For example the wooded areas of the Crown estates between St. Albans and Hemel Hempstead, and Prince's Coverts, south of Esher, are now in the hands of the Forestry Commission. Most of the remaining Commission holdings are either on the fringes of the Chiltern Hills or upon the North Downs.

Finally, there are the many areas shown in Figure 18 as public open space. Probably more than any of the other areas of publicly owned land, public open space has had a bearing upon the form of urban development. This is partly a result of its permanence and immunity to urban and industrial encroachment, but also of its position, often within, or on the immediate fringes of, urban areas. For example, Banstead Downs have trimmed the southward growth of Sutton, separated it from Banstead itself, and determined the line bounding both settlements. Cassiobury Park, private landscaped grounds which passed into public ownership between 1909 and 1930, has provided a green wedge penetrating to the centre of Watford. Hainault Forest, a very large public recreation ground, has effectively limited the further outward spread of the London County Council post-war out-county estate at Hainault. The most extensive areas of public open space lie first, in Essex, where Epping Forest, formerly a royal hunting preserve, provides a strip of public woodland about one mile wide and over five miles in length between Chingford and Epping, and secondly, upon the Chalk Downs and sandy Tertiary soils to the south of London. Here an irregular and discontinuous semicircle of generally quite large open spaces lie a little beyond the edge of London, stretching from Chobham Common in the west to Dartford Heath in the east. But public open spaces do more than mould urban development. They provide the bulk of the recreational land in the green belt and in this way contribute towards fulfilling one of its main functions, that of satisfying the outdoor recreational needs of London and its outliers. There is more open space available to the public generally than is indicated in the map. To that shown must be added the land secured under the Green Belt Act, over one quarter of which is open space with full public access, and the National Trust holdings, almost all of which are effectively public open space.

Unlike the land-use controls discussed in the earlier part of this chapter, the areas of publicly owned land do not always assist directly in the attainment of green belt aims. Some categories of public land are in opposition to present public policy and some, because of their siting, operate so negatively as to be ineffective. However, as has become clear, there are substantial areas of public land which support the green belt and which, together with the land, use controls already discussed, have added to its diversity and visual amenity. They are areas which have contributed sufficiently to the existing land-use pattern to be worthy of special note in any analysis of green belt landscape.

Part Three

THE EFFECTS OF LAND-USE CONTROL

5 · The Nature of the Approved Green Belt

The immediate future of London's green belt is far from clear. *The south east study 1961–1981* and its accompanying White Paper plainly indicated one line of development. *A strategy for the South East* has more recently outlined a quite different approach. The approved green belt, it seems certain, will be maintained without great change, though it will be recalled that local authorities have been asked to consider which limited areas, contributing little of value to the purpose of the belt, might be suitable for housing. In the course of time the approved green belt may be enlarged, but not, it is clear, by accepting in their present form those extensions provisionally agreed between the Ministry of Housing and Local Government and local authorities. At the present rate of development in the south-east the land allocated for building within the green belt extensions, is insufficient for long-term needs, and the areas themselves may be inappropriate if the proposed new urban forms are adopted.

While there is no certainty about the detailed adjustments to green belt boundaries, it seems likely that the effective green belt will undergo a change in both its shape and area over the next few years. Such changes must be based upon assessment of present land usage and landscape quality within the green belt and imply as much a knowledge of land-use trends as of current demands and needs. In the face of these impending alterations it is important to know what the present green belt is like, and, as far as possible, what recent changes have been taking place within it. The following chapter attempts to answer these questions.

The character of the green belt

Over a long period changes in land-use on the fringes of London have been modified or controlled. From 1935, under the London County

121

Council green belt programme and later under the Green Belt Act, considerable areas were reserved against development and much public open space created in the zone up to ten miles wide beyond the edge of built-up London. Since 1939 all developments in the same area have been restricted. During the Second World War and immediately afterwards all but essential building was prevented by shortage of materials and labour, then in 1947 the Town and Country Planning Act enabled local planning authorities to comply with Abercrombie's green belt proposals. From the middle 1950s green belt control has been in full operation.

Though the green belt is more open than it would now be if economic and social forces had been allowed to operate unhindered over the last thirty or more years, much of the green belt is still not green. The south-east (central London excepted) has long been subject to persistent population increases; agriculture and other rural activities have experienced great pressure from urban and industrial land uses, particularly on the fringe of London. Broadly three types of land use are found in the green belt. There are first the undesirable uses, many of which persist from before the time when planning permission was necessary and the green belt established, for example, housing, commerce, and manufacturing. Occasionally non-conforming uses have been introduced despite green belt control, though usually only where some special reason exists. Secondly, there are land uses which, though undesirable, are inevitable, for example, gravel digging, sewage plants, and water pumping stations. Thirdly, there are the approved uses, for example, agriculture, forestry, schools, hospitals, recreational space, and cemeteries.[1]

When studying the components of London's green belt it is necessary to distinguish between the land uses which occur in the areas shown as green belt in the approved development plans, and land usage in the general zone immediately beyond the outer edge of London, that is, in the green belt plus the excepted areas already shown in Figure 16. The first excludes, and the second includes, most of the major residential, commercial and industrial land. While it is of value to know the composition of the designated green belt, this presents a misleading picture of the zone fringing London unless set against an estimate including all land in that area. Brentwood, Leatherhead, and Watford, for example, are completely surrounded

---

[1] D. Thomas, 'London's green belt: the evolution of an idea', *Geographical Journal*, 129 (1963), 14–24. Figure 8.

by London's green belt, but are not covered in the development plan maps by the green belt notation. Towns such as Billericay, St. Albans, and Woking are excluded from the approved green belt by diverting its outer boundary inwards. These and many other urban and industrial areas exist in the green belt zone and they cannot be ignored or discounted.

There is another reason why land-use data for the green belt alone may tend to mislead. Local planning authorities, when they came to draw the boundaries of their county green belts did not all adopt the same methods, nor were they all inspired by the same motives. They were given overall guidance from the planning ministry, but in practice considerable inconsistencies appeared between authorities in the green belt maps which they produced, and which were eventually approved. It is instructive to compare the former county of Middlesex with Hertfordshire in respect of green belt designation. In Middlesex, isolated developments such as hospitals and water pumping stations are often excluded from the green belt in the development plan map, for example, Clare Hall Hospital, Potters Bar, and the pumping stations on Enfield Chase. Nearby in the Vale of St. Albans similar developments are shown wholly within the green belt in the Hertfordshire plan, for example, Shenley Hospital, and the pumping station at Water End. The small villages of Botany Bay and South Mimms in Middlesex are not scheduled as green belt; the larger villages of London Colney and Shenley, only a few miles away but in Hertfordshire, are so scheduled. The most striking example is the village of Elstree, which is astride the common county boundary. Middlesex Elstree is excluded from the green belt but Hertfordshire Elstree is within the belt. Any attempt at drawing a comparison between land use in Middlesex and Hertfordshire in the section of the green belt to the north of London from which the above examples have been drawn is inevitably in error unless supported by more broadly based evidence.

Clearly two sets of land-use data need to be studied. The first, relating to the approved green belt alone, while giving a true impression of what the belt as designated is composed, will be to some extent both unrealistic and inconsistent. The second, relating to all land fringing London, should give a more reasonable estimate of the uses of land, and therefore of the pressures likely to be exerted, in the green belt zone.

Measuring land usage

The use of land in London's green belt can best be derived from an analysis of vertical air photographs. For most areas the size of the approved green belt it would be necessary to piece together photographs from a number of overlapping flights undertaken at different dates to produce a complete covereage. Fortunately in June and October, 1959, on two clear and cloudless days, the Royal Aircraft Establishment, Farnborough, photographed the whole of the south-east of England on the 1: 90,000 scale.[1] By use of this air survey and with a ground check and revision, the land-use in the summer of 1960 of the areas of twenty-four 1:25,000 Ordnance Survey sheets

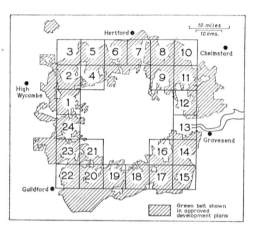

19.
The bounds of the twenty four 1: 25,000 Ordnance Survey sheets used in producing land-use statistics of London's green belt

in the green belt zone was recorded (Nos. 1–24 in Fig. 19). Eleven major land-use categories were employed, most of which were sub-divided in order to give a more precise picture of the activities which exist in the green belt. With a number of the categories it was possible, by comparing the results of the air and ground survey with published Ordnance Survey maps, to estimate the amount of land developed for that land use between 1955 and 1960. This is an important period over which to study developments of all kinds on the fringe of London because it represents broadly the first five years of green belt control following their approval in development plans,

---

[1] Royal Aircraft Establishment, Sortie Nos. D. 1312 (June 15, 1959), D. 1322 (October 6, 1959).

and also the five years following the Duncan Sandys definition of the purpose of a green belt.

The distribution of land uses among the eleven classes, and subdivisions of the classes, was determined from the 1 : 25,000 sheets by a sampling method relying upon systematic line traverses.[1] Line sampling is a technique which has hitherto been found well-suited to the production of land-use statistics. It seems to have been first used by Rosiwal in 1898 for petrographic analysis and later by Trefethen and the Tennessee Valley Authority for estimating the quantity and distribution of various types of land.[2] Osborne and Proudfoot, considering data very similar to those found in the green belt, outlined the procedures to be followed and also the likely error involved in line samples of different kinds.[3] Haggett has more recently shown how random line sampling is more accurate, though possibly a little slower, than random point or random block sampling methods when applied to studies of the woodland cover in the England-Wales border country.[4] In the study of green belt land-usage the distributions in the maps were sampled systematically rather than randomly, that is, the traverse lines were drawn parallel and equally spaced. Although the abandonment of randomness makes it impossible to calculate with accuracy the standard error of each sample, a systematic treatment ensures that every section of every map is adequately covered and that the highly clustered land-uses of the green belt are reasonably well represented. Past experience has indicated that random line sampling may be only one-half to one-fourth as efficient as systematic surveys of the same intensity.[5] The method adopted appears to be not only more practicable, but also much more accurate than any other available.

The experience of Trefethen and Proudfoot is important in deciding an efficient sampling design. They concluded that good results could

[1] W. Bunge, *Theoretical geography*, Lund Studies in Geography Series C, No. 1 (Lund, 1962), 97-100; S. Gregory, *Statistical methods and the geographer* (London, 1963), 94-5.

[2] A. Johannsen, *Manual of petrographic methods* (New York, 1918), 191-229; M. J. Proudfoot, 'Sampling with traverse lines', *Journal of the American Statistical Association*, 37 (1942), 265-70.

[3] J. G. Osborne, 'Sampling errors of systematic and random surveys of cover-type areas', *Journal of the American Statistical Association*, 37 (1942), 256-64; Proudfoot, op. cit.

[4] P. Haggett, 'Regional and local components in land-use sampling; a case study from the Brazilian Triangulo, *Erdkunde*, 17 (1963), 108-14.

[5] Osborne, op. cit., 264.

be obtained by line sampling when the total length of the traverse lines exceeded by 100 times the length of the average intercept of the field types traversed. For very limited land-uses it might be necessary to increase the ratio of total traverse to overall field intercept to rather more than 100 : 1. In order to ensure a highly representative sample ten north to south traverse lines have been used on each 1 : 25,000 sheet, the kilometre grid lines 0–9 being employed in each instance. Because of the fragmented land-use pattern around London this produced a ratio well in excess of 100 : 1.

Though no fully valid estimate of the sampling error of a systematic sample is possible, approximate estimates of the standard error of a line sample can be made in a number of ways. Following one of the methods, that proposed by Yates,[1] each line on a 1 : 25,000 survey sheet can be considered a separate stratum. The strata may be taken to contain pairs of successive land-use units. The error variance is then estimated from the successive differences between strata. Applying this method to the survey sheets it is possible to calculate an approximate value for the standard error, and hence assign confidence limits to the estimates for each land-use. In Table I 5 per cent limits have been calculated for the eleven major land-use categories shown in Ordnance Survey sheet TL 10 (St. Albans).

In the single sheet examined in Table I the standard error values for each land-use are relatively high and the confidence limits consequently widely spread. However, the same procedure can be adopted for all the survey sheets used in the green belt investigation, and, since the errors of the different maps are virtually independent, the standard error of the estimates for each land-use in the whole green belt can be taken as the square root of the sum of the squares of the standard errors for every sheet. In effect, the more sheets that are used in making estimations of green belt land usage, the smaller the standard error becomes in terms of the total area of land under examination, and the narrower is the range defined by the confidence limits. If the land-uses shown in the twenty-four sheets of Figure 19 are studied, then it is seen that, for example, category 10, which exhibited the largest standard error in Table I and which occupied 62·3 per cent of all land beyond the continuous inner edge of the green belt, has 5 per cent confidence limits of 61·3–63·3 per cent. Category 1, with the second largest standard error in Table I, has

[1] F. Yates, *Sampling methods for censuses and surveys* (3rd ed., London, 1960), 229–30, 232–3.

TABLE I

Estimates and 5 per cent confidence limits
for the areas of the major land-uses in Ordnance
Survey 1 : 25,000 sheet TL 10
(Per cent of map area)

Land-use category	Area occupied	5 per cent limits
1	16·35	11·53–21·17
2	0·56	0·00– 1·45
3	2·68	0·76– 4·60
4	5·35	3·01– 7·69
5	0·15	0·00– 0·37
6	2·60	0·51– 4·69
7	6·88	5·41– 8·35
8	0·43	0·00– 1·16
9	4·98	2·84– 7·13
10	59·73	52·52–66·94
11	0·30	0·00– 0·60

even narrower limits of 13·4–15·2 per cent, while the land-uses showing next greatest variance, categories 4 and 9, have limits of 1·6–2·6 per cent and 5·0–5·8 per cent respectively. At the other end of the scale the minor land-uses with very small standard errors in Table I, for example, category 5, when studied at the level of the whole green belt have 5 per cent confidence limits which are so narrow that they cannot be expressed in the first place of decimals. This result is completely consistent with the expectation that as any land-use approaches 50 per cent of the total land area the variance of the estimate increases; as a land-use approaches 0 per cent and 100 per cent the variance of the estimate decreases, being zero at 0 per cent and 100 per cent.

An investigation by Haggett confirms the accuracy of the sampling method.[1] Though Haggett was concerned only with random sampling techniques, as opposed to the systematic methods used here, his comparison of point, area and line samples with 'true' values reveals that, at all levels of sampling intensity, the mean error of the line sample is least, and at the higher sampling intensities, the mean error is extremely low. Using sixteen parallel lines, selected randomly, within a five kilometre square cell system, the mean error of sixty-four separate estimates was as low as 1·63 per cent. In terms of a given level of accuracy the line traverse method also proved to be quicker over the sample intensity ranges likely to be employed in practice. It is not surprising, therefore, in the present investigation into the land-use of Ordnance Survey 1 : 25,000 sheet TL 10 that ten line traverses selected systematically and with a ratio of total traverse length to average field intercept length of 288 : 1, have yielded such good results.

It could similarly be demonstrated that, despite the tendency of land-usage on the fringe of London to be aligned along main routes (in the selected survey sheet broadly north-west to south-east) the general assumption that traverse studies are most efficient when undertaken normal to the 'grain' does not seem in this instance to hold true. The land-use pattern is sufficiently broken and the equally-spaced traverse lines sufficiently selective to produce no significant differences between results whatever the alignment of sampling lines. This is fortunate because it means that sampling can, with confidence, be based on the north-south grid lines in all parts of the green belt.

The results of the sampling of the twenty-four 1 : 25,000 sheets shown in Figure 19 are presented in Tables II and III. In Table II the use of land in the approved green belt is distributed among the eleven categories, and subdivisions of those categories, while in Table III a similar distribution appears in which is included not only green belt land-use, but that of all other land lying within the selected Ordnance Survey sheets and beyond the continuous inner boundary of the green belt. Table II thus gives a picture of what the approved green belt, as designated, is composed in terms of the uses to which it is put by man; Table III gives an impression of the way in which

---

[1] Haggett, op. cit., 112-3. See also I. D. Read and A. T. A. Learmonth, *Applications of statistical sampling to geographical studies*, Occasional Papers No. 5, Department of Geography, Australian National University (Canberra, 1966), 3-6.

land is employed on the fringe of London irrespective of the notations which appear in the county development plans. During the air-photograph analysis, field work, and the compilation of statistics, it became evident that the balance between land-uses varied greatly from one part of the green belt to another. Consequently, in both tables, in an attempt to represent these differences, the percentage of land falling within every class, or sub-class, is shown for the whole area covered (sheets 1–24 in Fig. 19) and also separately for each quadrant of the green belt (N.W.–sheets 1–6, N.E.–sheets 7–12, S.E.–sheets 13–18, S.W.–sheets 19–24, in Fig. 19).

In any estimation of land-usage one problem invariably arises; that of the multiple use of land. It is one never easy to resolve. In London's green belt, because of the pressure upon land, probably more multiple use exists than is normal for the country as a whole. Woodland, for example, is sometimes used for recreation, playing fields are often grazed, and wet sand and gravel pits are frequently used for fishing and water sports, occasionally even before mineral working has finished. In such instances, where the use of land for more than one purpose is evident, areas falling into more than one category in Tables II and III have been apportioned equally between the different uses. There are, however, much less obvious multiple uses of land, such as the use of farmland and roadside spaces for weekend picnicking. These are transitory and irregular uses of land which no general survey is adequate to comprehend, and therefore they generally fail to be represented in the tables.

Green belt ingredients

The land-use categories shown in Tables II and III are a compromise. They represent a balance between what it is desirable to know about different types of land in the green belt, and what it is practical, given the techniques of data collection and analysis available, to discover about those different types of land. Broadly, the first five categories cover those uses which have already been characterized as being either undesirable, or inappropriate but inevitable, in a green belt as it is conceived by most people. Land devoted to dwellings, commerce, manufacturing and uses closely associated with those activities, such as the gardens of homes, or the yards and spaces surrounding factories, has been shown under the first two categories. Here, in green belt terms, are the clearly undesirable uses. In categories 3, 4 and 5 the

I   129

TABLE II

The use of land in London's approved green belt, 1960
(Per cent* of development plan green belt)

Land-use			N.W. (1–6)	N.E. (7–12)	S.E. (13–18)	S.W. (19–24)	Total (1–24)
1. Residential and Commercial	a. permanent	to 1955	6·3	3·7	5·7	7·9	5·9
		1955–60	0·4	0·3	0·3	0·3	0·3
	b. temporary		–	–	–	0·1	–
			6·7	4·0	6·0	8·3	6·2
2. Manufacturing		to 1955	0·3	0·1	0·3	0·2	0·2
		1955–60	–	–	–	0·1	–
			0·3	0·1	0·3	0·3	0·2
3. Extractive	a. sand and gravel		1·5	2·1	0·7	2·2	1·6
	b. chalk		–	–	0·5	0·4	0·2
	c. others		–	–	0·1	–	–
			1·5	2·1	1·3	2·6	1·8
4. Transport	a. road		1·2	0·4	0·6	0·6	0·7
	b. rail		0·4	0·2	0·5	0·5	0·4
	c. air		0·8	0·5	0·3	0·2	0·4
			2·4	1·1	1·4	1·3	1·5
5. Public Services	a. public utilities		0·2	0·1	–	1·4	0·4
	b. service and government		0·2	0·6	0·8	–	0·4
	c. cemeteries		–	0·1	0·1	0·1	0·1

6. Institutions standing in extensive grounds	a. schools, etc. to 1955	1.8	0.4	0.3	0.4	0.7
	1955–60	–	–	–	–	–
	b. hospitals	0.6	0.2	0.5	–	0.3
	c. others	–	0.1	0.1	0.1	0.1
		2.4	**0.7**	**0.9**	**0.5**	**1.1**
7. Woodland		**12.3**	**7.4**	**13.3**	**14.5**	**11.8**
8. Water		**1.1**	**0.1**	**0.7**	**0.8**	**0.6**
9. Recreational	a. playing fields	0.7	0.7	0.1	0.4	0.5
	b. golf courses	2.3	0.7	1.2	2.3	1.6
	c. race courses	–	–	–	0.3	0.1
	d. open spaces	2.7	4.0	3.1	5.6	3.9
	e. others	–	0.1	0.1	0.2	0.1
		5.7	**5.5**	**4.5**	**8.8**	**6.2**
10. Agricultural	a. grass and arable	65.3	76.8	66.6	60.6	67.5
	b. orchards	0.4	0.1	3.8	0.1	1.2
	c. nurseries	0.4	1.2	0.2	0.5	0.6
	d. allotment gardens	0.5	0.2	–	0.1	0.2
		66.6	**78.3**	**70.6**	**61.3**	**69.5**
11. Unused	a. cut over	0.3	–	0.1	–	0.1
	b. others	0.4	–	–	0.1	0.1
		0.7	**–**	**0.1**	**0.1**	**0.2**

* Percentages are rounded to one decimal place

(Based on O.S. 1 : 25,000 sheets TL 00, TL 10, TL 20, TL 30, TL 40, TL 50, TQ 05, TQ 06, TQ 07, TQ 08, TQ 09, TQ 15, TQ 16, TQ 19, TQ 25, TQ 35, TQ 45, TQ 46, TQ 49, TQ 55, TQ 56, TQ 57, TQ 58, TQ 59.)

TABLE III

The use of land in London's green belt zone, 1960

(Per cent* of area beyond continuous inner boundary of green belt)

Land-use			N.W. (1–6)	N.E. (7–12)	S.E. (13–18)	S.W. (19–24)	Total (1–24)
1. Residential and Commercial	a. permanent	to 1955	15·8	7·6	9·8	19·2	13·1
		1955–60	2·3	1·0	0·6	1·0	1·2
	b. temporary		–	–	–	0·1	–
			18·1	8·6	10·4	20·3	14·3
2. Manufacturing		to 1955	1·0	0·1	0·8	0·5	0·6
		1955–60	0·2	0·1	–	0·1	0·1
			1·2	0·2	0·8	0·6	0·7
3. Extractive	a. sand and gravel		1·1	1·8	0·9	1·6	1·3
	b. chalk		–	–	0·8	0·3	0·3
	c. others		–	–	0·1	–	–
			1·1	1·8	1·8	1·9	1·6
4. Transport	a. road		1·5	0·4	0·7	0·9	0·9
	b. rail		0·9	0·5	0·5	0·8	0·7
	c. air		1·0	0·4	0·2	0·2	0·5
			3·4	1·3	1·4	1·9	2·1
5. Public Services	a. public utilities		0·3	0·1	0·1	1·4	0·5
	b. service and government		0·5	1·2	0·6	0·3	0·6
	c. cemeteries		0·1	0·1	0·1	0·2	0·1
			0·9	1·4	0·8	1·9	1·2

	to 1955	1955-60		to 1955	1955-60
6. Institutions standing in extensive grounds					
a. schools, etc.	2·0	0·5	0·4	0·8	0·9
b. hospitals	0·1	0·1	0·1	—	0·1
c. others	0·5	0·3	0·4	0·1	0·3
	—	—	0·1	—	0·1
total	**2·6**	**0·9**	**1·0**	**0·9**	**1·4**
7. Woodland	**9·7**	**6·5**	**12·9**	**12·2**	**10·3**
8. Water	**0·9**	**0·1**	**0·4**	**0·7**	**0·5**
9. Recreational					
a. playing fields	0·7	0·6	0·2	0·5	0·5
b. golf courses	2·1	0·5	1·0	1·8	1·3
c. race courses	—	—	—	0·2	0·1
d. open spaces	2·9	3·3	2·6	4·8	3·4
e. others	0·1	0·1	0·1	0·2	0·1
total	**5·8**	**4·5**	**3·9**	**7·5**	**5·4**
10. Agricultural					
a. grass and arable	54·8	73·3	62·5	51·5	60·6
b. orchards	0·4	0·2	3·7	0·1	1·1
c. nurseries	0·1	1·0	0·2	0·4	0·4
d. allotment gardens	0·5	0·2	0·1	0·1	0·2
total	**55·8**	**74·7**	**66·5**	**52·1**	**62·3**
11. Unused					
a. cut over	0·2	—	0·1	—	0·1
b. others	0·3	—	—	0·1	0·1
total	**0·5**	**—**	**0·1**	**0·1**	**0·2**

* Percentages are rounded to one decimal place

(Based on O.S. 1 : 25,000 sheets TL 00, TL 10, TL 20, TL 30, TL 40, TL 50, TQ 05, TQ 06, TQ 07, TQ 08, TQ 09, TQ 15, TQ 16, TQ 19, TQ 25, TQ 35, TQ 45, TQ 46, TQ 49, TQ 55, TQ 56, TQ 57, TQ 58, TQ 59.)

undesirable uses are intermixed with activities which, though un-attractive in a green belt context, are difficult or impossible to locate elsewhere. Extractive industry is tied to its workable deposits, and, though some deposits, such as sand and gravel, are widespread, the economics of transportation often does not allow a location further removed from the markets in the conurbation. Much of the land devoted to transport must also necessarily occupy parts of the green belt if it is to serve the urban areas which the green belt encloses. Road and rail tracks, together with their ancilliary parks, stations, and depots, exist and are probably increasing within the green belt. On purely geometric grounds they must occupy a greater proportion of total land as they converge upon London. Civil airfields take large parts of the green belt already, and, with the lengthening of runways and the great expansion of air transport, it seems as if new airfield developments will take further sections of the green belt. Public services, too, because the population which they serve is so large, and because additional services are sometimes required to assist the functioning of London as a capital city, overspill into the green belt when available space within the urban area becomes fully used. Only cemeteries, of all the public service land, are fully accepted as a land-use which is appropriate for a rural area.[1]

The next five categories (6–10) shown in the tables are approved uses of land within a green belt. Institutions standing in extensive grounds form a category rarely found in land-use analysis. It is employed here simply because, cemeteries apart, it is the single major urban land-use allowed to develop in green belts. Schools, colleges, and hospitals make up the bulk of the institutions which appear in the category, but there are a large number of other institutions, less important in terms of the area which they cover, ranging from research units to convents. The woodland and water categories give an impression of the amount of amenity land in the green belt, particularly as the water category includes none of the water areas created by mineral working. Both currently operating quarries and pits, and disused workings not put to other use, are listed with the extractive industries. As recreational activity in the green belt is such a centre of interest a five-fold sub-division has been made of the land devoted to leisure pursuits. There seems less need to subdivide agricultural land. Though it is a major element in traditional green belt

[1] *Supra* p. 89.

philosophy, and though areally it is by far the most important ingredient of London's green belt, a detailed examination of variations in the proportion of grassland to arable, or in the composition of the arable area, along the lines of more generally applicable surveys,[1] is unnecessary in this investigation. The last category (11) is for land under no active use at the date of the survey.

Turning to the statistical distribution of land-uses among the categories, Table II reveals that, as had already been suggested by earlier, though less extensive, surveys,[2] when the approved green belt alone is considered, the picture which emerges is very satisfactory. Rural and open uses of land predominate. Residential and commercial activities occupy 6·2 per cent of the green belt, manufacturing 0·2 per cent, extractive industry 1·8 per cent, and land devoted to transport and the public services (cemeteries excluded) 2·3 per cent. Together the non-conforming activities, some of which are temporary and others inevitable, cover only 10·5 per cent of the approved green belt. There is as much land available for recreation as there is devoted to residential and commercial purposes, there is more open water than there is manufacturing industry, the amount of woodland exceeds the total amount of land taken up by all the undesirable activities, and dominating all other land-uses is agriculture, which occupies nearly 70 per cent of the approved green belt.

In those categories where recent changes in land-use can be measured, there is little which detracts from this favourable impression. Residential and commercial land expanded to occupy an additional 0·3 per cent of the green belt in the period 1955–60, manufacturing took insufficient land to enter into percentages rounded to the first decimal place, and schools, although an approved land-use, also occupied so little new land that the total does not appear in the table. It is true that in relation to the amount of such land in the green belt, the increment over the five year period is sizeable. For example, residential and commercial land increased by nearly 5 per cent and the area taken by manufacturing increased by over 17 per cent. But as all the quantities are so small these developments can hardly be regarded as significant of widespread encroachment upon the green belt.

[1] For example, see maps of Second Land Utilization Survey of Britain.
[2] D. Thomas, 'The green belt', in J. T. Coppock and H. C. Prince (eds.), *Greater London* (London, 1964), 300–6; 'The components of London's green belt', *Journal of the Town Planning Institute*, 50 (1964), 433–9.

The figures for the quadrants illustrate the extent to which land-use varies from place to place. But despite all variations, there is no sector in which the approved land-uses fail to dominate within the green belt. In the south-west, agriculture, though less prominent than elsewhere, still occupies over 60 per cent of the land, and it is supplemented by areas of recreational land (mostly golf courses and open spaces) which are well above the average. In the north-east, woodland is surprisingly sparse but this is compensated by the highest proportion of land under agriculture in all quadrants. A noticeable feature of the north-west is the area taken by schools and hospitals in the green belt. Of the non-conforming uses the south-west has more than its share of residential, commercial, and public utility land, while the north-west has much more than its share of land for transport, particularly of civil airfields. But perhaps the most remarkable aspect of Table II is the low proportion of land devoted to mineral working. In the south-east no more than 1·3 per cent of the green belt is used by the extractive industries, and at their maximum, in the south-west, they occupy only 2·6 per cent of the green belt.

Table III presents an estimate of land-uses in the zone up to ten miles wide beyond the outer edge of built-up London. It includes all land, whether green belt or not, which falls within the study area and which is beyond the continuous inner boundary of the green belt. The introduction of areas excluded from the green belt, many of them largely built-over, alters considerably the balance between land-uses. Residential and commercial land is now seen to occupy 14·3 per cent of the extra-metropolitan area, manufacturing 0·7 per cent, transport and public services (excluding cemeteries) 3·2 per cent. The figure for extractive working falls to 1·6 per cent as most of this activity is within the approved green belt. Together the non-conforming uses cover 19·8 per cent of the area, that is, very nearly one-fifth. It is a picture very different from that suggested by Table II. Of the approved green belt activities only institutions in extensive grounds appear more important in Table III, a result of the greater density of schools and hospitals within the built-up areas. The rest remain steady or decrease in importance, agriculture occupying 62·3 per cent of all land.

As might be expected, the changes in use, where they can be detected, are more marked in Table III than in Table II. Building upon land not designated green belt has proceeded vigorously in recent years. An additional 1·2 per cent of the extra-metropolitan area was developed for residential and commercial purposes in the period 1955–60, 0·1 per cent for manufacturing, and another 0·1 per cent for schools. These represent increases of over 9 per cent, over 16 per cent, and over 7 per cent respectively.

The most noticeable feature revealed by the data for the quadrants in Table III is the degree of urbanization to the north-west and south-west of London. In this part of the green belt zone residential, commercial, and industrial land occupies a fifth of the total area, and agriculture barely more than half. Associated with this development to the north-west and south-west of London other non-conforming uses, particularly those which fall under the transport category, are more prominent than elsewhere. In total the non-conforming uses in the north-west sector amount to 24·6 per cent of all land, and in the south-west to 26·4 per cent. Though in these areas the provision of recreational land is above average for the green belt zone it is clearly to the north-west and south-west that the green belt is least green. The north-east, with 74·7 per cent of its area devoted to agriculture and only 13·2 per cent to the non-conforming uses, and the south-east, with 66·5 per cent under agriculture and 15·1 per cent occupied by non-conforming uses, present a rather different picture and certainly a different problem. Whatever the aims of green belt policy might be, whether to prevent urban expansion or urban coalescence, to preserve agriculture, to reserve space for recreation, or to promote amenity, it is in the north-west and south-west of London's green belt that these ends will prove most difficult to achieve.

Land-use statistics compared

There are other methods of measuring land-usage and other means of determining the utilization of land. Having established the accuracy of the land-use survey adopted in this study and, in a broad way, discussed the land-use pattern which emerges, it is instructive to compare the results with those of another attempt to estimate land-uses within London's green belt, that made by the Standing Conference on London Regional Planning in 1964.[1]

Early in 1963, technical officers of the Ministry of Housing and Local Government approached individual members of the technical

[1] Standing Conference on London Regional Planning, *Agenda* (April 22, 1964), 9–10.

panel of the Standing Conference, that is, the chief planning officers of the constituent authorities, to seek their help in preparing a set of maps to show how land was used in the approved green belt. The purpose of the maps was said to be to enable the planning authorities to resist amendments to the green belt, and to ensure that if any boundary adjustments had to be made, these would be where least damage would result. The technical panel seems to have viewed these arguments cautiously. The White Paper, *London—Employment: housing: land*, had already suggested that areas of green belt would have to be built upon,[1] and after some discussion it was decided not to act upon the Ministry officials' requests. Instead, it was agreed that the Conference should make its own survey of green belt land-usage for the information of the authorities concerned.

The survey and analysis seems to have taken about a year to complete. It was confined to the green belt as it appeared in approved development plans and ignored the extensions which were currently being proposed. Land-usage was derived from the surveys which were undertaken between 1959 and 1963 in connection with development plan reviews. The information was plotted to a common notation on Ordnance Survey maps of the 1 : 25,000 scale, land-uses occupying less than five acres being ignored. Variations in the definition of land-use classes and variations in the practical application of those classes in the field as between local authorities gave rise to difficulties in producing the green belt map. These could not be wholly overcome and it was suggested that in future development plan surveys, standardized methods should be adopted. The land-uses were measured by planimeter and the resulting distribution among the classes tabulated for each county having a portion of the approved green belt, and also for the approved green belt as a whole. For presentation to the Standing Conference on London Regional Planning the acreages of each land-use category in each county were rounded to the nearest hundred. Acreages of less than fifty acres were not shown.

In Table IV a comparison is attempted between the land-use statistics produced by the Standing Conference and those shown earlier in this work in Tables II and III. Fortunately, the Standing Conference, like the present study, distinguished between land-usage in the approved green belt and that of all land beyond the outer edge

---

[1] *London—Employment: housing: land*, Cmnd. 1953 (H.M.S.O., 1963), 12-13; see also *supra* pp. 63-4.

TABLE IV

A comparison of land-use statistics produced by the Standing Conference on London Regional Planning (a) with those shown in Tables II and III (b)

Land-use category	Per cent of designated green belt		Per cent of all land		Categories in Tables II and III
	a	b	a	b	
1. Towns, villages and other land where surface development predominates	2·9	7·9	19·0	17·1	1 + 2 + 4a, b + 5a
2. Airfields, War Department land, reservoirs and water works, mineral workings, tips and other land of predominantly open character	5·0	3·2	4·1	3·2	3 + 4c + 5b + 8
3. Institutions in extensive grounds, cemeteries, playing fields, and other land-uses appropriate to the green belt	7·0	3·5	5·8	3·5	5c + 6 + 9a, b, c, e
4. Public open space	7·1	3·9	5·9	3·4	9d
5. Remainder, mainly agricultural and woodland	78·0	81·5	65·2	72·8	7 + 10 + 11

of London, but within the green belt zone. Despite this, the comparison is a difficult one to make because the land-use categories in each study are not directly comparable and cannot, even by grouping classes, be perfectly matched. However, an approximate correspondence can be achieved by combining suitable categories and subcategories in Tables II and III so that they equate broadly with the five land-use classes of the Standing Conference study. Given the inaccuracies of the method it would not be surprising if small discrepancies appeared between the two sets of statistics. But for statistics which refer to the same area, are of roughly the same date, and which have been compiled with some degree of rigour, the differences shown in Table IV, especially for land-usage within the approved green belt, are much greater than could have arisen by the method of comparison alone. It seems clear that both sets of figures are affected by the limits and restraints adopted, sometimes arbitrarily, during their compilation. The statistics can only be understood and interpreted against a background of knowledge about these conditions. A comparison of the compilation of the two sets of figures will therefore be pursued further.

To begin with, the areas covered by the two surveys are not identical. In this study the statistics were drawn from the area represented by twenty-four 1 : 25,000 Ordnance Survey sheets. Although these covered a substantial portion of the approved green belt certain small parts were not included, notably the outer sections of the Essex and Surrey green belts (Fig. 19). The Standing Conference survey, on the other hand, refers to the whole green belt. No great differences seem likely to have arisen from this lack of conformity as there is no reason to suppose that the areas of green belt omitted from the present survey are in any way unusual or atypical. The only possible exception is the Surrey green belt south-west of Dorking where the proportion of recreational open space is higher than average for the whole green belt.

Another aspect of the definition of study area, the green belt boundaries adopted, is likely to have been far more important a factor in producing differences in results. Both studies use the same outer boundary for the green belt, that shown in approved development plans. It is a relatively uncomplicated and easily traced line. The inner boundary, by contrast, is greatly involuted and many detached fragments of the green belt are completely surrounded by built-up land, particularly in the former county of Middlesex. In Table II, showing land-use in the approved green belt, all green belt land has been included, whether it is part of the continuous belt, or whether it is a detached portion. In Table III, showing the use to which all land is put in the area immediately outside London, the continuous inner edge of the green belt has been adopted as the boundary of the survey. Thus urban areas which are often thought of as being separate from the London conurbation and which are administratively quite distinct, such as Esher, Dartford, and Hoddesdon, are treated as part of continuously built-up London because they are joined to the conurbation by strips of development not scheduled as green belt. Similarly, other urban areas usually considered as part of the conurbation, but almost completely surrounded by green belt land, such as Enfield, Orpington, and Uxbridge, are also included with the main part of London in making the calculations. The logic behind this procedure is simply that the true London conurbation is composed of all those urban and industrial areas which have coalesced. Administrative boundaries, many of which were originally delineated when London was less than half its present size, should not be allowed to disguise the real extent of the continuously built-up land. The fringe of London in this study is what lies outside these areas. The inner green belt boundary adopted by the Standing Conference for both approved green belt and total area calculations is an arbitrary line approximating to, though by no means identical with, the inner boundary of the Green Belt Ring proposed in the *Greater London plan 1944.*[1] It is a line drawn rather tightly around London and leaving within the green belt study area many marginal towns which are today contiguous with London, including all those mentioned above. The different inner edges to the study areas can cause few discrepancies in the statistics on green belt land alone, because the fringe of London developments are almost all excluded from the green belt, but in the calculation of land-usage in the total area there is a large potential source of disagreement. Paradoxically, the percentage of all land under urban and other development shown by the Standing Conference survey is little larger than in the survey presented here (Table IV, category 1). This is because the large towns which lie on the outer edge of the green belt are excluded from the Standing Conference statistics, but included in Table III, because many of these towns fall within the 1 : 25,000 sheets which are the basis of the survey.

The discrepancy between the two percentage figures shown for urban and other development within the approved green belt (Table IV) points to another difference between the surveys. In the survey undertaken in support of this work every land-use parcel was measured, however small or large it might be. In the Standing Conference investigation land-use blocks of less than five acres in extent were discounted. As a good deal of the pre-green belt development on London's fringe was of scattered houses or cottages, and as local

[1] P. Abercrombie, *Greater London plan 1944* (H.M.S.O., 1945); see also Figure 12.

141

authorities have tended, in their drawing of green belt boundaries, to exclude the large urban blocks from the green belt, it seems as if the Standing Conference survey has missed much of this haphazard development. In addition, the areas of town maps in preparation, or submitted to the Minister of Housing and Local Government but not yet approved by him together with towns in Hertfordshire proposed to be excluded from the green belt zoning in the development plan review, have also been ignored in the green belt reckoning made by the Standing Conference. It is, perhaps, not surprising that their survey shows urban and industrial development in the green belt to occupy less than 3 per cent of the area.

A further source of discrepancy in the statistics is in the definition of land-usage. The difficulty of equating one land-use classification with another had already been stressed, but the problem is rather deeper. In preparing the statistics for this study a strict land-use categorization has been employed. That is, land has been allocated among the classes on the basis of the precise purpose for which that land was used at the date of the survey. The Standing Conference figures are based upon the areas shown in county development plan maps which do not always depict strictly land-use units. There is often an element of land ownership involved, particularly where the local authority is the landlord. For example, development plan maps show the areas of hospitals and schools. But often, not all the area outlined is used directly for the purpose of healing or teaching: frequently outlying areas, though administered from the institution, are devoted to agriculture. While it is possible that agricultural produce from this land may be consumed in the hospital or school, in terms of its use and appearance the land is agricultural. This difference in definition leads to the discrepancies shown in Table IV under categories 2 and 3. The differences shown under category 4 are almost wholly a result of the failure to match the two classifications.

The above comparison of the preparation of the two sets of statistics has brought to light once more a general point which is worth emphasizing. Land-use statistics, like any other quantitative data, are only as good as the techniques and methods used in their production, and are limited by the assumptions and restraints imposed in that process. It is only against a background knowledge of the accuracy and methods of preparation of the figures presented here that a more detailed examination of the land-use components of the green belt may be made in the following chapters.

6 · The Components of the Approved Green Belt—The Non-Conforming Uses

It has already been argued that the use of land in London's green belt falls into three broad groups. First, there are the plainly undesirable uses: land devoted to dwellings, commerce, manufacturing, and other areas of land closely associated with these uses, which detract from the greenness and visual amenity of the green belt. These activities are covered by categories 1 and 2 in Tables II and III. Secondly, there are those uses of land which, though undesirable because they give no support to green belt aims, are usually inevitable in the present state of planning organization and at the present level of social and technological development. The extractive, transport, and public service industries, with which most of these uses are connected, are covered by categories 3, 4 and 5 in Tables II and III. Thirdly, there are the approved uses: activities which do not require substantial buildings, or in which buildings form a small proportion of the total area occupied, so that land of a predominantly open character results. Schools, hospitals, woodland, water areas, recreation land, and agriculture clearly are important here, and these, together with the unused land, mainly cut-over woodland or grassland run to waste, are covered by categories 6 to 11 in Tables II and III. For the convenience of discussion the first two groups may be merged and considered as the non-conforming uses. The third group may be considered as the conforming uses.

Figures 20 and 21 represent cartographically the information shown in Tables II and III. They illustrate for both the approved green belt and for all land beyond the outer edge of the conurbation, but within the statistical frame, the distribution of land-uses by quadrants. To give emphasis to the maps, the portion of each non-quantitative divided circle in each quadrant occupied by the non-conforming uses is shaded. The maps highlight not only the great variation in the distribution of land-uses among the categories, but also the differences

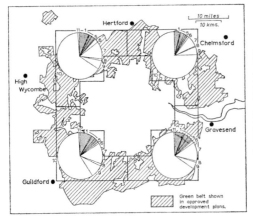

20.
The use of land in
London's approved green
belt, by quadrants, 1960.
The land-use categories
are those shown in Tables
II and III
(Source: Air photograph
and field survey)

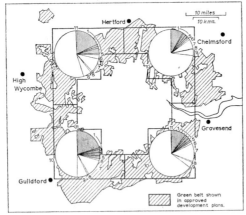

21.
The use of land in
London's green belt zone
beyond the continuous
inner boundary of the
green belt, by quadrants,
1960. The land-use
categories are those shown
in Tables II and III
(Source: Air photograph
and field survey)

which exist between quadrants and the differing results which stem
from the two separate methods of calculation. The Figures indicate
the land-use position in 1960. To understand the differences revealed
it is necessary to study the trends and underlying causes of the growth
of each use of land more closely. Each of the eleven land-use categories already adopted will thus be examined in turn. The non-
conforming uses are treated in this chapter, while a discussion of the
conforming uses is reserved for the following chapter.

Residential and commercial land (category 1)

From Figures 20 and 21 it is plain that housing and commerce hold by far the most important position as non-conforming occupiers of land in the green belt. Of the green belt as approved in development plans over 6 per cent is taken by these uses, and for the whole extra-metropolitan area covered by the statistical study, the figure exceeds 14 per cent. To the north-west and south-west of London, residential and commercial developments occupy about one-fifth of all land. Over the period 1955–60 the acreage of housing and commercial land increased by a little under 5 per cent in the approved green belt, and by a little over 9 per cent when all land is taken into account.

Fringing the conurbation and corresponding roughly with the area of the green belt there lies a zone of what is obviously semi-urbanized land. Pahl has recently described this fringe as 'urbs in rure', because not only is it substantially built-upon with settlements of all sizes, but it also has a population which is, or is rapidly becoming, oriented to urban ways of thought and living.[1] It is a zone in which urban development ranges from large industrial settlement, such as Slough and Watford, with populations of 75,000 or more, through smaller, largely dormitory settlements, such as Dorking, Gerrards Cross, and Potters Bar, to small villages and groups of houses scattered seemingly haphazardly in the countryside. The urban areas are now separated by the green belt, but in other circumstances they might well have acted as major growing points for the further expansion of the London conurbation, as did settlements such as Bromley, Enfield, Harrow, and Hounslow in the period between the wars.[2] Even so, it is clear from the statistics already cited that urban growth in the green belt is not eliminated. An increase in residential and commercial land of over 9 per cent in five years is considerable. While much of this was not upon land shown as green belt in county development plans, but was the result of development infilling spaces or replacing older buildings in existing towns, there is reason to suggest that the figure is very much less than the concomitant growth in population. The new developments were generally at a density far higher than is

[1] R. E. Pahl, *Urbs in rure*, London School of Economics and Political Science Geographical Papers No. 2 (London, 1965).
[2] See J. H. Johnson, 'The suburban expansion of housing in London 1918–39', in J. T. Coppock and H. C. Prince (eds.), *Greater London* (London, 1964), 142–66.

average in the green belt, and whether they were upon previously unoccupied spaces or upon redeveloped land, they contributed to the general intensification of land occupancy.

The Census figures for population changes in the Inner Country Ring of the Outer Metropolitan Region, as currently defined by the Ministry of Housing and Local Government, are interesting in this context.[1] The Inner Country Ring covers roughly the same area as the approved green belt, though it excludes all those areas which lay within Middlesex, and includes all the new towns around London. It does, in fact, correspond reasonably closely with the area used in compiling the statistics in this study. In 1951 the Inner Country Ring contained 10 per cent of the population of the south-east England study area (see Fig. 5). By 1961 the share of the Inner Country Ring had risen to 13·1 per cent, that is, an increase in population of 659,000, which represents a change of 39·7 per cent. Over three-quarters of the additional population of the Inner Country Ring was contributed by migration into the area. Over the same period the population of the London conurbation fell by 2·3 per cent while the population of the Outer Country Ring rose by 20·0 per cent, and that of the remaining outlying parts of the south-east England study area rose by 9·6 per cent. Population growth, and therefore the demand for residential and commercial land, has been greater in recent years in the green belt area than anywhere else in south-east England and has far outstripped growth elsewhere in the county. It should be remembered, of course, that more than one-third of this population increase has been in the new towns.

In order to study the components of the green belt in greater detail it is necessary to look more closely at land-use distribution. So far, discussion has been confined to a general consideration of the whole green belt area, or to the differences between the quadrants. To understand the complicated interaction of the various land-uses it is desirable to make an examination on a plot to plot basis. A manageable area for study is a quadrant of the green belt. The diversity within the London green belt is such that no single quadrant could be truly typical of the whole, a fact which Figures 20 and 21 have already amply illustrated. The north-western fringe of London, however, seems to contain all the major land-use elements and to exemplify all the major current trends, though not necessarily in

[1] Ministry of Housing and Local Government, *The south east study 1961–1981* (H.M.S.O., 1964) 121, 124.

precise proportion to their occurrence or importance throughout the whole belt.

The north-west quadrant is conveniently represented by the areas of ten 1 : 25,000 Ordnance Survey sheets[1] which provide a standard frame for the study of all land-uses. They cover an area stretching from Barnet, Edgware, Harrow Weald, and Ruislip in the north-western part of the conurbation through development plan green belt to provisional green belt and beyond. It is, in fact, the same area

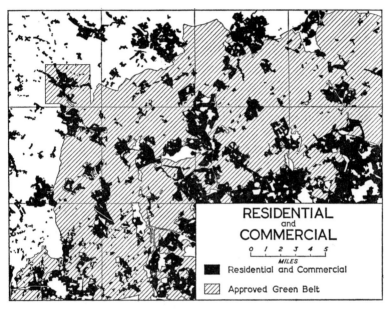

RESIDENTIAL
and
COMMERCIAL

```
0   1   2   3   4   5
        MILES
```

■ Residential and Commercial

▨ Approved Green Belt

22. **Land used for residential and commercial purposes in the green belt to the north-west of London, 1960**
(Source: Air photograph and field survey)

as that shown in the maps of the north-west section of the study area in Chapter 4 (Fig. 16a), where controls over land other than green belt were treated. Details of land-usage were derived, as before, from air photograph and field survey.

Figure 22 reveals the detailed distribution of residential and commercial land to the north-west of London against the background of the approved green belt. The semi-urbanized nature of the metropolitan fringe is immediately apparent. There are represented on the

[1] SP 90, SU 98, SU 99, TL 00, TL 10, TL 20, TQ 08, TQ 09, TQ 19, TQ 29.

map most of the major types of development. Of the sizeable urban agglomerations which appear in the green belt St. Albans and Watford may be taken as examples of old-established towns which have grown as a result of their commercial or industrial importance, though, of course, their proximity to London has been an important factor in their development. Towns such as Radlett and Rickmansworth are dormitory settlements, whose function is mainly to provide accommodation and services for workers travelling daily into the London conurbation and for their families, who usually remain behind. Other large settlements are London County Council housing estates, such as Borehamwood and Oxhey, which have grown as a result of planned population overspill from the former County of London during the inter-war and in the immediate post-war period, while a more recent stage of overspill planning is represented by the new towns, for example Hatfield and Hemel Hempstead. There are also a great number of smaller settlements, many of them too small to have been excluded from the green belt when it was first designated and therefore contributing substantially towards the 6 per cent of the approved green belt now covered by residential and commercial development (compare Fig. 16a).

The settlements vary greatly in character, but the differences are ones of degree, rather than of an absolute distinction of function. All settlements act as dormitories for those working elsewhere and almost all contribute daily to the workforce of the London conurbation. All but the smallest settlements provide goods and services for their own population and for those dwelling in neighbouring settlements. Therefore all but the smallest settlements are, to some degree, centres of employment. Most of the larger settlements also contain manufacturing industry. It is not surprising that as so many urban areas combine, albeit in different proportions, the functions of dormitory settlements, service centres and industrial towns, their orientation towards communication links is so marked. The processes of suburban growth described in Chapter 1,[1] of the accretion of settlement around railway stations and of the spread of settlement along main roads, operated with equal force in the extrametropolitan area and produced the very characteristic pattern of the present-day urban distribution. Its association with the main road and rail links to central London, which are also the main links with the north and west of the country, is so close that it is virtually

[1] *Supra* pp. 23–5.

possible to sketch the main transport lines into the settlement map without reference to a map of roads and railways.

Economic linkage is clearly an important factor in determining the growth and distribution of settlement on the metropolitan fringe. Manufactured articles must move freely to their markets, goods and services must be provided for what is a relatively affluent population, and journeys to work, some of them quite long, must be convenient and swift. But social linkage is also an important factor in associating urban areas with lines of communication. From its very nature the population of the green belt area is a mobile one. In a study of the growth of population and industry in Hertfordshire, Hooson has pointed out that only 40 per cent of the inhabitants of that county in 1951 had been born within its boundaries.[1] Over one-third of the migrants had originated in London and Middlesex and over one-fifth had come from other counties in south-east England. The bulk of the migrants settled in the southern part of the county. Hooson estimates that in the seven years before the Second World War, a period of rapid growth, 80 per cent of the county's immigrants came to that part of the area lying south of a line from Berkhamstead to Welwyn Garden City, that is, into what is now Hertfordshire approved green belt. Since the war it is this same general area which has experienced greatest gains by migration (see Fig. 2). Such a population not only has ties with family and friends in and near the conurbation, but it is also one accustomed to the services and entertainments of the central area of London, and financially able to enjoy its benefits. Road and rail communications form an important part of the life of these communities.

It is not surprising, given the population trends of the pre-green belt period and the fact that three of London's eight new towns lie to the north-west of the conurbation, that, despite green-belt control urban uses of land in the area covered by the survey maps have continued to expand. Neither is it unexpected that this new development should seek to follow the same patterns as before. In Figure 23 an attempt is made to show the scale and location of recent development to the north-west of London. The map shows, for the period 1955–60, the land occupied by fresh buildings and their immediately adjacent grounds under those land-use categories for which changes can be

[1] D. J. M. Hooson, 'The recent growth of population and industry in Hertford-shire', *Institute of British Geographers, Transactions and Papers*, 25 (1958), 197–208.

identified. As can be seen by reference to Tables II and III it shows new residential and commercial development, new manufacturing plant, and new schools and colleges. Of these, the Tables also show that residential and commercial expansion is by far the most important and must occupy most of the areas shown in Figure 23.

Despite the apparent scatter of recent developments closer examination of the map reveals the influence of planning and green belt control. While all the large urban centres such as Borehamwood,

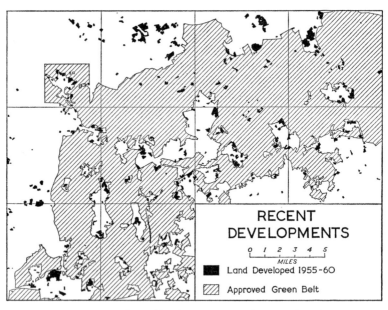

RECENT
DEVELOPMENTS

0 1 2 3 4 5
MILES

■ Land Developed 1955-60

▨ Approved Green Belt

23. Recent developments for residential and commercial, manufacturing, and institutional uses in the green belt to the north-west of London, 1955-60 (Source: Air photograph and field survey)

Gerrards Cross, Rickmansworth, and Watford, have grown considerably, their growth has been circumscribed. It has occurred either within the towns, where waste or open land has been developed, or on their immediate peripheries, where land left between the edge of the town and the surrounding green belt has since been converted to urban use. Such 'white' land developments have been commonplace within the green belt and in many towns, for example, Bushey, to the east of Watford, and in Potters Bar, almost all the peripheral land not scheduled as green belt has now

150

been built over. Beyond the outer edge of the approved green belt old-established towns, like St. Albans, have expanded greatly and the large 'white' areas left in the new towns of Hatfield and Hemel Hempstead have been substantially developed.

Building within the green belt proper has affected far smaller areas. This is exactly as expected, because, with the exception of school or college building, which may be allowed, there is a clear presumption against residential, commercial, or industrial expansion, particularly where it might create pressure for further building. Though the developments appear to be scattered and detached on the map, in fact no isolated building has been allowed. All recent development has been designed to 'infill' or 'round-off' existing settlements in the green belt. For example, the large villages of Bricketwood and Radlett, to the north-west of Watford, have large additions within the body of the built-up area and also on their peripheries, where the outer edges of the settlements have been smoothed. In other villages, land lying between the existing edge of the settlement and a line of communication has been developed. For example, in Brookman's Park a tract of land alongside a main railway line has been built over, while in London Colney areas of land between the village and a new by-pass road have been developed. Though 'infilling' and 'rounding-off' are elastic terms, great care has clearly been taken by the local authority planners in the area illustrated on the map to ensure that no development contributes greatly towards the merging of adjacent settlements. Sporadic developments and low density building, so characteristic of this area in the inter-war period, seems to have been vigorously excluded, while the large, established settlements have been consolidated.

Some further light is thrown upon residential and commercial developments in the green belt by a policy statement issued by the Hertfordshire County Council in 1960.[1] The Council accepted that the purpose of the Hertfordshire sector of the green belt was to preserve a stretch of mainly open country as near as possible to London to act as a barrier against further outward spread of building development and to prevent the merging of existing settlements. In order to achieve these aims the Council believed it essential to retain and protect the rural character of the area by implementing green belt policy strictly. The growth of existing settlements was to be severely restricted and new building was to be permitted outside such

[1] Hertfordshire County Council, *Building in the green belt* (Hertford, 1961).

settlements only in the most exceptional circumstance, unless required for agricultural or allied purposes. The detailed operation of the policy was based largely upon the views expressed in a letter sent by the Ministry of Housing and Local Government to the Clerks of the Councils of the Home Counties in March, 1959. In the letter the Minister did not favour the proposal of some county councils that natural increases in population and other future expansions should be accommodated upon 'white' land which would surround the development areas of towns and villages shown in development plans, and lie between the land zoned for building and the green belt. Such 'white' areas were inappropriate within the green belt and it would not be justifiable to agree to the reservation of land for so general and unspecified future demands. It was the Minister's view that villages and hamlets wholly within the green belt, and which were not covered by town maps, really fell into one of two categories. Either they were not distinguished from the 'green background' in development plans, in which case green belt policy should be strictly applied and no building should be allowed except for that usually acceptable in green belts, or they might be distinguished from their 'green background' by being listed in the development plan written statement, in which case the strict green belt policy might be modified to the extent set out in the approved development plans, that is, 'infilling' or 'rounding-off' might be permitted.

Accordingly, the Hertforshire County Council evolved a threefold classification of green belt settlements. Each type was to be differentiated in the development plan when it was next reviewed, and in each the allowable developments were to be clearly defined. The first category included small towns and certain of the large villages. These were to be excluded altogether from the green belt since many of them were in no way related to agriculture or strictly rural requirements. They were due mainly to inter-war suburban growth and their planning problems were much more akin to those of the town map areas. In due course a perimeter line for each was to be defined on a map and, consistent with the views of the Minister, it would closely encircle the existing limits of buildings so that little expansion could take place into the green belt. Within the settlement as delimited in the map infilling or redevelopment would be permitted in accordance with normal planning practice, but the boundary line would be firmly held. Since Hertfordshire, unlike its neighbour Middlesex, had in its first development plan excluded from the green belt only major urban areas, such as Borehamwood, Rickmansworth, and Watford,[1] it would be necessary in the development plan review to redraw the green belt map.[2] Little change was envisaged on the inner limit of the green belt, but new internal boundaries would appear and town maps would be prepared to cover these 'excluded' villages, some of which, like Brookman's Park, London Colney, and Radlett, were quite large. In the proposed extensions to the approved green belt identical methods would be adopted.

The second category was that of 'listed' villages. Generally they would be large villages, but not sufficiently large to warrant their exclusion from the green belt. Though in the green belt map they would be ruled over by the standard notation, they would be distinguished from the general run of green belt villages by their appearance in a list included in the development plan written statement. It was proposed that a certain amount of 'infilling' might take place, provided that it occurred in the central core of the settlement and not in ribbons of development spreading out along roads from the village. In most instances sites to be developed would be reserved to meet essential local needs, including council housing needs. Great attention was to be paid to the preservation and enhancement of the character of the village and therefore only genuine 'infilling' on suitable sites would be approved. The fragmentation of gardens, or the demolition of old houses of character in order to develop their sites at higher density, would not normally accord with the county council's policy.

Villages in the third category would be shown in the development plan maps as wholly within the green belt, but no exceptions would be entered in the written statement to the strict application of green belt control. Building, or change of use of buildings, would not normally be allowed other than for purely green belt purposes. The council took the view that essential development might include not only dwellings for agricultural workers, but also the provision of accommodation for others, such as a village policeman or school-teacher, whose presence was essential to the local village community and for whom no suitable existing housing was available. In order to simplify control in such settlements and in the green belt generally a clear instruction was given to district council officials upon how they should deal with applications for permission to develop. They

[1] *Supra* p. 123.
[2] *Infra* pp. 217–18.

should first satisfy themselves that an applicant met the essential requirements laid down by the council. He should be able to show that he was unable to find suitable accommodation in an existing building. He should also be able to show either that refusal to allow development would injure the local rural community, local agriculture, or some other essential local interest, because the applicant was employed in the village or in the district for which it formed the logical centre, or alternatively that there was some quite outstanding reason why the district council should recommend that the application for a new house in the green belt be considered. The onus of proving conclusively that the proposal should be treated as an exception to the normal policy of refusing permission for development within the green belt was upon the applicant. Only when these essential points were satisfied should the district officials forward the application to the county council's divisional planning officer for a recommendation. If the points were not met then the district council officials were empowered to reject an application outright, without consulting the county's divisional planning officer.

The policy statement was issued in 1960, and has strongly influenced decisions upon developments in the Hertfordshire green belt since that date. However, the document was no more than a formalization of methods, attitudes, and opinions already strongly held. It therefore does much to explain the pattern of recent developments shown in Figure 23, which occurred in the five years preceding 1960.

A rather different approach to the study of land-use arrangements within the green belt is to examine the variations in the occurrence of particular uses and activities with distance from the edge of the metropolis. The approach has interest on two different planes. First, it is closely linked with a set of ideas, originally outlined by von Thünen in 1826,[1] which have now come to occupy much of the attention of land-use theorists. The notion that distance from a market, or central place, may influence economic and other activities and hence the uses of land which result from those activities, is now widely held, and forms the basis of central place theory. This theme has recently been employed very effectively by Chisholm in the analysis of purely rural settlement and land-use, where distance is shown to be an important variable on a quite small, as well as on a

[1] J. H. von Thünen, *Der isolierte Staat* (Rostock, 1826). See also P. Hall (ed.) *Von Thünen's isolated state* (Oxford, 1966).

larger, scale.[1] But London is large and its influence is powerful, while the green belt is relatively narrow and in addition its land-use is complicated by heavy urban and suburban development. It is unlikely that a study of land-use differences with distance from London will contribute much to the testing of such theories. It is at the second, more practical, level that greatest interest lies. Any planning decisions about the future arrangement of green belt land-use must be made on the basis of what exists at the moment and upon an estimate of how flexible, in terms of location, different uses are. Therefore in looking at the green belt as a whole it is important to

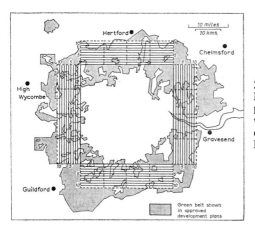

24.
Line samples used in producing statistics of variations in land-use with distance from built-up London

know which of the land-uses cluster around the immediate metropolitan fringe, which are further out, and which are evenly spread through the belt.

In order to study the variation of land-usage with distance from built-up London, sixteen of the 1 : 25,000 Ordnance Survey sheets used in the earlier calculation of land-use were employed.[2] These are so disposed that four sheets cover each of the northern, southern, eastern and western sections of the green belt (Fig. 24). Within every sheet the data were resorted so that line samples were produced as far as possible normal to the outward spread of activities from London. Line one, which represented the one kilometre distance, was composed of a boundary line in each sheet, that nearest to central

[1] M. Chisholm, *Rural settlement and land-use* (London, 1962).
[2] Nos. 1, 2, 5–8, 11–14, 17–20, 23, 24, in Figure 19.

London. Line two, the two kilometre line, lay one kilometre further away, and so on through to the ten kilometre line, which lay one kilometre from the edge of the sheet furthest away from central London. The lines one to ten thus represent the land-use pattern at distances increasing by one kilometre from the inner to the outer edge of the approved green belt. The kilometric distances themselves are very approximate. As can be seen in Figure 24, the complexity of the outer edge of London is such that line one only roughly corresponds with the inner edge of the green belt. But despite its deficiencies the method is the simplest and most practical means of estimating land-use differences with distance away from London.

In Figure 25, showing variations in residential and commercial land with distance from London, two curves are shown. The one

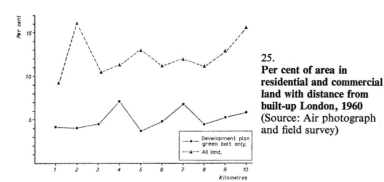

25.
Per cent of area in residential and commercial land with distance from built-up London, 1960 (Source: Air photograph and field survey)

represents differences within the area designated as development plan green belt, the other shows differences in all land beyond the continuous inner boundary of the green belt. As with all green belt statistics, those relating to development plan green belt alone are to some extent a product of local authority draughtmanship and, since all planning offices excluded large urban areas from their green belts, no matter at what distance from the edge of London, it is not surprising first, that the values are low, and secondly, that they are erratic, bearing little relationship to the overall distribution of such land through the green belt. For this reason the variations in all commercial and residential land expressed as a percentage of all land are more revealing. There is a very pronounced 'peak' of settlement at the two kilometre distance, that is, only a little beyond the edge of London, and a distinct hint of intensifying development towards the outer edge of the approved green belt. The pattern which emerges in an idealized transect of the green belt is of a fairly clean edge to built-up London followed by a narrow settlement-free zone. Beyond this lies a band of dense settlement, perhaps commuters' towns and villages which, but for the green belt, might have already become part of the London conurbation. Through the remainder of the green belt there is a fair scatter of settlement but as the outer edge is approached the amount increases to match the peak of the inner zone. This outer fringe of settlement is composed of rapidly growing towns and villages, including new towns, which have been forced to grow at some distance from London by the green belt, and which accommodate much of London's current overspill.

All the above comments on the quantity and distribution of residential and commercial land in the green belt must be viewed against the background of the position of that land generally. Such perspective is given by the statistics produced by Best.[1] He showed that in 1960–1, 10·6 per cent of the total land area of England and Wales was devoted to urban uses. This study has shown that in 1960, which is virtually at the same time, 6·2 per cent of the approved green belt and 14·3 per cent of all land on the fringe of London was developed for dwellings and commerce. Best's figure was based largely upon an analysis of development plan maps and his urban category appears to include not only residential and commercial uses, but also industry, urban open space, educational areas, and a wide range of other uses found within towns and cities.[2] The categories in this study are limited; the miscellaneous uses subsumed by Best here appear under their own separate headings. It is thus possible to speculate that, making allowances for such uses, urban development within the carefully drawn approved green belt at least approaches the national average. When all metropolitan fringe land is accounted, urban development clearly greatly exceeds the national average. Such are the pressures of people upon land that characterize the far from rural fringe of London.

---

[1] R. H. Best, 'The future urban acreage', *Town and Country Planning*, 32 (1964), 352; 'Extent of urban growth and agricultural displacement in post-war Britain', *Urban Studies*, 5 (1968), 1–23.

[2] R. H. Best, *The major land-uses of Great Britain* (Department of Agricultural Economics, Wye College, 1959), 23–5.

Manufacturing (category 2)

The second of the non-conforming land-uses, manufacturing industry, is far less important in terms of the area which it occupies in the green belt (Figs. 20, 21). Of the green belt as approved in development plans only 0·2 per cent is used for manufacturing, and for the whole extra-metropolitan area covered by the statistical survey the figure is only 0·7 per cent. In the north-west alone does the amount of land taken by manufacturing exceed 1 per cent. Over the period 1955–60 the acreage devoted to manufacturing increased by over 17 per cent in the approved green belt, and by over 16 per cent when all land is taken into account. But these are rates of increase based upon small absolute values and consequently represent very small increases in acreage. The acreage increases, when expressed as a percentage of approved green belt land, are insufficient to enter the first place of decimals; when all land on London's fringe is examined the increase over the period amounts to an additional 0·1 per cent of the area. Of all land-uses, manufacturing industry is probably that most strongly resisted by local authorities in their green belts.

But despite the small acreage occupied by manufacturing and the apparently insignificant increases of recent years, it is a land-use which has an impact far greater than its area would suggest. Large numbers of people find their employment in these small areas and small increases in area can accommodate a substantial number of additional workplaces. Extra workers need housing and they also require the facilities to travel to work daily. Indeed, one of the noticeable features of manufacturing industry on the fringe of London is the degree to which it generates traffic, both journeys to work, which are composed largely of 'cross movements' in contrast with the 'radial movements' more typical of central London industry, and also the movement of goods and other industrial trips. Existing industry, and increases in that industry, within and adjacent to the green belt exerts pressure upon land and expresses itself in land-usage other than that strictly definable as manufacturing.

As part of the investigation which supported *The south east study 1961–1981* an analysis was made of the employment statistics derived from the Ministry of Labour's annual June estimates of employees.[1] Although there are many difficulties in the use of such data, for

1 Ministry of Housing and Local Government, op. cit., 131–40.

example, the fact that some large firms exchange the national insurance cards of some of their employees in local employment office areas other than that in which they work, or the fact that the boundaries of Ministry of Labour local office areas do not always coincide with those of local authority areas, the figures produced are interesting in this context. They show that in 1955 the Inner Country Ring of the Metropolitan Region, as currently defined by the Ministry of Housing and Local Government and which approximates closely to the approved green belt,[1] contained 8·9 per cent of the employees of the south-east England study area. As the same area in 1951 included 10 per cent of the population of the south-east England study area, the region on the fringe of London is clearly not far below average in the south-east in its provision of employment. Between 1955 and 1962 numbers employed in the Inner Country Ring increased by 24·7 per cent. Over the same period employment in the London conurbation rose by 6·6 per cent, in the Outer Country Ring by 16·7 per cent, and in the remaining outlying parts of the south-east England study area by 10·9 per cent. By 1962 the Inner Country Ring contained 10·1 per cent of the employees of the south-east England study area. The statistics are indicative of the fact that the rate of employment growth in the green belt has exceeded population growth in recent years. It should, of course, be recalled that the Inner Country Ring is defined by the Ministry of Housing and Local Government so as to include the new towns.

All the above data refer to employment generally. An examination of the structure of that employment in 1962 reveals that only 2·6 per cent of those enumerated in the Inner Country Ring were engaged in the primary industries, that is, in agriculture, forestry, fishing, mining, or quarrying (Orders 1 and II in the *Standard Industrial Classification* of 1958). As many as 44·6 per cent were employed in the manufacturing industries (Orders III to XVI) and 52·8 per cent were engaged in the service industries, including construction (Orders XVII to XXIII). It is notable that the proportion of workers engaged in service industries is lower than elsewhere in the south-east England study area, and that the proportion employed in manufacturing is higher. This anomaly is not likely to be corrected quickly. An analysis of the changes in employment over a recent period shows that while numbers engaged in the primary industries in the Inner Country Ring are falling, service employment is growing slightly

[1] *Supra* p. 146.

faster than average for the south-east and manufacturing industry very much faster than average. The growth in manufacturing work-places in fact outstrips both absolutely and relatively similar expansion in any of the other major areas of the south-east. The types of manufacturing which appear to be expanding most rapidly are mainly the lighter growth industries, such as radio and electronics, plastics, precision engineering, toys and sports equipment, shop and office fitting, and mechanical handling equipment.

Using the same source of material Martin was able to identify for three separate periods, 1951–56, 1956–58 and 1959–62, changes in manufacturing employment in a broad zone of south-east England outside the London conurbation.[1] The inner boundary of the area coincided closely with the edge of built-up London, while the outer boundary was drawn at sufficient distance to include Bletchley and Colchester in the north, Reading in the west, and the whole of the sout coast east of Havant. It is an area which includes both the Inner and Outer Country Rings of the Ministry of Housing and Local Government and also substantial areas outside their limits. Within each sector of his area Martin showed that there had been continual increases in industrial employment in every period. Greatest absolute increases were in the north-west sector, followed by the north-east, south-west and south-east. In the period 1951–56, for example, increases in manufacturing employment ranged from 52,000 in the north-west to 24,000 in the south-east sector, and in the period 1959–62 the range was from 33,000 in the north-west to 19,000 in the south-east. Expressed as percentage increases the figures reveal that the rate of change was consistently highest in the north-east sector, with the south-west sector usually in second place. The existing, substantial industrial nuclei of the north-west sector depressed its growth rate to a lower position.

As a result of his study of industry and its growth in the extra-metropolitan area Martin was able to suggest three different types of manufacturing expansion. The first occurred in the eight new towns. Here, the manufacture of electrical goods and mechanical engineering were predominant. In 1963 these industries employed together almost half those engaged in manufacturing in the eight towns. The vehicle, chemical and food industries were also important, employing an additional 30 per cent of the industrial work force. The

[1] J. E. Martin, *Greater London: an industrial geography* (London, 1966), 217–37.

second type of expansion was that typical of estuarine areas, notably of lower Thames-side. Around towns such as Coryton, Grays, and Northfleet, and upon the Isle of Grain, oil refining, petrochemicals, paper and cement were the industries which had led the growth. Expansion in the remainder of the area constituted the third type. Away from new towns and lower Thames-side growth had taken place mainly in established centres. Much of it involved the extension of existing factories and hence, here again, engineering was the most important element. One marked feature of all this growth, both inside and outside the conurbation, is that industry appears to be becoming more labour intensive. Throughout the period 1951–62 Martin's study area contained over one quarter of British manufacturing employment, percentage increases in the labour force consistently exceeded the national average rate, and yet it received less than a quarter of the new industrial floor space. The increasing density of industrial workers helps to explain the inconsistencies between their increasing number and the rather smaller increases in the land which they occupy.

Though there is much detail in the statistics derived from the Ministry of Labour estimates they should be viewed with some caution. The recent publication of the 1961 Census Industry and Occupation tables has drawn attention to their shortcomings.[1] The Census figures themselves, it is true, are liable to some small error, since they are derived from a 10 per cent sample survey, but they seem to indicate that the Ministry of Labour returns overemphasized the growth of employment in central London, and tended to understate the growth in extra-metropolitan areas. For example, the Census revealed that the employment increase in the City of London and in the five central metropolitan boroughs of Finsbury, Holborn, St. Marylebone, St. Pancras, and Westminster in the period 1951–61 was 55,000 or 4·6 per cent, about one-third of the estimate based upon the labour exchange data. In Berkshire, Buckinghamshire, Essex, and Hertfordshire over the same period the numbers of employees increased by 20 per cent or more. The errors in the Ministry of Labour statistics arose presumably because some employers with head offices in central London exchanged the national insurance cards of employees who worked elsewhere in city centre labour exchanges. The effect on the discussion above of this new data is to

[1] Standing Conference on London and South East Regional Planning, Paper L.R.P. 721 (1966).

emphasize the importance of manufacturing in the green belt. Employment, and increases in employment, are not likely to be less important relative to other areas than has already been suggested, and are probably more important.

Figure 26 shows the detailed distribution of land devoted to manufacturing to the north-west of London. Apart from the rather limited areal expression of the industrial land, which has already been revealed in the statistics, there are two obvious features. First is the

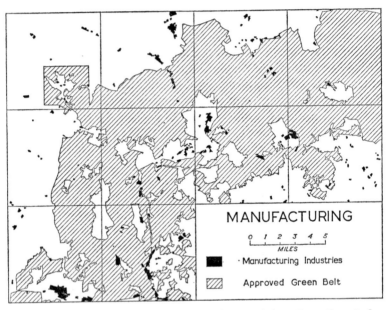

MANUFACTURING

0 1 2 3 4 5
MILES

■ · Manufacturing Industries

▨ Approved Green Belt

26. **Land used for manufacturing purposes in the green belt to the north-west of London, 1960**
(Source: Air photograph and field survey)

way in which industry clusters in the larger settlements, such as in Borehamwood, Slough, Uxbridge, and Watford within the green belt, and in Hemel Hempstead and St. Albans immediately beyond the green belt. Industry has not only been attracted to these towns, but in large part has also contributed to their growth. A location near the metropolitan market and at the same time with access to the consuming centres of the Midlands and the North has clearly been a distinct and continuing advantage. The second feature of the map stems directly from this factor. It is that industry has tended to

develop along lines of communication—along main roads and railway lines—exactly as it did in the outer suburbs of Greater London.[1]
The obvious example here is to the north-west of Watford, where
industry has spread along the valley of the Gade; a valley also
occupied by the main railway from Euston to the Midlands, by the
A41 road connecting London with Birmingham and beyond, and by
the Grand Union Canal.

In his study of the recent growth of population and industry in
Hertfordshire, Hooson examined closely the expansion of manufacturing in what he described as the 'focal area' of the county, that is,
in the section in the south-west lying south of a line from Berkhamsted
to Welwyn Garden City.[2] He found that in 1951, roughly two-
thirds of the employment of Hertfordshire was in the 'focal area'.
Thirty years earlier, in 1921, making all allowances for discrepancies
in the data, he estimated that the proportion of the county's
employees working in the same area could have been no more than
one-half. This points to the conclusion that there was a notable shift
of emphasis in the employment pattern within Hertfordshire during
the inter-war period; a shift caused largely by the growth of manufacturing, particularly in the towns of Borehamwood, Hatfield, St.
Albans, Watford, and Welwyn Garden City, within, or close to, the
green belt. That such a powerful growth has now been contained in
terms of area, if not in terms of numbers employed, is indicative of
the working of green belt controls.

The graph showing variations in land devoted to manufacturing
in the green belt with distance from London (Fig. 27), like that relating

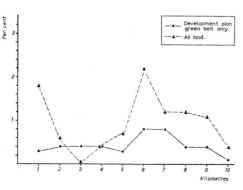

27.
**Per cent of area in
manufacturing with
distance from built-up
London, 1960**
(Source: Air photograph
and field survey)

[1] *Supra* p. 24.
[2] Hooson, op. cit., 201–4.

to residential and commercial land, contains two, quite contrasting curves. Differences within the green belt as defined in development plans are small and the overall level of values low. Local authorities have been careful to draw green belt boundaries where practical so that manufacturing, and undesirable land-use, is excluded. Differences in manufacturing over the whole extra-metropolitan area are greater. There are distinct 'peaks' at the one and six kilometre distances and a pronounced 'trough' at the three kilometre distance. Comparing this graph with the previous one (Fig. 25) it is interesting to note that although the lack of manufacturing industry at three kilometres from the edge of London corresponds with a zone of sparse settlement, at the one and six kilometre distances there is no marked intensification of residential and commercial land. Though industry rarely occurs without settlement, settlement in the form of small villages and even quite substantial dormitory towns does exist in the absence of industry.

Very little can be said with confidence about how industrialized the green belt is in comparison with the country generally since there are no certain national statistics. Almost all recent land-use surveys have been biased heavily in favour of rural activities. For example, the Land Utilization Survey of 1931–9 did not isolate manufacturing as such, but subsumed it under the general heading of 'land agriculturally unproductive', a category which included all urban uses other than houses with gardens. In England and Wales in the pre-war years land agriculturally unproductive amounted to 3·2 per cent of all land.[1] However, in the course of a later survey in 1950 Best estimated roughly that built-over land in England and Wales accounted for 9·7 per cent of the total, and that of this no more than 6 per cent was devoted to manufacturing.[2] In other words, less than 0·6 per cent of all land seems to have been taken by industry in 1950. It has been demonstrated above that in 1960 0·7 per cent of all land on the fringe of London and within the study area was given over to manufacturing. Here again, as with the first non-conforming land-use, the conclusion is unavoidable that in the general area of the green belt, despite the very small areas recorded in the survey, it is probable that a greater proportion of land is occupied by industry than is average for England and Wales.

[1] L. D. Stamp, *Land of Britain, its use and misuse* (2nd ed., London, 1950), 196.
[2] R. H. Best, 'The composition of the urban area in England and Wales', *Journal of the Town Planning Institute*, 44 (1957–8), 160–4.

Extractive (category 3)

Extractive industry occupies far more land than manufacturing industry in the green belt (Figs. 20, 21), though as a use of land it tends to be more transitory. Of the green belt as approved in development plans 1·8 per cent is under extractive working, or not yet returned to other uses following extractive working. A slightly smaller proportion of the whole extra-metropolitan area covered by the statistical survey is taken for extractive industry, namely 1·6 per cent. This is presumably because a high proportion of all the land in this category falls within the green belt. Most of the working is concerned with the extraction of sand and gravel but in the south-east, and to a lesser extent in the south-west, chalk quarrying is an important element. Of the four quadrants all except the north-west are remarkably consistent in the amount of extractive working which they contain, 1·8 to 1·9 per cent of all land. In the north-west only 1·1 per cent of all land is used for extractive purposes. The figures, by quadrants, of green belt land alone are very variable, a result of differences between local authorities in the drawing of green belt boundaries.

There are three main factors which control the distribution of extractive working. The first is the location of the workable deposits, the second is the location of the area of consumption of the end-product of the extractive industry, the third is the economics of the extraction and marketing of the material. In the vicinity of London, as has already been shown above, workable deposits are of two major types, either sands and gravels, or chalk. The sand and gravel deposits occur in the terraces of the Thames and its major tributaries, notably the Colne and Lea. They are found in the form of higher level glacial or plateau deposits in the Vale of St. Albans, in the country around Beaconsfield, and fairly generally throughout south Buckinghamshire and south Hertfordshire, and they also exist as 'solid' deposits in the Lower Greensand, particularly as exposed in its Wealden outcrop between Dorking and Maidstone. The terrace, glacial and plateau deposits yield gravel and also varying amounts of 'sharp' sand, that is, sand which is relatively coarse-grained and angular, and which is therefore suitable for concrete aggregates. The Lower Greensand, in contrast, yields mainly 'soft' sands which, because of their finer nature, are better suited to building and other more refined work. The chalk is derived exclusively from

165

the 'solid' Cretaceous beds which form a rim to the London basin. The Chiltern Hills, to the north-west, and the North Downs, to the south of London, are the main zones of working, though it should be noted that one low-lying area, around Dartford and Purfleet, where the lower Thames and Darent have revealed chalk, has developed as a zone of cement production.

The markets for these products are nearby. Large-scale rebuilding in the London conurbation and extensive new urban development outside its boundaries have, since 1945, exerted enormous demands upon the extractive industries. New road works and the maintenance of existing roads, which are much more heavily used now than hitherto, have also increased the demands for these materials. But sand, gravel, and chalk are bulky commodities of relatively low value and, in this sense, are quite unlike other minerals extracted in this country, such as coal, china clay, or iron ore. They are usually covered by only a thin overburden of river alluvium, brick earth, or boulder clay and are worked by highly mechanized open cast methods. This means that the cost of transport forms a far higher proportion of total costs than is true of the higher value minerals, and transportation over anything other than short distances leads to a rapid percentage rise in total costs. Sand, gravel, and chalk rarely travel far from their point of production, unless they are in some highly specialized form, a situation which is, of course, made possible by the fact that sand, gravel, and limestone deposits are widespread throughout most of the country. It has thus become a widely accepted economic argument that these materials must be extracted as close as possible to the point where they are to be used, and if they are to be used in cities then it is inevitable that deposits not far beyond the city's edge should be worked.

At this point it is worth recalling the immediate post-war period when the debate about the place of mineral working in London's green belt raged most vigorously. The case against the continued widespread and uncontrolled extraction of minerals was put most firmly by Sir Patrick Abercrombie. He argued, in his plan for Greater London,[1] that the working of sand and gravel, and also of chalk was the cause of growing concern. In the past, fertile agricultural land had been laid waste, and little or no effort had been made to reinstate the land for any profitable use following excavation. As a result of sand and gravel working, abandoned pits, some half filled with water,

[1] P. Abercrombie, *Greater London plan 1944* (H.M.S.O., 1945), 59-60.

irregular heaps of spoil and overburden, disused excavation plant, and old buildings littered the countryside. The areas were not only untidy, they also represented a great waste of national resources. In a number of instances, particularly at Feltham, the proper development of settlements had been impeded because urban land-uses had been forced to spread over a wide area, utilizing any odd pieces of land left over from mineral working. In the future, while it was of great importance that adequate supplies of good sand and gravel should be available as near as possible to the centre of London, since the likelihood was that greater use would be made of concrete than ever before, it would almost certainly be found that deposits existed in such quantity that a permanent prohibition against the working of part of these deposits would be feasible, and that working in other areas could be postponed for many years. In some places the working of the higher-level plateau gravels would not only preserve the agriculturally rich valley land, but might also lead to an improvement in the agricultural value of the higher areas. In order to maintain and improve the amenity of the areas fringing London Abercrombie recommended that appropriate after-treatment should become a condition of working, and that before extraction began the ultimate use of each area should be decided. If necessary a levy should be imposed upon the developer to ensure that funds were available for restoration when mineral working was over. In areas of high agricultural value the controlled filling of pits with builder's debris and domestic refuse should be undertaken, and top soil replaced. In other areas the creation of playing fields or amenity open spaces might be more useful, and sometimes little infilling would be necessary—the natural growth of vegetation and the judicious planting of tree belts would soon merge the excavations with their surroundings. Some pits would be too extensive for filling in, and these, if properly treated and their surroundings preserved against development, should make excellent reservations for boating, bathing, and fishing, on the model of the Rickmansworth Aquadrome. But in all areas old plant, such as huts and gravel-crushing machinery, should be removed and spoil heaps levelled.

The working of chalk, argued Abercrombie, though less widely scattered than the excavation of sand and gravel, resulted in a more widespread interference with amenity. The quarrying was on a vaster scale, often involving cutting away whole hillsides, and closely associated with it was the growth of giant cement works. In Abercrombie's view the chalk areas were intrinsically of great natural beauty. Any factory was inappropriate, and particularly those which covered surrounding areas with a grey deposit of cement dust. The principal cement works were located on lower Thames-side, and Abercrombie noted with regret that another area of chalk quarrying to the north-west of London near Dunstable and Luton had opened up, worked mostly by the same firms and oriented to the same market. It appeared that here was an instance where the centralization of an industry, rather than decentralization, was necessary. By increasing the scale of working on lower Thames-side all the cement required for the London market for many years could be produced without encroaching further upon the Chilterns. Even so, such action would not, so Abercrombie thought, absolve quarrying firms of the responsibility of after-treatment, if it were possible. Infilling was possible in some situations, and, where this was not practicable, a considered scheme of landscaping might be undertaken, and certainly derelict buildings and old plant could be removed.

The major opposition to Abercrombie's line of argument came from the Advisory Committee on Sand and Gravel at the Ministry of Town and Country Planning.[1] The committee was unable to accept the view that the extraction of sand and gravel could be prohibited or postponed for a long period on the fringe of London. Deposits were far from scanty and the exhaustion of the known reserves was not so imminent as to preclude the reservation for agriculture of any gravel land at all, nevertheless, the assumption that reserves were abundant, or that it would be practicable to meet all requirements by working deposits further afield, were not borne out by the evidence which had accumulated since Abercrombie prepared his report. While output costs at more distant pits might remain more or less the same, difficulties might arise in attracting sufficient labour, and the greatly increased costs of haulage from pit to market would inevitably lead to a far higher selling price. If more distant areas, such as those around Beaconsfield and Burnham Beeches, were developed the extra transport costs might raise the market price of gravel by between 20 and 40 per cent. As the terms of reference of the committee required them to consider the need for maintaining supplies of sand and gravel 'at a cost which is reasonable in all the circumstances', they were forced to discount the suggestion

---

[1] Ministry of Town and Country Planning, *Report of the Advisory Committee on Sand and Gravel* (H.M.S.O., 1948), 30–6, 61–8.

that sand and gravel working should be diverted away from the fringe of London. The committee was not prepared to reject any land for mineral working solely on the grounds that it was included within the green belt.

If this conclusion were accepted then, the committee argued, several things followed. Further damage to amenity would be unavoidable. Proper after-treatment was essential, but the amount of existing dereliction together with the scale of present working meant that there might well be delays in the restoration of worked land. Though there might be no serious permanent damage to the green belt, the urgent national need for sand and gravel should take precedence over the amenity interests. Another matter was that of damage to agriculture. Gravel-bearing land, especially where the gravel was overlain by brick earth deposits, had developed over the years into areas of high agricultural productivity which were intensively worked. Mineral working would destroy the agricultural value of these areas and hence the committee felt that it was necessary to reserve the pick of the market gardening areas for agriculture, while allowing development elsewhere. A balance had to be struck between the locational and physical needs of the two industries without prejudicing any future change of policy with changing circumstances. Meanwhile on the one hand, the available reserves of gravel would not have been permanently sterilized, on the other, the losses to agriculture would have been minimized. The competition with other forms of land-use appeared less easy to accommodate, since, once development had taken place, the sand and gravel reserves were permanently sterilized. Often developments, such as for housing, schools, playing fields, roads, cemeteries, trunk sewers, airfields, and reservoirs, were so urgently needed that they could not be postponed long enough to allow underlying sand and gravel to be extracted. But wherever possible, urged the committee, the development of sand and gravel fields should be phased so that the mineral could be extracted and the worked-out site reconditioned before it was handed over to its ultimate non-agricultural use. When such a use involved building it would probably be necessary to wait for between two to five years after the completion of filling before construction could begin.

In such debates there are rarely outright winners or losers but as time passed it became clear that it was the economic argument which carried most weight and which determined public policy. No mention was made of mineral working in the green belt circular, issued by the

Ministry of Housing and Local Government in 1955,[1] though it may, even at that time, have been considered a 'land-use appropriate to a rural area'. However, when shortly afterwards Duncan Sandys, the Minister, asked the Town and Country Planning Association to prepare a memorandum on green belts the official attitude to mineral working on the metropolitan fringe was clarified. In the course of its observations on green belt policy the Executive of the Town and Country Planning Association introduced the problems of surface mineral working and its subsequent restoration. The Minister's comments upon the memorandum were published,[2] and he also gave his permission for his notes to be circulated to local planning authorities together with the memorandum, which he thought was 'well worthy of study'. As in these notes he explicitly agreed to the after-treatment of areas of mineral working, and therefore implicitly to the existence of the extractive industry in green belts, it seems that short-term sacrifices of amenity were fully acceptable in order that the costs of building material should not rise inordinately. Later official statements[3] conspicuously fail to challenge the necessity of mineral working in green belts and there is ample justification for describing the land-use as one which is, in the present climate of thought, undesirable but inevitable.

But despite the continual insistence upon the after-treatment of worked areas, in practice considerable tracts remains derelict for long periods. A calculation undertaken by the Civic Trust upon statistics for the year 1958 revealed that during the year 11,990 acres in England and Wales had been made derelict by surface and underground mineral extraction.[4] The total area restored in the same year was 8,395 acres leaving an increment to past dereliction of 3,595 acres. Of the acreage unrestored well over one-quarter was contributed by sand and gravel working, which had a restoration rate of as low as 50 per cent. Compared with the restoration rates for open-cast coal and open-cast ironstone working of about 95 per cent, the sand and gravel industry emerges as both a short-term, and a long-term contributor to dereliction. The reasons for this are not difficult to see. Unlike coal and ironstone extraction, sand and gravel is

[1] Ministry of Housing and Local Government, *Green belts* (H.M.S.O., 1955), Circular No. 42/55; *supra* pp. 88–9.

[2] 'Green belts: Minister's reply', *Town and Country Planning*, 24 (1956), 151–3.

[3] For example Ministry of Housing and Local Government, *The green belts* (H.M.S.O., 1962), 8.

[4] Civic Trust, *Derelict land* (London, 1964), 21–4.

usually recovered from very thick deposits which have a thin over-burden. At coal and ironstone sites it is a fairly simple matter after the thin seams have been worked to replace the thick overburden and cover this with top soil, but where relatively large quantities of material are extracted the worked-out pits inevitably remain as holes in the ground, and where working has cut the water-table, as wet holes. The same applies with even greater force to the extraction of chalk where cliff faces and bare-rock floors are the consequence of quarrying and are extremely difficult to restore, or even to screen.

In such circumstances the provisions first enacted in the planning legislation of 1947 become hard to apply. Development control was intended to refer as much to mining operations as to building or engineering, and all mineral operators (with the exception of the National Coal Board) need to seek planning permission for the extension of existing working or for the opening up of new sites. The local planning authority in giving its consent is empowered to make such conditions 'as they think fit', that is, the authority may grant permission to develop subject to some appropriate after-treatment when mineral working has ceased. However, the term 'as they think fit' has not been interpreted by the courts to mean 'just as they please'.[1] The conditions must be 'fit' or proper in terms of the development for which planning permission is being given. In the words of Lord Denning in his judgment in the Court of Appeal in 1958, 'Conditions, to be valid, must fairly and reasonably relate to the permitted develop-ment. The planning authority are not at liberty to use their powers for an ulterior object, however desirable that object may seem to them to be in the public interest. If they mistake or misuse their powers, however bona fide, the court can interfere by declaration and injunction'. One of the tests of reasonableness which is usually applied is that the cost of complying with a condition must not be so great that it makes unprofitable the individual working to which it is attached. A condition which does not satisfy this test would either be removed by the Minister on appeal, or, if accepted initially by the developer, might safely be ignored when mineral working is com-pleted. Sand and gravel extraction, working thick beds of low value material, and chalk quarrying, producing substantial scars on the land surface, are both sectors of the mineral industry in which, unless by chance filling material is available at little cost, planning conditions relating to restoration of the site are largely ineffective.

[1] D. Heap, *An outline of planning law* (4th ed., London, 1963), 66-9.

171

Some of the results of this lack of control appear in Figure 28. Here, for the area to the north-west of London, all land used actively for extractive working together with those sites no longer worked but not yet adopted for other purposes, are shown as they were in 1960. The importance of the Vale of St. Albans and the Colne valley is immediately obvious, and particularly striking is the area on the southern edge of the map between Hayes and Slough. These are areas which have long been worked for sand and gravel and they contain

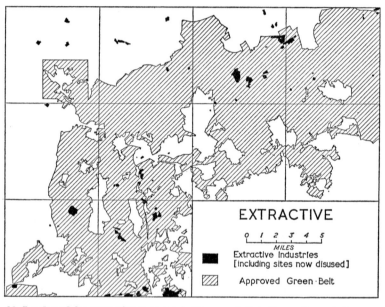

28. Land used for extractive purposes in the green belt to the north-west of London, 1960
(Source: Air photograph and field survey)

many disused as well as active pits. In fact, the signs of mineral working are even more pronounced in this zone than the map suggests, because many of the older pits, although clearly recognizable in the field as such, have now been converted to other uses, for example, for recreation, and therefore do not appear in this map. Between Beaconsfield and Gerrards Cross rather newer areas of sand and gravel working appear and in the extreme north-west of the map the areas shown are devoted to chalk quarrying. One fact emerges very clearly from this detailed view of the distribution of the extractive industry: almost all of it occurs on land which is approved green belt. Local authorities drew their green belt boundaries so as to leave the extractive industry within the green belt, and the subsequent development of the industry has continued largely unhindered.

Variations in the amount of land devoted to the extractive industry with distance from London are shown in Figure 29. Unlike the two previous graphs of this kind there is a fair degree of consistency between the two curves. As expected from the statistics shown in Tables II and III the curve for development plan green belt is generally the higher. Only at the eight and nine kilometre distances does the curve for all land exceed the green belt curve, suggesting that at this distance beyond the edge of London a higher proportion of non-green belt land is devoted to extractive working than of land

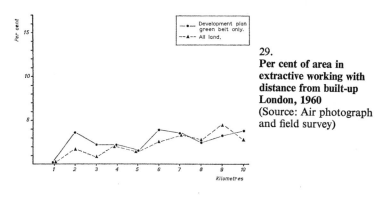

29.
Per cent of area in extractive working with distance from built-up London, 1960
(Source: Air photograph and field survey)

within the green belt. Close to the edge of London the graph indicates that little extraction is underway. Thereafter, between 1·5 and 3·8 per cent of all land is taken for mineral working and there is the slight suggestion of a 'peak' at the six and seven kilometre distances, doubtless caused by the location of the Vale of St. Albans, the valley of the River Colne, and the Chalk and Lower Greensand outcrops to the south-east and south of London.

With ample reserves of sand, gravel, and chalk available in the green belt, and pressing demands from throughout the south-east of the country, it is to be expected that the amount of land taken is relatively high. Though the figure is a little uncertain, Best estimated that 0·4 per cent of England and Wales was devoted to opencast mineral working in 1950.[1] As this figure includes the extraction not

[1] Best (1959), op. cit., 97.

only of sand, gravel, and chalk, but also of such materials as brick clay, china clay, coal, and ironstone, substantial consumers of land in those areas where they are worked, the proportion of all land taken by mineral extraction on the fringe of London, 1·6 per cent, is clearly greatly above expectation. Consistent with the conclusions which have been derived from the study of the two previous land-use categories, this disparity can only indicate the great pressures and demands which are exerted upon land on the fringe of a large conurbation.

Transport (category 4)

Land devoted to transport is another undesirable, though inevitable, use (Figs. 20, 21). Transport and its associated activities occupy 1·5 per cent of the approved green belt, and, as might be expected from the greater density of roads, railways, terminals, and transport parks within towns, they occupy 2·1 per cent of all land beyond the edge of London and within the survey area. Main roads, together with uses intimately linked with them, such as bus garages, car parks, and roadside paths and verges, are the most important occupiers of land taking 0·7 per cent of the approved green belt, and 0·9 per cent of all land on London's fringe. Of the four quadrants, the south-east and the south-west are close to average in the area taken by roads, but the north-east is markedly below, and the north-west markedly above, the norm for the green belt as a whole. Railways, together with their stations and goods yards, occupy 0·4 per cent of the approved green belt, and 0·7 per cent of all land. The distribution by quadrants is much more even but here again the north-east emerges with less than its share. The third sub-category contains those uses associated with civil air fields (Royal Air Force stations are included under the Public Service category). Uses linked with air transport take 0·4 per cent of the approved green belt and 0·5 per cent of all land. The north-west quadrant is dominant containing as much land under these uses as any other two quadrants combined, but this position is achieved with the aid of two large airfields at Hatfield and Radlett, which are used for the testing of aircraft manufactured in adjacent plants. This, together with its higher than average proportion of roads, has created in the north-west quadrant a heavy clustering of land utilized for transportation.

The history of the development of the road and rail systems of the

London area is detailed and intricate. It has been more than adequately treated elsewhere and will therefore not be pursued at any length here.[1] It is sufficient to note, as Hall has pointed out, that the road pattern of London and its surrounds was the product of five sets of planners: the Romans, the private estate builders working from the seventeenth century through to the present day, the turnpike builders of the late eighteenth and early nineteenth centuries, the agencies which rebuilt London in the second half of the nineteenth century, and the arterial road planners of the period since 1918. The railways developed from the 1830s onwards. Their route pattern was controlled by two main factors: first, the relief of the London basin and its surrounding chalk rim, and secondly, the disposition of the existing urban development. Neither high ground, nor already developed land, were insuperable barriers to railway building, but their influence is quite marked upon the present map of railways in the London area. The important fact which emerges from a study of the history of road and rail construction is that the main radial routes came to have two main functions. On the one hand they provided trade links and communication for other purposes between London, the capital, and other parts of the country; that is, they possessed a long-distance, inter-regional function. On the other hand they carried suburban traffic (though the railways in the early part of the nineteenth century were slow to develop their passenger-carrying potential) and they acquired an important intra-regional function.

Because of their essentially radial pattern both road and rail transport increase their occupancy of land as London is approached, and in their second, intra-regional, rôle particularly they create great pressures upon undeveloped land. They generate development and they also hinder the use of adjacent land, especially of farmland, by introducing non-conforming activities into rural fringe areas. In the green belt, as elsewhere, there exists the paradoxical situation that roads and railways encourage urban, industrial and other developments and thus help to establish the land-use pattern: these land-uses in turn generate the traffic by road and rail upon which the communication system depends. It is difficult and probably unwise, to distinguish too clearly between cause and effect in the study of the distribution of land devoted to transport. The three land-use categories already studied have provided abundant examples of the close

[1] See, for example, P. Hall, 'The development of communications', in J. T. Coppock and H. C. Prince (ed.), *Greater London* (London, 1964), 52–79.

interconnections between transport and other uses of land, and the same point has emerged in many other studies.[1]

Though they depend upon the radial road and rail system for access to the central parts of London, civil airfields create different land-use patterns. Of the airfield sites available for development in 1945, and Abercrombie proposed one major airport and nine others with supporting or specialized functions,[2] only Heathrow airport has developed fully, with Gatwick airport as a supplementary field handling some short-haul and medium-haul services. At a far lower level in terms of passenger and freight services are the airports of Luton, Southend, and Stansted, while at a lower level again are a large number of small airfields from which mainly private flying takes place. These airfields tend to be nodes of non-conforming land-use as they often generate about them other uses of land, such as manufacturing and the airport service industries, like catering and laundering. This exterior influence is, of course, roughly commensurate with the size and activity of the airfield. At one extreme, at Heathrow for instance, in addition to the considerable development of airport buildings for passengers, for freight, for servicing, and for administration, there is a substantial agglomeration outside the limits of the airfield of economic activities which are directly oriented to the airport. A large proportion of such development fails to be represented in the statistics quoted earlier, because all the major airfields of the London area fall outside the boundaries of the approved green belt. Heathrow airport is joined by continuous development to Greater London, and hence, though it projects well into the green belt zone, in the statistical study of green belt land-usage the airport and its associated economic activities do not register. Gatwick, Luton, Southend, and Stansted airports, on the other hand, lie well beyond the outer edge of the approved green belt, though they are within, or very near to, the extensions of the green belt which have been proposed by local authorities. They too are unrepresented in the statistics. At the other extreme a small private airfield might have no more than a few hangers and service buildings on the field and no extra activities beyond its bounds. Many fields of this type do exist within the approved green belt and generally little concern is felt about their inappropriateness. Indeed, such air-

---

[1] See, for example, D. L. Munby's paper reprinted in D. Senior (ed.), *The regional city* (London, 1966), 158–66.
[2] Abercrombie, op. cit., 77–81.

fields, if they are devoted largely to recreational flying, might well be considered as conforming land-usage.

Land devoted to strictly transport uses is shown in Figure 30. Here, for the area to the north-west of London all 'A Class' roads, railways, and airfields are shown against the background of the approved green belt. Dominating the map is the radial alignment of main roads and railways. Ring roads are present, and, it is true, carry

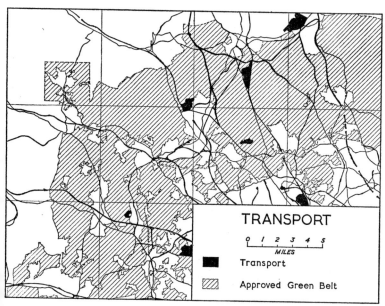

30. **Land used for transport purposes in the green belt to the north-west of London, 1960**
(Source: Air photograph and field survey)

substantial flows of local and long-distance traffic, but it is the radial road and rail links which connect London through this area with the north, midlands, and west of the country. The radials are also important for more local communication—for the movement of goods and people. The close correspondence already noted earlier in this chapter between road and rail routes on the one hand, and the location of settlement and manufacturing on the other, is partly a reflection of these important interconnections[1] (compare Figs. 22 and 26). Certainly those areas of the approved green belt which are

[1] *Supra* pp. 23–5.

distant from main roads and railways have the least urban and other development. The influence of airfields is more difficult to detect in the map. None of the major airports occur in or near this north-west sector of the green belt, but there are medium-sized airfields with adjacent development and also small fields with little or no building around them. The airfields of Hatfield and Radlett are closely associated with the aircraft manufacturing industry, that at Leavesden, to the north-west of Watford, is almost completely surrounded by urban, industrial, and other development, while the two smaller fields at Denham and Elstree, though they may have had many close links in the past with the film studios nearby, remain isolated in largely rural settings.

Variations in the amount of land devoted to transport with distance from the edge of London are shown in Figure 31. There is a fair degree

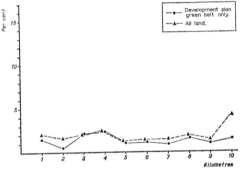

31.
Per cent of area in transport land with distance from built-up London, 1960
(Source: Air photograph and field survey)

of consistency between the two curves in the figure, and, as expected, the curve representing transport land as a percentage of all land is, at almost every point, above that showing transport land within the green belt as a percentage of the green belt. In the non-green belt areas, and particularly within towns, the density of roads, railways and also airfields, which are often excluded from the green belt, is higher. The expectation that the amount of land under transport uses would be greater on the immediate fringe of London and would decrease with distance into the green belt is not clearly supported by the graph. When all land is taken into account there is a suggestion of decreasing transport percentages outwards from London's edge, but the anomalies in this trend are sufficient to warrant closer investigation. The basic point is that though the radial pattern of roads and railways is the dominant one, it is not the only factor determining the amount of transport land. There are at least three other important variables which have a bearing upon the distribution of land given over to transport. The distribution of extra-metropolitan settlement is the first. It has already been shown in this chapter that there is a thickening of urban development a few kilometres beyond the edge of London[1] and this may be part explanation of the rather high values for transport land at the three and four kilometre distances. Part of the explanation also may be the second factor, the existence of ring roads, which usually interconnect the settlements on London's fringe. The third factor is the location of airfields. The very unusual value at the ten kilometre distance and the rather high value at the eight kilometre distance are both largely attributable to the effect of airfields. In a land-use category where the percentage of land occupied is rather small, the fairly large acreages taken by even small airfields can have a pronounced influence upon the statistics for transport land.

There is a strong presumption with this land-use category, as with those already studied, that the amount of land occupied in the green belt exceeds the national average. Best produced no estimates of the area devoted to roads and railways in England and Wales as a whole, but he gives 0·1 per cent as the proportion taken by civil airfields in 1950.[2] Despite the fact that no major airfield falls within the statistical area used in this study, 0·5 per cent of the extra-metropolitan zone so defined is devoted to civil airfields. Given that the main roads and railways which focus upon London also produce a heavier than normal distribution of land under these uses—and this is not an unwarranted assumption—then yet again a non-conforming land-use emerges as being more extensive in the green belt than generally in England and Wales.

Public Services (category 5)

The last of the undesirable uses of land which appear in the green belt is public service land. As Figures 20 and 21 have already shown it is another relatively minor occupier of space taking 0·9 per cent of the approved green belt and 1·2 per cent of all land beyond the edge of London and within the survey area. Three sub-categories have been distinguished. First, there are the public utilities; land

[1] *Supra* pp. 156–7.
[2] Best (1959), op. cit., 97.

taken up by gas, water, electricity, and sewage installations account for 0·4 per cent of the approved green belt, and 0·5 per cent of all land. Secondly, there is the land occupied by service and government departments—the War Department, the Air Ministry, the General Post Office, the British Broadcasting Corporation and many others. They take 0·4 per cent of the green belt, and 0·6 per cent of all land. Thirdly, there are cemeteries, strictly speaking a conforming land-use since they were specifically mentioned as a permissible development in the 1955 circular on green belts.[1] Cemeteries occupy 0·1 per cent of the green belt and the same proportion of all land. Variations between the sectors are not great. Nothing useful can be said about differences in development plan green belt devoted to the public services since some local authorities deliberately excluded such land from their green belts, while others did not. When all land is considered, the south-west quadrant appears to have much more than an average amount of public utility land, a fact to which the large reservoirs in that area are largely contributory. The north-east is above average in its service and government land, mainly as a result of the Royal Air Force airfields in that sector. Cemeteries, as might be expected, are fairly evenly distributed around London.

Many public services are essentially overspill land-uses. As towns and cities grow, or as development within their boundaries becomes more intensified, public services, particularly the public utilities, have to meet the needs of an increasing population. Eventually they require more space and often migrate to the edge, or beyond the edge, of the urban area. Though many of the public utilities which move into the country fringes of towns and cities are undesirable uses in a rural context, they are often no more conforming within the urban area. A sewage plant or an electricity transforming station is difficult to accommodate aesthetically whatever its location. Other of the public services require large amounts of land, or demand special sites, and this often means that they are attracted at the outset to areas beyond the boundaries of towns and cities. But since they serve, or are very closely connected with, the life of urban areas they tend to predominate in those rural areas adjacent to towns. Water supply installations and storage areas, and much of the service and government department land falls into this group. The only major category of public service land which is not positively linked with urban areas is that used for military exercises. For this purpose exten-

[1] Ministry of Housing and Local Government (1955), op. cit.

sive, relatively unoccupied, and preferably cheap areas seem desirable.

Figure 32 shows the extent of public service land to the north-west of London. It reveals very clearly the way in which land under public service use clusters in and about London and the towns of the green belt. A detailed examination of each use seems to suggest that the clustering really operates at two levels. First, there is the clustering to supply purely local needs. Along the fringe of London and in and around such towns as Watford, domestic gas plants, electricity

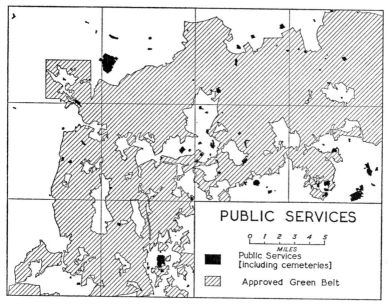

PUBLIC SERVICES

0 1 2 3 4 5
MILES
■ Public Services
[including cemeteries]
▨ Approved Green Belt

32. **Land used for public service purposes in the green belt to the north-west of London, 1960**
(Source: Air photograph and field survey)

stations, sewage works, water supply installations, cemeteries, and rubbish dumps occur frequently. Where they lie outside the built-up area they are usually at no great distance. More than a mile or two from the larger towns in the green belt public service land of this type is virtually non-existent (Fig. 32). Secondly, there seems to be a more general scattering of public service land in the green belt which has little connection with local settlement, other than that it may derive its work force locally, but which has obvious links with London's metropolitan function. These uses are more widely distri-

181

buted and they include government research stations, General Post Office relay installations, and transmitting stations of the British Broadcasting Corporation. A number of the uses linked with London's metropolitan function were evacuated to the green belt during the 1939–45 war and have since never returned to the more central locations. Only a very few of the areas shown in Figure 32, such as the airfield at Bovingdon in the north-west, have no direct functional links with London or with the surrounding towns.

Figure 33 shows variations in the amount of land devoted to public services with distance from the edge of London. The two curves, the one for green belt land only, the other for all land, are not greatly different, both showing a maximum at the three to five kilometre distances, with a sharp drop in the percentage of land occupied by the public services up to the nine kilometre distance. There is a

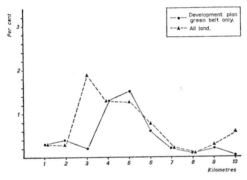

33.
Per cent of area in public service land with distance from built-up London, 1960
(Source: Air photograph and field survey)

fairly close correspondence with the comparable curves for residential and commercial land (Fig. 25), a correlation which is completely consistent with the conclusions drawn from the distribution map of the area to the north-west of London (Fig. 32).

Despite the very close clustering of public service land around London and the towns beyond its fringe, the percentage of the green belt occupied by this land does not nearly match the national average figure. The reason for this is that land used by the service departments for training and other purposes, and by water undertakings as water gathering grounds, is very extensive, particularly in the uplands. Hence in the green belt study area all public service land together takes only 1·2 per cent of the whole, while Best calculated that in England and Wales in 1950 2·3 per cent of the total land area was occupied by the service departments alone, and another 1·3 per cent by water undertakings.[1] Best makes no estimate of other types of public service land but it can be safely assumed that, in the green belt they take more land than is general in the country.

Figures 20 and 21 have already given some idea of the importance of the non-conforming land-uses. The statistics quoted in the above chapter have emphasized that impression. Taken together the land-use categories discussed above (though omitting cemeteries which are an allowable development) occupy 10·5 per cent of the approved green belt and 19·8 per cent of all land on London's fringe. It is impossible to arrive at an accurate figure for the same uses in the country as a whole using Best's estimates, but making generous allowances for those sub-categories which he does not define, it cannot exceed 17 per cent. Even so this figure is greatly inflated by military and water gathering land. The conclusion is clear, and it has emerged from the study of each individual non-conforming land-use. Within the general green belt area, that area which Scott, Abercrombie, and others emphasized should be dominated by agriculture, forestry, and recreation, the undesirable land-uses occur more frequently and cover more area than they do in the country at large.

[1] Best (1959), op. cit., 97.

7 · The Components of the Approved Green Belt—The Conforming Uses

Despite all that has been written in the last chapter about the uncommonly high proportion of non-conforming uses of land within the green belt zone, it is, of course, the conforming uses which occupy the bulk of the land on the fringe of London. Together, categories 5c through to 11 in Tables II and III, which define the conforming uses, take up 89·5 per cent of the approved green belt and 80·2 per cent of all land on the metropolitan fringe and within the study area. That is to say, nearly nine-tenths of the green belt as shown in approved development plans and over four-fifths of all land in a comparable narrow zone beyond the edge of London is composed of land-uses which, in descending order of importance in terms of the acreage which they occupy, may be listed as agriculture, woodland, recreation land, schools and hospitals, water areas, unused land (mainly cut-over woodland or grassland run to waste), and cemeteries. All these are uses which do not require substantial buildings, or in which buildings form only a small proportion of the total area occupied. They lead, in fact, to a landscape of a predominantly open character, which is why they have become generally acceptable in green belts.

As in Chapter 6 each land-use will be considered in turn, and in the order in which they appear in Tables II and III.

Institutions standing in extensive grounds (category 6)

As explained earlier, institutions standing in extensive grounds form a category rarely found in land-use analyses. It is employed here simply because it is the single major urban land-use allowed to develop in green belts and was specifically listed as an approved use in the green belt circular of 1955.[1] The category includes schools, colleges, hospitals and a large number of other institutions, less

[1] Ministry of Housing and Local Government, *Green belts* (H.M.S.O., 1955), Circular No. 42/55.

important in terms of the area which they occupy, ranging from research units to convents. It should be clearly understood that the statistics quoted below referring to this category relate only to land-usage directly connected with the institution. For a school or hospital the figures would include the buildings, together with those grounds which are used by the pupils or patients. The figures do not include land in other uses, such as agricultural or residential, which might occur on land owned by the institution, even if such land is contiguous with the grounds included in the statistics.

From Figures 20 and 21 it can be seen that the institutions hold a relatively minor place among the conforming uses. Of the green belt as approved in development plans only 1·1 per cent is devoted to them, while for the whole extra-metropolitan area covered by the statistical survey the figure is barely higher at 1·4 per cent, and signifies little more than that the density of institutions within the urban areas is greater than in the surrounding green belt. Schools and colleges occupy well over half the land taken by institutions. They take 0·7 per cent of the approved green belt and 1·0 per cent of all land on London's edge. Of the four quadrants, the north-west has markedly more than a normal share of land devoted to educational uses. As much as 1·8 per cent of the green belt and 2·1 per cent of all land is taken by schools and colleges in that sector. It is possible within this sub-category to identify increases in land occupance over the period 1955–60. But despite the permissiveness of green belt control in respect of this use, increases over the period within the approved green belt were insufficient to appear in percentages rounded to the first place of decimals. When all land on the fringe of London is accounted there appears an overall increase in land taken for schools and colleges amounting to 0·1 per cent of the total area, and a similar increase is recorded for all quadrants except the south-west, where the increase is too small to be registered. Hospitals are far less important as consumers of land. They occupy 0·3 per cent of the green belt and an identical proportion of all land. The north-west is again the out-standing sector with the south-east also showing an above-average acreage under hospitals. The south-west sector, in contrast, has a marked dearth of land devoted to hospitals, and no figure can be recorded under this quadrant for the green belt, or for all land. In the hospital sub-category it is again possible to identify changes in area occupied over the period 1955–60. In fact, the changes are so small that nowhere do they enter the first place of decimals. Under the third sub-category, in which a wide range of other institutions is included, 0·1 per cent of both the green belt and of all land is recorded. Differences between the quadrants are so small that they can be disregarded. Studying all the sub-categories together, the most remarkable feature to emerge is the dominance of the north-west quadrant. Within the green belt to the north-west of London there exists well above twice the green belt average of land devoted to institutions in extensive grounds, and even when all land is accounted, the amount of institutional land is little less than twice the average.

The widespread distribution of the institutions listed under this category is a fairly recent phenomenon. Until the late nineteenth century, schools and hospitals were not primarily a public responsibility; they were the outcome of individual initiative and of co-ordinated voluntary effort and subscription. Since such a method of sponsorship had practical limits, the number of schools and hospitals was itself limited. It was not until 1888, when elected county councils were established with control of local affairs and taxation, that the troubled social conscience of the time began to be assuaged on a broader front. Thereafter local authorities attempted to supply a wide range of communal services, including schools and hospitals, paid for out of rates, and out of loans charged upon the rates. The number of institutions increased enormously and some, particularly those which required large amounts of land and in which daily accessibility was not an over-riding factor, were located where land could be acquired most cheaply, outside towns and cities. So it came about that hospitals were scattered widely on the outskirts of urban areas, and mental hospitals more than most other types. At the end of the nineteenth century a new and more humane attitude was being taken to mental illness, which, together with local authority financing accounts for the large number of mental institutions dating from this period, but the attitude was not so humane that it was thought desirable for such hospitals to be too closely associated with the major towns and cities.

Figure 34 shows land used for institutional purposes on the urban fringe to the north-west of London. It illustrates the distribution of schools, colleges, hospitals, and other institutions for the year 1960 in that section of the green belt where it has already been shown such uses are most frequent. Within the urban areas and inside the Greater London conurbation there is a fairly dense scatter of small institutional areas. These are composed mainly of schools and

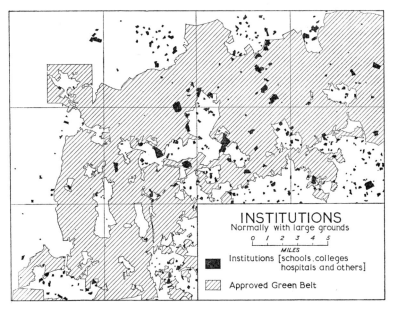

34. Land used for institutional purposes in the green belt to the north-west of London, 1960
(Source: Air photograph and field survey)

hospitals which serve the urban population. In the more recent settlements, such as the new towns of Hatfield and Hemel Hempstead, or in Borehamwood and Potters Bar, the areas given over to institutions are larger, a result of the more liberal provision of playing fields and grounds in recent times. But the largest areas lie within the approved green belt. These, in contrast with the areas inside the urban blocks, are composed mainly of private schools and mental hospitals. The contrast, however, is more than one of scale; that is, it is more than a straightforward distinction between the large isolated units of the green belt and the small, but densely distributed, units of the towns and cities. As has already been suggested there exists a contrast in origins which, more important in this context, appears to have led to a contrast in functions. The areas within the towns and cities supply directly urban needs and there is a day to day movement of children and adults to and from them; those in the green belt are not so immediately connected with the built-up areas, and, unlike the urban oriented institutions, have shown no recent tendency to expand in their present locations. It seems most probable

187

that it is in these functional links that the reasons for the lack of expansion of institutions into the green belt must be sought.

The graph showing variations in the amount of land devoted to institutions standing in extensive grounds with distance from the edge of London (Fig. 35) reveals one quite clear trend. The area taken by institutions decreases markedly through the green belt from a peak in the first few kilometres to low values from the sixth kilometre outwards. There is no correlation with the similar graph for settlement (Fig. 25), but since there are two quite distinct components in the distribution, the one urban-oriented, the other not, this is hardly surprising. It seems plain that the major overall influence is of London itself and that the trend has been dictated largely by the overspill of

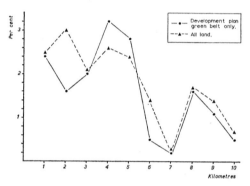

35.
Per cent of area in institutional land with distance from built-up London, 1960
(Source: Air photograph and field survey)

institutions, such as hospitals, from the conurbation, and also by the attraction of other institutions, such as some of the private schools, to the conurbation. In both these processes distance from London is an important determining variable.

No national land-use survey has ever distinguished institutions standing in extensive grounds as a separate category or sub-category. It is therefore not possible to compare the percentage of all land on London's fringe which institutions occupy (1·4 per cent) with the position in the country generally. Observation in the field suggests that institutions are far more frequent in the green belt area than they are in the country at large and this impression has some comparative support from Best's statistics.[1] For example, the area occupied by all small towns and villages of under 10,000 population in England and

[1] R. H. Best, *The major land-uses of Great Britain* (Department of Agricultural Economics, Wye College, 1959), 97.

Wales is the equivalent of 1·9 per cent of the total area, while all isolated dwellings together occupy only 1·4 per cent of England and Wales. In this light the amount of land taken by institutions in the green belt area is very substantial.

Woodland (category 7)

Woodland is perhaps the easiest of all the land-use categories adopted in the statistical survey of green belt activities to define and measure. Trees have a long life and the boundaries of woodland blocks are relatively stable compared with those of many of the other uses of green belt land. Areas held and administered by the Forestry Commission usually remain permanently in timber production, while Tree Preservation Orders issued by local authorities and Forestry Dedication Covenants entered into with Forestry Commission aid the durability of the two-thirds of national woodland in private ownership.[1] However, a major problem of definition does arise. Though woodland represents in most parts of the country an exclusive use of land, on the fringes of cities and in other special instances it is subject to multiple use. Most often the second use is as recreation land. Consistent with the methods adopted throughout the survey in respect of the multiple use of land, in order to avoid double-counting, areas have been divided equally between all categories represented in any unit of land.

Woodland is a major occupier of land in all parts of the green belt (Figs. 20 and 21) and is one of the more important conforming uses. Of the green belt as shown in approved development plans 11·8 per cent is under wood, while in the whole extra-metropolitan area covered by the statistical survey 10·3 per cent is woodland. The south-east and south-western quadrants of the green belt contain most woodland, and here over 13 per cent of the approved green belt and over 12 per cent of all land is so occupied. The north-east quadrant surprisingly, when it is remembered that it contains most of Epping Forest, has a very low proportion of its total area under wood, little more than half that of the south-east and south-west quadrants.

It has already been suggested that there are two main factors which have determined the present distribution of woodland on London's fringe.[2] The first, in a sense, is a negative factor, and the second, a

[1] *Supra* pp. 109–10.
[2] *Supra* p. 110.

189

positive factor. It is clear from field inspection and from the land-use distribution maps of the survey area that all but a few of the larger tracts of woodland are located in areas which have been considered unsuitable for agriculture, because of their slope, soil, or drainage. As Willatts pointed out in his Land Utilization Survey memoir of Middlesex and the London region, the prosperity of British agriculture before the age of steam-ships was sufficient to ensure that woodland was seldom allowed to remain near such a great agricultural market as London except in those areas where cultivation was judged to be unprofitable.[1] But although much woodland remains as a result of the negative operation of physiographic factors, that is, the land was unsuited physically to agriculture and has not since been developed for urban or industrial purposes, it is far from being exclusively land in a natural condition. Timber is often grown as an economic crop and the woodland areas from which it is produced are tended and improved. More positive than the long-term effects of the economics of agricultural production is the second factor, the use of woodland in the past as an integral part of landscape gardening. Prince has shown that, particularly through the nineteenth century, beyond the existing suburbs of London and stretching into the present green belt and further, landscaped parks were laid out as settings for the country residences of statesmen, merchants, bankers, and officers of the crown.[2] The parklands contained numerous tree-lined avenues, blocks of exotic trees, and belt plantations, as well as larger areas of woodland. Up to 1920 such parks occupied a higher proportion of the surface areas of the fringe of London than of any other district of England. Since that time some of the parkland has been developed for building, but a good deal of the area which is no longer strictly parkland still remains in open uses, such as for golf courses, or has been acquired by institutions, such as schools, hospitals, and teacher training colleges. Here much of the woodland has been retained and, together with the plantations of the areas still surviving as parkland, now contributes to the wooded fringe of London.

The composition of the woodland varies greatly from one part of the green belt to another. In the western portion of the Chiltern Hills, for example, at the edge of and beyond the green belt to the

[1] E. C. Willatts, *Middlesex and the London region* (*The land of Britain*), 79 (London, 1937), 144.

[2] J. T. Coppock and H. C. Prince (ed.), *Greater London* (London, 1964), 333–52; H. C. Prince, 'Parkland in the Chilterns', *Geographical Review*, 49 (1959), 18–31.

north-west of London, beech high forest is predominant. In many places the woodland consists of pure beech stands but elsewhere there are small blocks of conifers, usually larch. Other types of woodland, such as coppice, are virtually absent. To the south of the Burnham gravel plateau woodland is more diverse, with oak joining beech as the most important element. In Surrey, by contrast, high forest composes only a small proportion of the woodland. On the clayland of the north of the county coppice with standards is the dominant type of woodland, but on the sandy areas in the west, pinewoods, particularly of Scots pine, give a distinctive character to the landscape. The woodland of all these areas contrasts sharply, to take yet another example, with the rough scrub belt which often marks the steep, south-facing scarp of the North Downs.

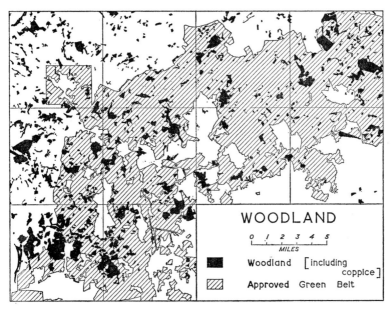

WOODLAND

0 1 2 3 4 5
MILES

■ Woodland [including coppice]

▨ Approved Green Belt

36. **Land used as woodland in the green belt to the north-west of London, 1960**
(Source: Air photograph and field survey)

The detailed distribution of some of these wooded areas is shown in Figure 36, which covers the north-west quadrant of the green belt. To the north and west of a line through Gerrards Cross and Watford lies the fairly dense scatter of woodland on the chalk back-slope of the Chilterns. The distribution is a very fragmented one, and

results from the haphazard clearance of the timber cover for agricultural, urban or industrial purposes. Until relatively recent times
these woods gave full or partial employment to thousands of wood
turners, known locally as 'bodgers', who produced furniture parts
from the larger trees. Today all the furniture industry is centred in
factories, mostly at High Wycombe, a little off the western edge of
the present map, but local Chiltern beechwood continues to be used.
To the south-west of Gerrards Cross lie the compact woodland areas
of the Burnham gravel plateau. Here, coarse glacial sands and gravels
produce a soil which drains very freely and which is not only exces-
sively dry, but also deficient in lime, phosphate, and potash. Little of
the timber in the Burnham area seems to be maintained primarily
for commercial purposes. Amenity and recreation are the main considerations. A third major area of woodland lies north and east of
Potters Bar. This represents the western extremities of Broxbourne
Woods, which woodland has been supplemented by that associated
with a number of landscaped parks, notably in Hatfield and North
Mymms.

Variations in the amount of land devoted to wood with distance
from the edge of London are shown in Figure 37. The two curves
run fairly closely together but, as expected, the curve representing

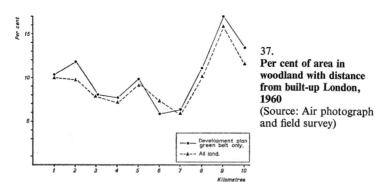

37.
Per cent of area in
woodland with distance
from built-up London,
1960
(Source: Air photograph
and field survey)

woodland as a percentage of development plan green belt is, at all
but one point, above that showing woodland as a percentage of all
land. On the immediate fringe of London woodland occupies a little
over 10 per cent of the area. Outwards through the green belt the
amount of land under timber tends to decrease, but after the seven
kilometre point the proportion rises sharply. The form of the curve

192

is simply a reflection of the fact that close to London greatest pressure has been exerted upon woodland by other uses of land. Beyond the seven kilometres distance the beginnings of the woodland associated with the gravels around Burnham, the Bagshot Beds of west Surrey, the Chilterns, and the North Downs produces a sharp increase in the amount of land devoted to this use.

With so many heavily wooded areas fringing, and sometimes lying within, the green belt it is not difficult to see why the amount of woodland far exceeds the national average. Best, in his calculation of land-usage for England and Wales for 1950, showed that high forest occupied 3·4 per cent of the total area and other woodland 3·0 per cent.[1] His total of 6·4 per cent is, it is true, now well out of date, being based upon the last census of woodland in 1947–9. Substantial and continuous planting, particularly of state forests, has been underway since that date, but by the year 1960, the date of the present survey, the area occupied had reached only 7 per cent.[2] The bulk of the Forestry Commission holdings lie in East Anglia, Hampshire, and in the upland areas of England and Wales, and it is in these areas where the major recent expansions of acreage under woodland have occurred. Recent trends in private woodland, which it will be recalled, accounts for two-thirds of the total woodland area, and almost all of that in the zone around London, is not as well documented, but any increases in acreage are unlikely to bear comparison with state planting. With the exception of East Anglia and Hampshire, it is in the uplands of the country, where large state forests supplement private woodland, that the proportion of land under woodland is highest, and the spread of woodland fastest. In this light, the fact that 11·8 per cent of the approved green belt and 10·3 per cent of all land in the narrow zone bordering London is devoted to woodland is significant of the particular importance of this land-use in establishing the landscape character of the area under study.

Water (category 8)

Water is a minor occupier of surface area in the green belt (Figs. 20 and 21). As defined in the statistical study used in this work it covers

[1] Best, op. cit., 97.
[2] J. T. Coppock, 'A decade of post-war forestry in Great Britain', *Economic Geography*, 36 (1960), 127–32.

0·6 per cent of the green belt shown in approved development plans, and 0·5 per cent of all land on the edge of London. The total area occupied is so small that too much reliance cannot be placed upon the small differences which exist between the four quadrants, but it appears that the north-east quadrant has far less surface water than any of the other three. The water areas which these statistics include are those which have no other major specific uses. Where they have one major use the water areas are normally included within the appropriate land-use category. For example, those water areas which form an integral part of active extractive working are shown under the Extractive land-use category, reservoirs which serve only or mainly for public water supply are listed under Public Services, and those water areas which are used mainly for fishing and water sports are recorded under the Recreational category. In effect, only the water areas which are used for a variety of different purposes, or which are virtually unused, are under study in this section.

Most of the surface water in the green belt is, of course, associated with rivers and streams and lies in valley bottoms. The major streams themselves are very variously used. They serve for navigation, recreation, as sources of water for public and industrial use, and also for the disposal of waste. Where the river valleys contain sand and gravel deposits, mineral working in the past has left suites of wet pits and quarries where the excavations have cut the water table. Fairly frequently in the London area streams have been dammed to create lakes. Occasionally these water bodies were needed to store and supply water for industry, and sometimes they were constructed for the replenishing of canals, but most frequently artificial lakes were produced to assist in the landscaping of the grounds of country houses.[1] These lakes and ponds are usually small in area, but they are very widely scattered in the green belt.

Some examples of each of the three types of water area appear in the map showing the distribution of surface water in the north-west quadrant of the green belt (Fig. 38). In the south-west corner of the map is a small section of the Thames, that running between the villages of Cookham and Bray, and skirting the eastern edge of Maidenhead. In these upper reaches the Thames is not, of course, as heavily used for the transportation of fuel, raw materials, and finished goods as it is within and below London, but it does have another major commercial use. It supplies a high proportion of the conurba-

[1] *Supra* pp. 110, 190.

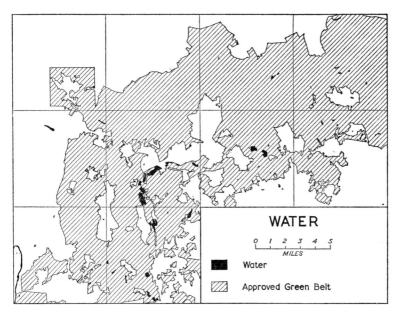

38. Land covered with water in the green belt to the north-west of London, 1960
(Source: Air photograph and field survey)

tion's water. One of the main extraction and storage areas lies a little
downstream of the section shown in the map, between Staines and
Walton-on-Thames. At the same time the river serves as the main
drain for London and other towns in the Thames basin. But perhaps
the most obvious use of the Thames above London is for recreation.
Fishing, boating, and swimming are major activities, as indeed, are
the industries which supply and service these pursuits. The second
type of water area, that produced by past mineral working, is much
in evidence in the map. The Colne valley, between Staines and
Watford, was an area of early development for sand and gravel
working, and many of the pits on the valley floor now lie derelict
and filled with water. Some are currently being used for leisure
activities and serve to meet the rapidly growing demand for facilities
for water sports of all kinds, but many remain as unused watery
monuments to a past extractive industry. The third type of water
area is that which results from the landscaping of country estates.
Since the land to the north-west of London experienced more of this
activity than almost any other part of the country it is not surprising
195

that artificial lakes, set in parkland, abound. They range from the very large water areas, such as those in Latimers, east of Amersham, where works on the river Chess in the mid-nineteenth century created an elongated lake and a series of waterfalls, or in Shardeloes, a few miles to the west, where in the eighteenth century a little known landscape gardener, Richmond, improved the grounds and dammed the Misbourne to form a 40-acre lake, to the small lakes and ponds in much more modest parks, such as in Camfield Place and Nyn Park, between Hatfield and Potters Bar, where the water areas are almost too small to appear in Figure 38.[1]

Since the area covered by water is so small no graph showing variations in the amount of water with distance from London has been produced. The sampling error is relatively large and the possibility of chance fluctuations is high. But there does appear to be a real increase in water area at the five, six and seven kilometre distance. This, it will be recalled, corresponds with a similar 'peak' in land devoted to the extractive industry (Fig. 29) and is doubtless a product of the location of worked sand and gravel fields close to London.

The best estimate available of the acreage of inland water in England and Wales is provided by the Ordnance Survey. In statistics compiled in 1966 they showed that in a total area of over thirty-seven million acres only 208,000 acres were under inland water.[2] The figure excludes all tidal water. Putting it another way, 0·56 per cent of the country as a whole is covered by water, a proportion which is almost identical with the figures produced above for the green belt and for all land surrounding London.

Recreational land (category 9)

Recreation land is the third most important conforming occupier of land in the green belt (Figs. 20 and 21). It takes 6·2 per cent of the green belt shown in approved development plans and 5·4 per cent of all land beyond the edge of London and within the study area. Because of the particular interest in this form of land-use in the green belt a five-fold subdivision was adopted in the statistical enquiry. Of the five sub-categories by far the most important in terms of land occupied is open space; that is, formal park and rough open land

---

[1] Coppock and Prince (ed.), op. cit., 33–57; Prince, op. cit., 18–31.
[2] *Annual Abstract of Statistics, No. 102 1966* (H.M.S.O., 1966), 1.

over which the public is free to wander at will, but which is not laid out for any organized games or recreation. The term 'open space' as defined here is not quite synonymous with 'public open space'. Some publicly owned recreation land is laid out for formal games, while some open space to which the public has access is, in fact, privately owned. Open spaces occupy 3·9 per cent of the approved green belt and 3·4 per cent of all land. In each case they make up well over half the total land devoted to recreation. The second most important sub-category is that containing golf courses—very extensive users of land. In the green belt they cover 1·6 per cent of the surface, but when all land is considered the figure falls to 1·3 per cent, largely because most golf courses lie on the edge of, or outside, towns and were almost all designated as green belt by local authorities. Playing fields rank in third place and are better balanced between town and country. They occupy 0·5 per cent of the green belt and also 0·5 per cent of all land. The fourth category, composed of race courses, takes 0·1 per cent of both approved green belt and all land, while in the fifth category a miscellaneous group of other recreational uses together achieve 0·1 per cent of the areas of green belt and of all land.

Variations in the amount of recreational land between the quadrants are substantial. In the south-western part of the green belt recreation land reaches its maximum. Nearly 9 per cent of the development plan green belt and 7·5 per cent of all land is devoted to recreation, all but 0·9 per cent in each instance being occupied by golf courses and open spaces. The abundance of areas of uncultivated and undeveloped land upon the Chalk of the North Downs and upon the sandy heaths of the Bagshot and other series, many of which have been preserved as commons, is the major contributor to this ample provision of recreation space. In the north-west and north-east, where large commons and extensive areas of otherwise unused land are less frequent, spaces open to the public occupy less land, though in the north-west, golf courses are a prominent feature of recreation land-use. In these quadrants the amount of recreational land is close to average for the green belt as a whole. It is in the south-east that recreation land is at a minimum. It occupies 4·5 per cent of the green belt in that sector and only 3·9 per cent of all land within the south-east survey area. It thus contains little more than half the recreational area enjoyed by the best endowed south-west quadrant.

Further light can be thrown on the recreation land of the south-west quadrant as a result of the work of Lovett.[1] Working within the Ministry of Housing and Local Government, but stimulated largely by a private, rather than a strictly professional, interest in the green belt, Lovett carried out an investigation in the late 1950s into the use of land for leisure activities within the green belt, and also though not so intensively, into such activities in the conurbation and in the area beyond the green belt. However, most of his work was concentrated upon the area represented in the Ordnance Survey One-Inch sheet No. 170 (London, S.W.), that is, roughly the same area covered by the south-west quadrant as defined in this study.

Lovett stresses the importance in this area of 'the oldest of public land, the commons'. These, he argues, attract people into the green belt to enjoy the scenery and, for the more academically minded, provide a field laboratory. But in many ways, man has added to the natural attractiveness of the Surrey hills and heaths. As well as under-taking extensive landscaping around country residences there are numerous sites and buildings of historic value and visual beauty, many of them now designated as ancient monuments or acquired by the National Trust. An intricate network of footpaths, bridleways, and by-roads provides attractive access to these points of interest, though the only evidence of their use that Lovett could produce was provided by the publication of walks and drives in evening news-papers and in guide books. Judged by these indices the Surrey hills seemed to be the most popular, as one might expect. Recent experi-ence suggests, and a number of studies confirm, that serious country walkers now form a very small minority group among those enjoying the passive recreational areas described above.[2] Most people reach the open spaces by motor car and only a small proportion of those seem to wish to stray more than a short distance away from their parked vehicles.

The more active leisure pursuits proved far easier for Lovett to identify and map. The activities associated with horse riding were well distributed; the various water sports—swimming, fishing, canoeing, water ski-ing, and sailing—were concentrated along the Thames and its tributary rivers; the grounds for the more formal

---

[1] W. F. B. Lovett, 'Leisure and land-use in the metropolitan green belt', *Journal of the London Society*, 358 (1962), 1–16.

[2] T. L. Burton and G. P. Wibberley, *Outdoor recreation in the British country-side* (Department of Agricultural Economics, Wye College, 1965), 35-6; T. L. Burton, *Windsor Great Park: a recreation study* (Department of Agricultural Economics, Wye College, 1967), 29.

sports, such as tennis, cricket, golf, and football, though widely spread, tended to cluster most thickly around the fringe of London, to which position many of them had come because of lack of space in the conurbation. Other leisure activities are impossible to record though they undoubtedly exist, for example bird watching, cross country running, cycling, or camping in other than established camp sites. Such pursuits are not great and permanent consumers of land space and they fail to be represented in Lovett's maps as they also fail to appear in the statistics presented here.

Outdoor recreation in the rural areas of this country has, of course, a long history. Large tracts of open country and woodland were preserved for hunting by the Norman and Scottish kings, and the killing of animals for sport has been a prominent recreation activity for a number of centuries. But as Burton and Wibberley, and Coppock have pointed out in complementary studies,[1] the impact of mass recreation upon the countryside has not been felt until relatively recently. The rural sports were the preserve of a privileged few. The bulk of the population found its recreation in or near the market place. It was only from the mid-nineteenth century onwards that leisure time became sufficiently long and sufficiently widespread to allow industrial and agricultural workers to range any distance from their places of work and dwelling. It is noteworthy that it was in the middle of the last century that legislative action was taken to prevent the further enclosure of common land in and near large cities, unless the recreational needs of the population could otherwise be met, and that it was the same period which saw the foundation of such groups as the National Trust, the Commons, Open Spaces and Footpaths Preservation Society, and a very large number of local societies whose aim was the preservation of rural areas for recreational and other purposes.

Burton and Wibberley describe four main stages in the growth of outdoor recreation in Britain.[2] From the mid-nineteenth century to the First World War mass recreation was confined largely to excursions and day-outings on Sundays and other holidays. The majority of the recreation trips were to the coast, and it was the period in which the seaside resorts, to which rail access was usually fast and

[1] Burton and Wibberley, op. cit.; J. T. Coppock, 'The recreational use of land and water in rural Britain', *Tijdschrift voor Economiche en Sociale Geographie*, 57 (1966), 81–96.
[2] Burton and Wibberley, op. cit., 1–3.

cheap, flourished and grew. In the second stage, between the two World Wars, increases in the numbers of workers who received holidays with pay increased the flow to recreation areas and the habit of spending holidays away from home became established. The period was also marked by a considerable growth in purely urban recreation. Theatres and concert halls were visited by a much wider range of society than previously, and the dance hall and cinema became important features of the urban scene. In the third stage, running from the Second World War to the mid-1950s, paid annual holidays were received by almost all workers and the spending of a week or a fortnight away from home became widespread. Spectator sports and recreations, such as football and the cinema, attracted their peak attendances, and the television set became as common-place as any other item of furniture in the home. Finally, in the fourth stage, mass recreation has entered a new phase. The largely passive entertainments so popular immediately after the war began to decline in their ability to attract spectators and they are being replaced by more active pastimes. Water sports, ten-pin bowling, climbing, pony-trekking, camping and caravanning, and above all, motoring for pleasure, have all shown very rapid growth rates over the past ten years.

Looking to the future, Burton and Wibberley have studied the changes in a number of factors which can be shown to be closely related to the growth of outdoor recreation.[1] Making estimates for changes over the period 1960–85 they showed that the number of private cars in use in Britain was likely to increase by 290 per cent, numbers engaged in full-time higher education by 220 per cent, the average length of annual holidays with pay by 100 per cent, real income per head by 75 per cent, population by 20 per cent, and that the length of the average working week was likely to fall by 25 per cent. The existence of so many interrelated variables precluded further analysis, but the magnitude of the projected changes suggested that the total number of annual holidays and of day or weekend trips would more than double over the twenty-five year period. The increasing number of people who will seek land space for recreational activities, combined with the fact that an increasing proportion of them will wish to be active participants, has clear implications for the use of London's green belt in the future. The green belt is not likely to have to accommodate many people on their annual holiday, but

[1] Ibid., 38–9.

it is likely to become the supplier of most of the space needed for weekend recreation simply because, to the population of the conurbation, it is the most accessible reservoir of undeveloped land.

Some notion of the detailed distribution of recreation areas at present in the green belt may be gained from Figure 39, which shows land devoted to recreation to the north-west of the conurbation. The most marked feature of the map is that the bulk of the recreation land lies in the outer parts of the conurbation and, more typically,

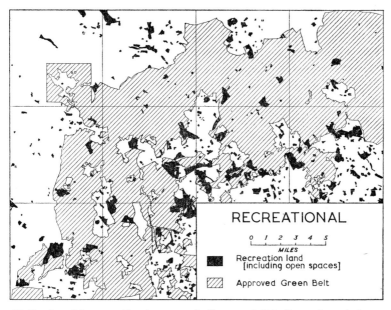

RECREATIONAL

0 1 2 3 4 5
MILES

■ Recreation land [including open spaces]

▨ Approved Green Belt

39. Land used for recreational purposes in the green belt to the north-west of London, 1960
(Source: Air photograph and field survey)

in the inner parts of the green belt. It is a peripheral distribution which is repeated, though less obviously, around other large towns within and beyond the green belt, such as Gerrards Cross, St. Albans, Slough, and Watford. Though road travel gives a high degree of flexibility to those seeking recreation areas, and though 'driving for pleasure' is one of the single most popular weekend recreation activities, it seems from the present distribution that there is some demand for recreational land close at hand, presumably because the use of nearby areas minimizes travel time and cost. There is some fragmentary evidence to support this contention in other surveys. For example, the British Travel and Holidays Association survey of Whitsun travel in 1963 revealed that, of all holiday travellers, nearly 45 per cent had remained within twenty-five miles of their homes and a further 25 per cent had reached a point no more than fifty miles from their homes; of those making day trips to Teignmouth in 1957 65 per cent had travelled less than twenty miles;[1] of the visitors to Windsor Great Park in June 1966 well over 70 per cent had journeyed less than twenty miles, despite the obvious attractions of the park;[2] and of the people travelling to take recreation on the thirty commons studied by Wager in 1962–3 in various parts of England, the majority had journeyed less than twenty miles and the median distance was ten miles.[3] From these observations it seems likely that the bulk of the users of the more ordinary open space or formal recreation land on the fringe of London originate less than ten to fifteen miles distant. The motor car may give mobility, but it is a potential which is only infrequently fully employed.[4]

Sylvia Law, studying similar evidence, has attempted in a recent paper to define different types of outdoor recreation areas on the basis of the intrinsic qualities of the facilities they possess.[5] She concluded that local and intermediate facilities would draw the bulk of their visitors from five to ten miles away, sub-regional facilities from up to twenty to thirty miles away, and regional facilities from up to fifty miles. Facilities of national significance have, of course, no distance limitations. The local, intermediate, and sub-regional areas would lie within the range of the half-day visitor, the regional areas would lie within day-visitor range. Most of the green belt recreation areas thus seem to fall into the sub-regional categories.

Confirmation that recreational land clustering upon the fringe of the conurbation is not particular to the north-west is given by Figure 40. Here variations in the amount of recreational land with distance from London are shown for the whole extra-metropolitan area and,

[1] Cited by Burton and Wibberley, ibid., 34–5.
[2] Burton, op. cit., 8–12.
[3] J. Wager, 'Outdoor recreation on common land', *Journal of the Town Planning Institute*, 53 (1967), 398–403).
[4] The implications for future urban growth of the great increase in short journeys from urban areas for leisure purposes are discussed in B. Cracknell, 'Accessibility to the countryside as a factor in planning for leisure', *Regional Studies*, 1 (1967), 147–61.
[5] S. Law, 'Planning for outdoor recreation in the countryside', *Journal of the Town Planning Institute*, 53 (1967), 383–86.

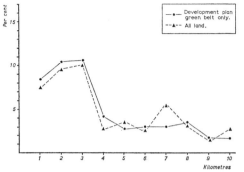

40.
Per cent of area in recreation land with distance from built-up London, 1960
(Source: Air photograph and field survey)

as usual, one curve refers to green belt land, and one to all land within the statistical frame. The very high values in the one to three kilometre range from the edge of London are a pronounced feature of both curves, as is the very sharp fall in the amount of recreation land beyond the three kilometre distance. The graph not only throws light upon the distribution of recreation land, it also indicates one of the land-uses most likely to be eroded by unrestrained and unplanned urban expansion.

No accurate record exists of the amount of land in England and Wales which is available for public recreation. Estimates of urban recreation land may be derived from the work of Best, where it appears that open space varies from about 15 per cent of the total urban area in London and in the new towns to over 21 per cent in other large settlements of over 10,000 population.[1] Figures are also available for the net losses of agricultural land to sports grounds, derived from the Ministry of Agriculture, Fisheries and Food June 4 returns.[2] Though the statistics are a little uncertain it seems that the annual gain in the area of sports grounds was between 9,000 and 10,000 acres, or 0·026 per cent of the total area of England and Wales, during the inter-war period when rural land was easily obtained. In the war years there were net gains to agriculture from recreation land, but as soon as the war was over sports grounds once more gained land from agriculture, and at not much below the pre-war rate. Since that time the acreage gained per annum has fallen.

[1] R. H. Best and J. T. Coppock, *The changing use of land in Britain* (London, 1962), 175; R. H. Best, *Land for new towns* (London, 1964), 26.
[2] R. H. Best, 'Recent changes and future prospects of land-use in England and Wales', *Geographical Journal*, 131 (1965), 1–3.

Through the 1950s the average annual gain was 3,500 acres, that is, 0·01 per cent of England and Wales each year, and the current figures are well below this.

Faced with a dearth of firm statistics Burton and Wibberley in their study of outdoor recreation in the British countryside were forced to make estimates based upon such material as was available.[1] By studying the areas occupied by the Statutory Access Areas of National Parks, the areas of nature reserves to which there was public access, National Trust properties, common lands, woodland, inland water, and other areas, they came to the conclusion that the area of rural land available for public recreation in England and Wales ranged between a minimum figure of 1·5 million acres and a maximum figure of 4·3 million acres, that is, between 4 per cent and 11·5 per cent of the country. They eventually settled on a figure of three million acres, which represents 8·5 per cent of England and Wales. Against this figure, however rough and ready it may be, the percentages of green belt land devoted to recreational use appear rather low, especially when it is remembered that playing fields and golf courses, two of the major contributors to the green belt totals, are largely unaccounted in Burton and Wibberley's calculations. Indeed, the figure for recreation land as a percentage of all land in the green belt (5·4 per cent) is identical with the figure calculated by Burton and Wibberley for the whole of the south-east, defined as the area lying south-east of a line drawn between the Wash and Bournemouth.

The comparison of the green belt and national statistics for recreation land seems to have revealed a contradiction. The figures do not appear to support the argument, already advanced, that recreation land clusters about the fringes of the large urban areas. But the contradiction is more apparent than real. There are substantial differences in scale in the areas to which the two sets of figures refer. The green belt statistics relate to a zone of about fifteen miles in width on the edge of London. The Burton and Wibberley calculations are based on data for major regions of the country, which they aggregate to arrive at national statistics. But it is interesting that these latter figures show not only that the national average of land occupied by recreation is higher than in the green belt, but also that the differences between regions in the provision of recreational land are very great. It would not be surprising if the distribution within

[1] Burton and Wibberley, op. cit., 5–19.

regions was also very uneven. Again, different types of recreation land are also involved. In the south-east, and especially around London, recreation land has to compete with many other land-uses; the areas are limited and because of the population density, heavily used, very often for formal recreation in organized sports or for activities which demand specially constructed facilities. In the north and west of the country, particularly in the uplands, larger areas are available, but they are often under-used because of their inaccessibility to centres of population. They remain largely as rough open spaces.

Agricultural land (category 10)

To the-man-in-the-street the green belt is an agricultural preserve, and it is a view which has some firm basis. Many of the authors and most of the committees which have pronounced upon green belts over the last seventy-five years have insisted that a viable agriculture is essential if green belts are not to become what Hugh Gaitskell years ago described as 'green ditches separating subtopias'. The Scott Committee, reporting in 1942, went so far as to suggest that in green belts the farmer should be the normal custodian of the land, and only the Ministry of Housing and Local Government circular of 1955 made no specific mention of agriculture in green belts.[1] The view is one which finds support not only in the orthodox principles of green belt design, but also in practice (Figs. 20 and 21). Agriculture is by far the single most important occupier of land in any of the English green belts, and in the London green belt it takes 69·5 per cent of the areas designated in development plans, and 62·3 per cent of all land in the same zone.

In the statistical survey of green belt land-uses four sub-categories were adopted. The first, easily the most important in terms of area occupied, included all grass and arable worked under normal farming conditions together with the farm buildings and dwellings directly associated with such working. No attempt was made to distinguish in detail different farming land-uses nor differences in the farming system from place to place since a number of other surveys have focused upon this particular aspect of land-use, including the field-by-field land utilization survey of Britain carried out in the 1930s and also the rather more detailed national land-use survey underway at this moment. Normal farming occupied 67·5 per cent of the approved

[2] *Supra* pp. 88–9.

green belt and 60·6 per cent of all land in the same area. In relation to this, the other uses listed under the Agricultural heading are minor, though they do bear comparison with some of the land-uses discussed already. The second sub-category contains orchards. In the approved green belt they take 1·2 per cent of the total area and when all land is considered they occupy 1·1 per cent of the area. Nurseries compose the third sub-category. They occupy 0·6 per cent of the approved green belt and 0·4 per cent of all land. Finally, allotment gardens (though, perhaps, a semi-urban use of land they seem most appropriately included here), because they are distributed more evenly between those areas designated as green belt and those not, occupy the same proportion of green belt and of all land, 0·2 per cent.

Variations in the amount of agricultural land between the quadrants are substantial. Agriculture reaches a maximum in the north-eastern section of the green belt where 78·3 per cent of development plan green belt and 74·7 per cent of all land is devoted to it. Here the area under grass and arable is very high, over ten percentage points higher than in any other quadrant of the green belt, obviously because urban, manufacturing, and other developments are greatly less than elsewhere on London's fringe. The amount of land devoted to nurseries is also very high, but since this quadrant contains the market gardening areas of the Lea Valley, the fact that 1·2 per cent of the green belt and 1·0 per cent of all land is so occupied is hardly surprising. In the south-east quadrant the proportion of agricultural land both in development plan green belt and in all land included within the statistical survey is close to average for the whole green belt ring, with orchards a particularly important element, but in the north-west and south-west, where built-over land is at a maximum, the proportion of agricultural land falls quite low. In the north-west 66·6 per cent of the green belt and 55·8 per cent of all land is given over to agriculture while in the south-west 61·3 per cent of the green belt and as little as 52·1 per cent of all land is under agricultural working. Grass and arable in the south-west occupies only 51·5 per cent, that is, very little over half, of the land fringing London.

It is plain that in the past agriculture has persisted as an occupier of space on the edge of London only where the demands for urban land have not been exerted. In very much the same way as agriculture, over many centuries, has reduced the areas devoted to woodland,[1]

[1] *Supra* pp. 110, 190.

so urban land-uses, because of their strong competitive positions in economic terms, have encroached upon farmland.[1] But it is clear that urban land-uses have not only overrun agricultural land, they have also influenced the remaining agricultural landscape over wide areas by their proximity.

Some years ago Wibberley indicated a number of ways in which the influence of towns might lead to the wastage and deterioration of surrounding farmland.[2] As towns grow they take over agricultural land. But the process of change is often neither smooth nor immediate. Farmland is zoned in a development plan for urban purposes. Objections are heard to the plan and after some modification it is approved by the planning Minister. If the land is to be developed within a short time the farmer may well begin 'farming to quit', that is, putting less into the soil than he removes so that fertility declines, productivity falls, and the farm begins to run down. At a later stage delays in development may lead to the land lying completely idle. Other problems arise when urban expansion absorbs parts of farms only. Farms, like any other economic enterprise, are composed of inter-dependent parts. Remove some of the parts and the whole operates much less effectively or, alternatively, the system has to be changed radically. In either case there is a tendency towards farm decay. Physical proximity to urban land-uses also causes difficulties for the farmer. Human beings and their domestic pets encroach onto farmland, cause damage to crops and hedges, and disturb stock. Such interference with the farming system is greatest where population pressure upon land is high, and where towns are expanding. There are two main reasons for this. First, it is evident that most damage to farming occurs where a purely urban population abuts the agricultural area, such as occurs when a new housing estate is built on the edge of a town to receive population from nearer the town centre. There is usually no disruption to farming where the agricultural area adjoins a long-established settlement the population of which has adjusted to its rural setting. Secondly, towns undergoing rapid expansion often cannot provide all the service needed by their inhabitants within the town boundaries. Activities such as recreation, the public utilities, cemeteries, schools, and hospitals thus overspill into the surrounding

[1] For a general consideration of the pressures upon agricultural land see J. Weller, *Modern agriculture and rural planning* (London, 1967), 109-54. But see also R. Best, 'Extent of urban growth and agricultural displacement in post-war Britain', *Urban Studies*, 5 (1968), 1-23.

[2] G. P. Wibberley, *Agriculture and urban growth* (London, 1959), 65-9.

countryside and carry the urban influence well byond the edge of the town.

The establishment of a green belt around London has in some way modified these effects upon the rural fringe. The possibility of urban development in many farming areas is now remote and the piecemeal take-over of farms has been considerably reduced. In other ways, however, London's rural surround is more susceptible to urban influence than the position as generally described by Wibberley. London is the biggest city in the country. Its physical limits are fixed and yet pressures within are enormous. Overspill has to occur and those activities which are allowable, like recreation, find their way into the green belt and there attract urban population. London is also the centre of the communication network of the country. It has already been noted that the closer one approaches the outer edge of London the more the radial communication routes converge and the smaller the intervening agricultural sectors. Often the routeways bisect farms and cause accessibility problems within the farm units, but their greatest effect is that, since urban and industrial development frequently follow roads and railways, they introduce ribbons of non-conforming land-uses into the agricultural fringe.

A more detailed view of the impact of urbanization on farming beyond the edge of London has recently been given by Ruth Gasson, one of Professor Wibberley's team of investigators at Wye College.[1] In her book she describes how six areas, each composed of one to five parishes, were chosen at different distances along the main road and rail routes from London to Hastings in order to test the hypothesis that urban-influenced change in rural areas varies with distance from the dominating city. From the National Farm Survey of 1941 it was possible to reconstruct a picture of farms and types of occupiers in those areas at that date. To give a comparable record of conditions at present a short questionnaire was sent to the 599 occupiers of agricultural land in the same parishes during the winter of 1964–5. The aim was to establish whether 'the occupiers were owners or tenants, full-time, part-time, or retired farmers, how long they had been in occupation and whether they had made any changes in farm size during that time'. The response rate of the survey was 78 per cent. In four of the areas a further random sample of 154 was drawn from the respondents to the postal enquiry and they were visited to

[1] R. Gasson, *The influence of urbanization on farm ownership and practice* (Department of Agricultural Economics, Wye College, 1966).

obtain additional information about types of farming; in the two other districts all the respondents in two parishes were interviewed.

The first major point to emerge from Miss Gasson's investigation was the swing from tenant farming to owner-occupation between 1941 and 1964–5. In 1941 the proportion of farms worked by owner-occupiers in all districts covered by the survey was 39 per cent. By 1964–5 the figure had risen to 69 per cent. There is a fair indication in the statistics of a link between urbanization and owner-occupancy in the area around London, but the real importance of the swing to owner-occupation lies in the financial resources of the person who has replaced, and will probably continue to replace, the tenant and small family farmer. As the landlord's capital is being withdrawn from agriculture so that of the farmer himself becomes more important, and it is often drawn from the wide range of urban economic activities in which the new owner-occupiers have their base. As might be expected, the statistics show that part-time farming is on the increase where urban influences are strong. Between 1941 and 1964–5 the proportion of farmers in the survey areas with another substantial source of income rose from 30 to nearly 50 per cent. There are also some clear differences with distance from London. Apart from the area nearest to London, where in 1964–5 the proportion of part-time farmers was rather low at 46 per cent, the number of part-time farmers decreases as distance from London increases.[1] However, since the owners of the larger part-time farms tend to live at some distance from London the proportion of land held by part-time farmers reaches its maximum at about fifty miles from the centre of London. It is at this same distance from London that the greatest swing to owner-occupation and part-time farming is currently taking place. This suggests that the effects of the urban influences have already been fully experienced by farms in the green belt and are now being felt in areas well beyond the green belt.

All but 8 per cent of the part-time farmers in Miss Gasson's survey of 1964–5 were primarily engaged in occupations other than agriculture, and 69 per cent were in occupations quite unrelated to agriculture. Such a large group of recreation farmers will clearly have an impact not only on the farming system, but also upon the landscape. The survey produced strong evidence to suggest that part-time

[1] See also A. Harrison, *The farms of Buckinghamshire—some features of farm business in a county adjoining Greater London* (Department of Agricultural Economics, University of Reading, 1966).

farming leads to greater specialization and simplification on farms. The part-time farmer is unlikely to pursue a management-intensive enterprise, such as dairying, unless he is able to employ a full-time manager, and the survey confirmed that part-time holdings were most often associated with beef, pigs, poultry, cereal growing, and fruit production, and usually concentrated upon one or two of these only. As many as 30 per cent of full-time farmers in the same areas engaged in five or more enterprises. While there is little difference between part-time and full-time farmers in the intensity of land-use or in the efficiency of their use of labour, there is great contrast between the criteria they adopt to judge their farming practice. Full-time farmers naturally tend to have economic efficiency as their goal; many part-time operators seemed more concerned with technical optima, such as higher yields or better livestock, or with the general appearance of their farms.

Another distinction between full- and part-time farming is in respect of farm size. Full-time farmers nearby large urban areas are under direct economic pressure. Opportunities of non-farm employment hasten the drift of workers from the land—in the green belt areas of Miss Gasson's survey regular farm labour in 1964–5 was half of what it had been in 1941. This forces farmers to take a larger share of the manual work upon themselves, make better use of existing labour through mechanization, and leads to an increase in farm size where farmers are able to meet the economic pressure, and to the disappearance of the smaller operators who cannot cope, or who are attracted to less exacting means of earning a living. Shortage of farm labour also affects the part-time farmer, but for him it is not so critical. Most part-time farms are small—50 per cent in the survey areas were under 20 acres while only 11 per cent of full-time farms fell into this category—and it is not as necessary for them to show a profit since most occupiers are assured of an income from their urban business or profession. This financial stability leads to a fairly stable size distribution. Two-thirds of the part-time farms in the survey had not changed in size during the tenure of the present occupier.

The effects of urban proximity are therefore two-fold. Large farms and small farms are increasing in number; the family farm of 20 to 100 acres, a size-group particularly vulnerable to economic pressures, is beginning to disappear. Miss Gasson summarizes the present trends as follows: 'On one side, competition from the urban sector, reinforced perhaps by contact with urban values and standards of living, compels the full-time commercial farmer to expand, both in acreage and in output. On the other side, urban pressure creates a demand for more small farms which are never intended to be self-supporting. This process is taking place continuously in all parts of the country and the survey suggests that, rather than causing any new departure, urban influences are hastening the inevitable evolution of agriculture.' It is within the green belt that these urban influences are greatest and their effects best developed. Together with the wider

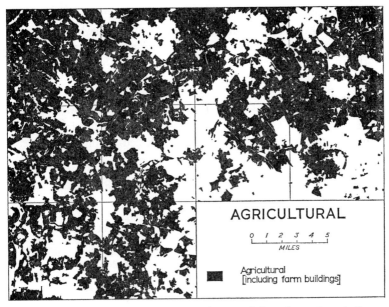

AGRICULTURAL

0 1 2 3 4 5
MILES

■ Agricultural
[including farm buildings]

41. **Land used for agricultural purposes in the green belt to the north-west of London, 1960**
(Source: Air photograph and field survey)

influences discussed earlier, they lead to the particular character of agriculture on the fringe of London.

As with all the previous land-uses, the detailed distribution of agricultural land is shown for the north-west quadrant of the green belt (Fig. 41). The map emphasizes the point already made that al-though the proportion of land devoted to agriculture is quite high within the green belt, farmland is, nevertheless, greatly fragmented. There is a scatter of alien activities throughout the agricultural area, but they are grouped particularly along the radial communication routes from London to the Midlands, the North, Wales, and the West, and also in a circumferential zone around the outer edge of the green belt where most overspill developments tend to be sited and where new towns are growing rapidly. It is possible to traverse the green belt outwards from London by one or other of the major trunk roads, for example, by A4 to the west, by A40 to South Wales, by A5 or by A41 to the Midlands, and catch only the briefest glimpse of agriculture before reaching the outer edge, and the same is rapidly becoming true of the orbital roads, such as the A414 running through Hemel Hempstead, St. Albans, Hatfield, and Hertford, which skirt the edge of the green belt. In fact, it is not until well beyond the green belt, in areas such as those which only begin to appear on the northern and north-western edges of the map, that uninterrupted blocks of agricultural land exist.

Though the north-west quadrant is not altogether typical of the complete green belt and has much more scattered development than either the north-east or the south-east quadrant, the impressions gained from Figure 41 are generally confirmed by Figure 42. Here

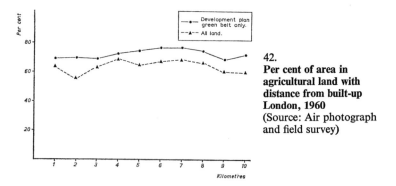

42.
Per cent of area in agricultural land with distance from built-up London, 1960
(Source: Air photograph and field survey)

variations in the proportion of land devoted to agriculture in the green belt as a whole are shown with distance from London. Of the land designated in development plans as green belt a consistently high proportion, about 70 per cent, is under farming. This is not surprising since most of the non-conforming activities have been excluded in the drawing of green belt boundaries. It is the curve showing agriculture as a proportion of all land within the statistical survey area which reveals the true balance between agriculture and the other land-uses. Agriculture is least well represented a little beyond the edge of London, where at the two kilometre distance only a little above 55 per cent of all land is devoted to farming. This is the zone in which residential and commercial, recreational, institutional, and a number of other uses of land are strongly represented. Agriculture reaches a peak in the four to eight kilometre range where least competition seems to be experienced from other activities, but begins to decline in importance towards the outer fringe of the green belt, that is, at the nine and ten kilometre distances, where rapid recent development in the new town zone has encroached upon the agricultural area.

With the exception of the public services and recreation land, all the categories of land-use studied so far, whether conforming or non-conforming, occupy a greater proportion of the land area of the green belt than they do in the country at large. Since most of these uses expand at the expense of agriculture it follows that the agricultural area of the green belt must be well below average. And so it appears upon a comparison of Best's figures[1] and those produced in this study. Best estimates the proportion of land occupied by agriculture in England and Wales in 1960 as 79·3 per cent. Apart from about 4 per cent under common rough grazing it is all land in sole occupation which is exclusively or primarily used for farming. Most of the common grazing land lies in upland areas, distant from London, but even if the total amount is discounted the gap between the national average and the figures for the green belt is substantial. In the development plan green belt 69·5 per cent of the land is agricultural, and when all land is included in the calculation, the proportion under agriculture falls to 62·3 per cent. Since these figures include orchards, nurseries, and allotment gardens, the amount of farmland in the green belt cannot be less than 15 percentage points below the national average and may be much more.

Unused land (category 11)

As might be expected in an area where there is such competition for land of all kinds, Figures 20 and 21 show that land completely unused occupies a very small proportion of the green belt. It takes 0·2 per cent of the approved green belt and exactly the same percentage of all land within the survey area shown in Figure 19. The area taken by this land category is so minor that too much attention must

[1] Best (1959), op. cit., 97; Best (1965), op. cit., 5.

not be paid to the slight variations from one quadrant to another. But it does seem that the north-western part of the green belt has more unused land than any other, with over 0·5 per cent of the area occupied, and the north-eastern part has least, the percentage figure being so small that it cannot be represented in the first place of decimals. Two sub-categories of unused land were defined in the survey, cut-over land and all other unused land. The values here are even smaller, and therefore differences are even less reliable, but it appears that cut-over land is most important in the north-west and south-east, and other unused land in the north-west and south-west.

Little is known of the general distribution of unused land in the past. One may assume that, because in the period before 1939 the pace and direction of development on city fringes was much less certain than it is today in green belts, there existed more unused land awaiting development. However there is little evidence to support this assumption. In the Land Utilization Survey prepared in the 1930s one of the categories employed was *Heathland, commons and rough pasture*. In the London area this category included four main types of land: rough hill pasture, rough marsh pasture, public or manorial commons and heaths, and finally, enclosed land formerly improved, but reverted to a poor condition and supporting a coarse vegetation of little agricultural value.[1] All these areas were shown on the Land Utilization Survey one-inch maps in yellow. Since the colour shadings were over-printed on Ordnance Survey sheets which generally use either a marsh or a heath and rough grassland symbol to depict the first three of the four types of land, it follows that the last category is represented by clear yellow shading. In fact, when the sheets for the London area are examined,[2] very little reverted land is revealed. The greatest concentration is upon the North Downs, where clearly it has nothing to do with urban expansion, and most of the rest can be identified as golf course, rough recreation land, or land on the fringes of gravel workings or reservoirs. Only a tiny proportion, for example in a few scattered patches near Watford and Rickmansworth or in the Lea Valley, appears to be agricultural land awaiting development, and has subsequently been built upon. The absence of this land on the survey maps may simply be due to the rapid growth of London in the early 1930s, which left little opportunity for land to lie idle.

[1] Willatts, op. cit., 147.
[2] Sheets 106 (Watford), 107 (North-east London and Epping Forest), 114 (Windsor), 115 (South-east London and Sevenoaks).

More likely it is due to the methods of classification used by the surveyors, mostly schoolchildren, who either left land upon which development was imminent in the agricultural, or other category it had occupied to that date, or placed the land in its new category— *Houses with Gardens* or *Land Agriculturally Unproductive* (that is, industry, yards, cemeteries, tips, etc.).

The detailed distribution of unused land at present is indicated by Figure 43, which covers the north-west quadrant of the green belt.

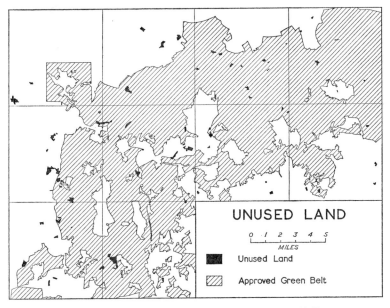

43. **Unused land in the green belt to the north-west of London, 1960**
(Source: Air photograph and field survey)

It will be recalled that the north-west contains more unused land than any of the other areas on London's fringe. Of the unused land shown in the map the larger tracts within the approved green belt, and in the countryside beyond it, are almost always cut-over land. They are areas which have been woodland, and will nearly all be replanted with timber, for example, the areas to the south-west of St. Albans, or the large area to the west of Iver Heath. Other tracts of unused land lie near the River Colne. Here they are either associated with the mineral working of this area, or they are stretches of marshy or waterlogged land. Only one or two very small areas, lying in 'white land', such as the tiny area in the north of Potters Bar, are unused because they are awaiting development. Land-use planning, reinforced by green belt control, combined with the intense demand for land of all kinds, seems virtually to have eradicated that unused land which can reasonably be employed for some purpose.

Since the area covered by unused land is so small it is not possible to construct a reliable graph showing variations in the amount of land lying idle with distance from London. There seems to be a concentration of unused land on the immediate fringe of London and also at the outer edge of the green belt, but it is possible that this result could have arisen by chance in the sampling.

There are no national statistics on unused land. It is not therefore possible to compare the amount of idle land in the green belt with that in the country as a whole, though the proportion of the green belt unused can hardly lie above the national average.

The last two chapters have been devoted to a detailed study of the land-use components of London's green belt. The general point to emerge from this examination is that all but one of the non-conforming uses in terms of their acreage are more strongly represented in the green belt than in the country at large, and the same holds true for a number of the more important conforming uses, such as institutions standing in extensive grounds and woodland. Only agriculture, and possibly, recreation land, are greatly under-represented in the green belt. In effect, there is a substantial clutter of urban and semi-urban land in the narrow zone immediately beyond the edge of the conurbation.

To some extent, it is true, the green belt has fossilized the land-use pattern which was in existence at the time its boundaries were designated. 'Development control', the main implement of statutory planning, is exactly what it appears. It enables local authorities to prevent undesirable changes, but does not easily allow them to rectify undesirable developments from the past. Green belt areas are simply those in which development control operates more stringently. Hence, while the pressure from current non-conforming uses of land can readily be resisted, little can be done about the consequences of past urban pressures upon rural land.

While the fossilization of pre-existing land-uses is a marked feature of the green belt, it by no means precludes change. As the survey of land-usage has already shown, small increases in non-conforming

216

land-uses took place between 1955 and 1960, and when the 'white land' within the survey area was accounted, the increases revealed were fairly substantial, for example, over 9 per cent in the area of residential and commercial land and over 16 per cent in the area of manufacturing.[1] Neither is the green belt itself static. There has already been some discussion above of the 400 acre tract in the Lea Valley, composed largely of disused greenhouses, which, though originally lying fully within the development plan green belt, was approved as building land.[2] The circumstances, it must be admitted, were rather special. The nature of the land was such that it could not, without great difficulty and expense, be returned to a rural use, and the links with central London made the area particularly suitable for overspill development. One further example of changes in the green belt itself will suffice to make the point.

It will be recalled that Hertfordshire County Council in its first development plan was one of those councils which sought to draw relatively uncomplicated green belt boundaries. Small patches of

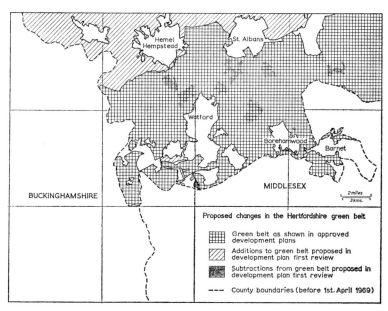

44. **Proposed changes in the Hertfordshire green belt to the north-west of London**
(Source: Ministry of Housing and Local Government)

[1] *Supra* p. 137.
[2] *Supra* pp. 93–4.

development within the green belt were generally not excluded and the green belt notation in the plan was used to cover even some quite large settlements like Abbots Langley, Brookman's Park and Radlett. When the first quinquennial review of the plan was prepared for submission to the Ministry of Housing and Local Government the opportunity was taken to propose changes in the area already designated as green belt. Figure 44 compares the original outline of the green belt in the quadrant to the north-west of London with that suggested in the review, and highlights those areas which it is proposed should be added to, as well as those areas which it is proposed should be subtracted from, the existing approved green belt.

Few changes are proposed at the inner edge of the green belt. In Figure 44 the inner edge of the Hertfordshire green belt is mostly defined by the boundary with Middlesex, but where it does correspond with the edge of the conurbation, at Barnet, it is clear that there is no relaxation of control. At the outer edge of the green belt substantial extensions are proposed. In effect, these are a re-statement of the earlier position taken by Hertfordshire, and most of the other counties fringing London, that the green belt should be extended well beyond its present limits. No final decision has yet been taken on these extensions, though, of course, they are now at variance with the proposals outlined in *A strategy for the South East*. A number of small additions to the green belt are suggested around settlements which lie wholly within its boundaries. These are almost exclusively designed to protect open spaces and recreation land which is at present left 'white' in the development plan, for example, the area to the south of Croxley Green, part of Oxhey Wood on the western side of South Oxhey, and an open space in north-east Bushey (compare Fig. 22). Most of the subtractions proposed from the green belt, occur towards its centre. They are either small extensions of the 'white land', as at Borehamwood, presumably to allow for some further expansion of the settlement, or they are simply exclusions from the green belt of the urban areas which previously were under green belt restriction, in order to comply with a policy already adopted and described earlier in this work.[1] In the second instance it appears as if the areas have been so 'rounded-off' that a little extra building space has been produced at the edges of the existing settlements.

The green belt has therefore in some way maintained the land-use

[1] *Supra* pp. 151–4.

pattern which was in existence at the time of its establishment, and in other ways it has encouraged change, but along certain specific lines. It has undoubtedly deeply affected the development of land-use in the fringe of London by excluding some uses over broad areas, and consequently allowing other uses to expand. But one important question remains: 'To precisely what degree has the green belt affected land-use on London's fringe?' To answer this a further question must be posed: 'What would have been the land-use pattern today if the green belt had not been created?' An attempt, if not to answer these questions, then to suggest the general lines along which answers might be sought, is made in the final chapter.

8 · The Green Belt in Perspective

The effects of the green belt upon the countryside of the metropolitan fringe are clearly profound. Quite how profound can only be established when the green belt as it exists is compared with what might reasonably have been expected to exist had the green belt never been designated. To define what might have been is the real problem. There seem to be two principal paths along which the predictions of land-use patterns on an uncontrolled urban fringe can effectively be approached. The first is by use of theoretical reasoning, the second, by analogy with what has happened in the rural surrounds of other large cities where growth has been less controlled than in London's green belt. The two paths are not as divergent as they may at first sight appear, since most of the theory treating of urban growth has a substantial element of comparative empiricism incorporated within it. But for the convenience of discussion the two approaches will be dealt with successively.

The contribution of theory

Of the two methods of approach, theoretical reasoning seems to have less to offer immediately than the empirical studies to an analysis of what the green belt area might have been like without a green belt. This has nothing to do with the intrinsic merits of the methods, but is simply a product of the fact that urban description and analysis by empirical means has attracted very many more scholars, over the years, than has urban theorizing. Until quite recent times British work on urban form and growth has been particularly long on fact and remarkably short on theory. It was not until about five years ago that serious attempts were first made to theorize about city development and to express that work in the form of mathematical models,

220

as, for example, in the research currently being undertaken by the Joint Unit for Planning Research.[1] Fortunately American and Scandinavian workers have concerned themselves much more with urban theory,[2] and it is from their work that such theoretical conclusions as exist upon city development must be derived.

It is now conventional to discuss the American models of city structure under three heads, concentric or zonal models, sector models, and multiple nuclei models.[3] Concentric or zonal theory depended essentially upon the supposition that cities developed outwards from their central areas more or less consistently in all directions. Since land values and accessibility to the centre were assumed to decline regularly with distance from the central business district, land-use types arranged themselves in regular concentric zones. The best known of the concentric theory models was that proposed by Burgess in the 1920s and based largely upon his study of Chicago.[4] Burgess postulated that within any city land usage was so organized that zones differing in age and character occurred, always in the same order from the centre outwards. The central business district was surrounded by a transition zone of mixed land-uses in which deteriorating residential property was being converted into smaller units, or to other uses, such as offices or light industry. Around this zone lay a working-class residential belt in which the dwellings were mostly old, but where the population was more stable than in the transition zone. A zone of middle-class dwellings completed the continuous built-up area of the city and was interspersed with pockets of high-cost development. Beyond the edge of the city lay the commuter's zone. This fringe area was dominated by suburban communities living in dormitory settlements. Much of the zone might still be open country, but the villages found within it would be undergoing a change in character and becoming functionally oriented towards the city, in which a considerable proportion of the population would be employed.

Though a number of more recent authors have claimed to recognize

[1] P. Cowan, J. Ireland, and D. Fine, 'Approaches to urban model building', *Regional Studies*, 1 (1967), 163-72.
[3] B. J. Garner, 'Models of urban geography and settlement location', in R. J. Chorley and P. Haggett (ed.), *Models in Geography* (London, 1967), 303-60.
[3] See, for example, J. H. Johnson, *Urban geography: an introductory analysis* (Oxford, 1967), 163-72.
[4] E. W. Burgess, 'The growth of the city', in R. E. Park, E. W. Burgess, and R. A. McKenzie (ed.), *The city* (Chicago, 1925), 47-62.

a concentric pattern in the land-use of a city which they have studied,[1] it is plain that to produce concentric zones there must be more than simply a strong radial emphasis in the transport system. There must be a large number of radial routes and they must be closely spaced. The further from the city centre, the less likely it is that these conditions will be met, since radial routes diverge with distance from the central point. The tendency, observed by many of Burgess's critics, of cities to assume a star-shaped form with more rapid developments taking place particularly along main radial roads than in the interstices, is therefore even more applicable to the areas beyond the city's fringe. It is thus likely that concentric models provide no more than a very moderate description of what green belt areas might otherwise have been like.

It was largely the unsatisfactory description of reality provided by the concentric model which encouraged further theories based upon different assumptions. One of the most important of these was the sector theory. All sector models are developed on the premise that the land-use of a city is mainly determined by the positioning of routeways radiating from the centre (that is, an assumption quite the opposite of that adopted by the concentric models which require all areas of the city at equal distance from the centre to be equally accessible). Differences in accessibility, for example, as between a point on a radial route and one distant from a main route to the city centre, lead to variations in land value, and hence variations in land-use. Probably the best known sector model was that advanced by Hoyt in 1939.[2] Hoyt suggests that similar land-uses agglomerate about particular radial routes from the city centre. Once contrasts have arisen in land-usage near the centre, these are perpetuated as the city grows to form distinctive sectors. Thus a high-class residential district, or a light manufacturing area, would extend itself by new growth on its outer arc.

The sector model appears to provide a better approximation to reality than the concentric model. Industry is more realistically treated and it seems very appropriate to the development of residential areas, particularly to the expansion of high-class dwellings. Hoyt, himself, was able to demonstrate, in an examination of thirty

[1] For example, H. Blumenfeld, 'On the concentric circle theory of urban growth', *Land Economics*, 25 (1949), 209–12.

[2] H. Hoyt, *The structure and growth of residential neighbourhoods in American cities* (Washington, 1939).

American cities, how the fashionable residential districts had emigrated outwards between 1900 and 1936,[1] while Jones, in his study of Belfast, found that the distribution of high-class residential areas was consistent with the sector theory.[2] All this seem to indicate that to predict possible developments in London's green belt area, it is necessary to pay most attention to present land-uses in the outer sections of the conurbation and to assume that they would, if allowed, develop further outwards. Growth would be focused upon the main radial communication arteries, and the rural land in between would be occupied much less quickly by urban uses of land.

The concentric and sector models offer a simple explanation of the way in which the land-use of a city develops. But cities are complex organisms and often do not conform with the assumptions upon which these models are based. For example, one of their main postulates is that each city has a single centre from which all outward growth takes place, whereas it is observable that cities are usually multi-centred, having different land-use nodes in which different urban functions are performed, each centre tending to act as a growth nucleus. It was to accommodate this feature that Harris and Ullman advanced their multi-nuclei model in 1945.[3]

Harris and Ullman suggested that cities had a fundamentally cellular structure, built around growth points. The number and position of the growth points depended upon the size of the city, its precise function, the peculiarities of its site, and upon its historical development. The larger the city the greater in number and the more specialized were its nuclei, but regardless of city size there were certain features which tended to create nuclei and to differentiate land-uses. Some activities had specialized requirements which limited their locations and hence contributed to their clustering upon particular sites. Others had a tendency to agglomerate in order to reap the economies of shared services or contacts with suppliers or markets. Like land-uses also tended to become grouped for a very different reason—that some activities repel others. Inconsistent land-uses were thus not found in close juxtaposition, but were inclined to gather in homogeneous districts. Finally, some activities were excluded from the high-rent areas because of their rent-paying ability

[1] Johnson, op. cit., 168-9.
[2] E. Jones, *A social geography of Belfast* (London, 1960), 276-8.
[3] C. D. Harris and E. L. Ullman, 'The nature of cities', *Annals of the American Academy of Political and Social Science*, 242 (1945), 7-17.

was low. They thus became confined to the low-rent districts of cities. Harris and Ullman were able to identify five distinct types of district in American cities which were associated with particular nuclei: the central business district, a wholesaling and light manufacturing area, a heavy industrial zone, residential districts of various classes, and peripheral suburbs, either dormitory or industrial. As Johnson has pointed out, the incorporation of the effects of historical and site factors into the model has produced unique elements which make it difficult to apply the model universally.[1] But for particular cities, such as London, it does provide an indication of the way in which a city develops, of the precise nature of accretions at the city's edge, and of the expected developments which might take place in association with existing nuclei.

Many authors have insisted that the three types of model are not mutually exclusive.[2] In most urban or even rural areas elements of all three can be identified. For example, Keeble and Haggett, in a study of urban expansion in rural areas of southern Cambridgeshire since World War Two, showed how the growth-distance gradients varied with distance from Cambridge, with distance from a major highway, and with distance from village centres.[3] The results suggested support for all three models. The gentle gradient from the main city was consistent with the concentric-zone model, the steeper gradient about the main road was in line with the sector model, while the steepest gradient about the outlying villages lent substance to the multiple-nuclei model. Even in a city with as simple a structure as Calgary's, Smith was able to recognize concentric zones as well as sectors.[4] At a theoretical level the fusion of the models is not a difficult matter. Mann has attempted to illustrate the urban structure of a typical medium-sized British city by combining the concentric and sector models,[5] while Marble has proposed a model of a star-shaped city which contains ingredients derived from the concentric, sector, and multiple-nuclei models.[6] As Haggett has stressed, in urban or rural areas, the use of all these models provides a better

[1] Johnson, op. cit., 171.

[2] For example, Garner, op. cit., 343.

[3] P. Haggett, *Locational analysis in human geography* (London, 1965), 180-1.

[4] P. J. Smith, 'Calgary: a study in urban pattern', *Economic Geography*, 38 (1962), 315-29.

[5] P. Mann, *An approach to urban sociology* (London, 1965), 95-6; see also Johnson, op. cit., 169.

[6] W. Garrison, B. J. L. Berry, D. F. Marble, J. D. Nystuen and R. L. Morrill, *Studies of highway development and geographic change* (Seattle, 1959), 144.

explanation of the growth of land-use zones, than of one alone; an eclectic rather than a selective use of location models may be the better overall policy in analysing geographic distributions.

The great contribution of the Scandinavians in the field of urban theory has also been in the production of models of settlement evolution. However, their models are less descriptive of the form of urban structure than the American examples described above, and are directed more to the simulation and prediction of population spatial patterns. In this work growth and migration of population have been studied both within a deterministic and within a probabilistic or stochastic framework. The deterministic models make strict assumptions about behaviour. Given that these assumptions hold true in practice, it becomes possible to predict with some degree of precision the future development of population and settlement in time and space. Such a model was that developed by Bylund in the study of the urbanization of the central Lappland area of Sweden.[1] He sought to explain why, in the period up to 1867, settlers had failed to occupy the best land before bringing land of lower quality into cultivation. A model was developed to simulate the waves of settlement under the assumption that colonizers wished to minimize the distances between their new locations and their original settlement, between their new locations and a church, and between their new locations and a line of communication. The patterns which he was able to produce from an initial settlement distribution approximated reasonably closely, at each stage of development, the actual distribution.

Though deterministic models of many different kinds have been employed with considerable success[2] they do have certain disadvantages. They tend to be inflexible, they require a fairly thorough knowledge of the processes of change operating in any given situation, and they become extremely cumbersome when there is a large number of factors to be considered. The alternative is the probabilistic or stochastic model. These depend largely upon random behaviour patterns. Though the actions of each individual may be consciously determined, the aggregate effect is random and may be discussed in terms of chance variations. By and large stochastic models are more flexible, and often more realistic than deterministic models, but they

---

[1] E. Bylund, 'Theoretical considerations regarding the distribution of settlement in inner north Sweden', *Geografiska Annaler*, 42 (1960), 225-31.

[2] See, for example, D. Harvey in Chorley and Haggett, op. cit., 563-70.

can also become mathematically more difficult. The difficulties are normally overcome by use of Monte Carlo methods. Broadly speaking, growth and change are simulated by random processes which are determined by reference to a sequence of random numbers. The random processes are made more realistic by constraining their operation to conform with empirically observed trends.

Perhaps the most ambitious use of Monte Carlo methods in settlements studies has been made by Morrill.[1] Though an American, his work rests heavily upon the earlier ideas of Scandinavians such as Ajo,[2] Dahl,[3] Hägerstrand,[4] Kulldorf,[5] Lövgren,[6] and Wendel.[7] Morrill studied an inland area of roughly 6,500 square miles in southern Sweden, centred upon the towns of Ljungby, Värnamo, Växkö, and Vetlanda, in which industrial growth began at about 1865 but became marked after 1880. The work is concerned with tracing the growth of population from 1860 to 1960 by the use of census material, and then, by employing principles derived from central place, industrial location, and transport location theory, simulating population growth in order to predict future distributions.

The model runs in twenty year cycles. Within each cycle a number of processes are defined, and assignments made for the location of new activities. The location of new transport routes, the location of central place activities, the location of manufacturing and other non-central place activities, and the movement of migrants between areas are simulated by the Monte Carlo technique. Thus from a bench-

[1] R. L. Morrill, 'Simulation of central place patterns over time', in K. Norborg (ed.), *Proceedings of the I.G.U. symposium in urban geography*, Lund Studies in Geography, Series B, No. 24 (Lund, 1962), 109–20; 'The development and spatial distribution of towns in Sweden: an historical-predictive approach', *Annals of the Association of American Geographers*, 53 (1963), 1–14; *Migration and the spread and growth of urban settlement*, Lund Studies in Geography, Series B, No. 26 (Lund, 1965).

[2] For example, R. Ajo, *Contributions to social physics*, Lund Studies in Geography, Series B, No. 11 (Lund, 1953).

[3] Especially in D. Hannerberg, T. Hägerstrand and B. Odeving (ed.), *Migration in Sweden: a symposium*, Lund Studies in Geography, Series B, No. 13 (Lund, 1957), 206–43.

[4] Ibid., 27–158, See also T. Hägerstrand, *Innovation diffusion as a spatial process* (Chicago, 1967).

[5] G. Kulldorf, *Migration probabilities*, Lund Studies in Geography, Series B, No. 14 (Lund, 1955).

[6] For example, E. Lövgren, 'The geographical mobility of labour', *Geografiska Annaler*, 38 (1956), 344–94.

[7] B. Wendel, *A migration schema: theories and observations*, Lund Studies in Geography, Series B, No. 9 (Lund, 1953).

mark distribution where the pattern of routes, services, manufacturing, and population is known, a new distribution can be predicted for twenty years hence. The new pattern in turn becomes the benchmark for the following simulation cycle.

Of particular interest in this discussion of the possibilities of determining developments in London's green belt had the green belt controls not been in operation, is Morrill's procedure for assigning migrants in each simulation. He assumes that the propensity to migrate from any source area is a function first of the size of the population, and secondly of its character, for example, its age structure, or its normal rate of turnover in jobs. The probability of migration between two areas is assumed to be closely related to the distance between the areas, to the difference in the attractiveness of the areas, and to the previous migration links between the areas. Given these assumptions, the chances of migration taking place from a source area to any other area can be assessed and probability values assigned. The total number of migrants from the source area can then be distributed among the destination areas by means of numbers drawn from a random numbers table.

In a commentary upon Monte Carlo models, Harvey has considered the effectiveness of Morrill's methods.[1] He concludes that though the model devised by Morrill is extremely useful for pedagogic purposes, it is difficult to verify as a general predictive tool since there is only one real world pattern with which its results have been compared. Predictive models based upon probability distributions can produce a very wide range of results. The procedure only becomes meaningful where large numbers of events, quite independent of one another, are under consideration, and where these are capable of being aggregated to form an overall pattern. The stage of Morrill's model which is concerned with the assignment of migrants between places seems to meet these conditions because it treats of the net movement of a large number of people, and Harvey was satisfied that this section of the model was capable of producing results which approximated reality.

Monte Carlo simulation methods are not without their difficulties. But given that the theoretical assumptions which determine the operation of the random variable contained in the model are valid, that the model is based upon data which can be aggregated, and that

[1] Harvey, op. cit., 582-92.

no more direct method is available for solving the problem, stochastic models may well prove to be the most efficient means of simulating changing spatial patterns through time. Such models, particularly if they are of the type advanced by Morrill, seem to offer practical and realistic methods upon which to base a hypothetical extension of the built-up area of London into the green belt for the period since its designation. If the methods were to be pursued they would certainly produce abundant material with which to speculate about the growth of population and economic activity on an uncontrolled fringe of London.

Finally, in this section dealing with possible theoretical approaches to the definition of developments on city fringes, reference is made to a body of work generally known as gradient analysis.[1] This consists of attempts to describe various features of a city or of cities in terms of regular and logical sequences with distance from the city centre. Graphs can be constructed to illustrate the gradations revealed by a statistical analysis of the features under investigation, curves can be fitted to the sequence produced, and equations can be derived to represent the curves. It can be seen that gradient analysis is simply a method of describing and generalizing urban structure which has a broad predictive value because it seems that relationships identified in one city may often hold true for others. It is related to concentric zone and sector theory, but has a more pronounced and rigorous quantitative foundation.

Though widespread interest in gradient analysis is a recent feature, it is by no means a new method. Bleicher, as early as 1892, had observed a regular decline in population density between the inner and outer residential areas of Frankfurt am Main, Burgess in 1928 referred to the various social and economic gradients produced by the growth of a city, and C. R. Shaw, in 1929, commented upon juvenile delinquency by reference to zone gradients and also to radial gradients measured along streets leading outwards from the city centre.[2] By 1933 Colby had explored the forces which determined the various urban gradients. One set of forces, the centrifugal forces, drove out certain land-uses from the city centre because of the high costs and congestion to be found there; another set of forces, the centripetal forces, attracted other land-uses into the city centre in

[1] See Johnson, op. cit., 172–5.
[2] Ibid., 173.

228

THE CONTRIBUTION OF THEORY

order that they might maximize their accessibility to customers and to other closely related activities.[1]

Further recent attention has been paid to gradient analysis following the work of Clark.[2] As the result of a study of the population density gradients of thirty-six cities, and using statistics ranging in time from 1801 to 1950, Clark was able to argue that regardless of the particular land-use arrangement within a city and regardless of the time period upon which the study is focused, the distribution of population densities decline as a negative exponential function of distance from the city centre. Or put another way, if the logarithm of population density is plotted on a graph against distance from a city centre, then the curve showing the relationship between the two will approach a straight line. Two important points should be made about Clark's generalization. First, residential densities for the central areas of cities are extrapolated from the slopes derived from the outer residential areas. Since the central areas of most cities are occupied mainly by business and public buildings the hypothetical density used in deriving the equation for the gradient is often very much higher than the observed density. Secondly, the values used for densities outside the central business area are usually calculated by taking the mean of all administrative or census districts which lie at roughly equal distances from the city centre. Since large metropolitan areas particularly have highly complex structures, with many subsidiary centres in addition to the main central area, it is very possible that in most of the studies of large cities, apparently regular population density gradients disguise quite important differences in urban form.

More recent work has confirmed Clark's original observations.[3] Of the hundred or more cities so far studied in all parts of the world in respect of their population density gradients not one has provided evidence which seriously challenges Clark's claim that a negative exponential model adequately describes residential densities within cities. Of course, not all the gradients identified have the same slope. The density gradients of cities tend to become less steep through

[1] C. C. Colby, 'Centrifugal and centripetal forces in urban geography', *Annals of the Association of American Geographers*, 23 (1933). 1–20.

[2] C. Clark, 'Urban population densities', *Journal of the Royal Statistical Society*, Series A, 114 (1951), 490–96.

[3] See, for example, B. J. L. Berry, J. W. Simmons, and R. J. Tennant, 'Urban population densities: structure and change', *Geographical Review*, 53 (1963), 389–405; C. Clark, *Population growth and land-use* (London, 1967), 339–87.

time as their areas are extended, and it is also clear that the gradients of different cities differ markedly. Muth, for example, in a study of thirty-six American cities, showed that the density gradient coefficient varied between 0·7 and 1·2,[1] while Clark, in a compilation of density gradients drawn from all parts of the world, has revealed a range at the present time from London, with a very low coefficient of 0·09 and therefore with a density gradient of very gentle slope, to Okayama, with a coefficient of 1·32.[2] Muth was able to identify only four variables which were significantly related to differences in the slope of the density curves; car registration per capita, the proportion of manufacturing employment in the central area, the proportion of substandard dwellings in the central area, and the overall size of the urban area. This led Muth to the view that bigger cities with low transport costs, with dilapidated central areas and with dispersed centres of employment were the more likely to contain population of high densities and to produce gentle density gradients. This conclusion finds support in the work of Winsborough.[3]

No full explanation yet exists for variations in the density gradients, or indeed for the existence of the gradient itself, but recent investigations by Alonso have at least provided an economic rationale for declining residential densities with distance from a city centre.[4] It is suggested that the phenomena may be seen, to put it in its simplest terms, as the result of the substitution by family units of rents for transport costs. The land most demanded, and hence most expensive, lies close to the city centre, where there is maximum accessibility to city services. The further away a site lies from the city centre the lower its cost, because competition is reduced, but the higher the transport costs involved, since the distance from city centre services is increased. High land values in or near the centre encourage dense residential development in order that families may minimize their costs. Further away from the city centre lower land values lead to lower density development and to a thinning out of population in the outer suburbs of the city. High and low density developments often become associated with different social groups and this factor

[1] R. F. Muth, 'The spatial structure of the housing market', *Papers and Proceedings, Regional Science Association*, 7 (1962), 207–20.
[2] Clark (1967), op. cit., 349–51.
[3] H. H. Winsborough, 'City growth and city structure', *Journal of Regional Science*, 4 (1962), 35–49.
[4] W. Alonso, 'A theory of the urban land market', *Papers and Proceedings, Regional Science Association*, 6 (1960), 149–58.

tends to emphasize and perpetuate the differences between the inner and outer suburbs of cities. Overall, this is an argument which is inclined to support Clark's original supposition that population gradients in cities are related to transport costs.

Clark's ideas have been considerably extended since 1951. Gradient analysis has been applied to urban characteristics other than residential population density, such as employment densities in all or in selected industries, land values, wholesaling, retailing, and many other features. The investigations have not always yielded similar kinds of gradients and similar functions. The exponential relationship has appeared frequently, but it is not ubiquitous. For example, in his work upon population change in the area under London's influence Ajo fitted sine curves to describe observed conditions over a distance of eighty miles from the centre of the conurbation.[1] But whatever the precise relationship the fact remains that it becomes possible to predict, having established the form of the relationship, the way in which the features under study would be likely to develop given an extension outwards of the urban area such as would be implied for London in the absence of a green belt. Extrapolations of this kind might be quite realistically undertaken since they could be made against the substantial background of knowledge on urban and rural gradients provided by Bogue, in 1949, in a major survey of the hinterlands of sixty-five United States cities.[2]

The theoretical models discussed in this section form a logical basis for arriving at conclusions about what the present green belt area of London might have been like without the green belt. But as has been stressed already they are potential rather than actual sources of enlightenment. No one has yet applied techniques like, for example, those of Morrill or Clark, to this particular problem. While the possibilities are exciting, practical results do not yet exist. At the moment, therefore, the prediction of the possible landscape effects of an uncontrolled expansion of London must rest almost entirely upon field investigations undertaken in analogous situations.

[1] R. Ajo, 'London's field response in terms of population change', *Acta Geographica*, 18 No. 2 (1964), 1–19; 'London's field response II', *Acta Geographica*, 18 No. 3 (1964), 1–25.
[2] D. J. Bogue, *The structure of the metropolitan community: a study of dominance and subdominance* (Ann Arbor, 1949).

The contribution of empirical studies

The literature is rich in empirical investigations of urban fringe areas, many of them based upon field studies in America. But as with the use of theoretical models to predict London's growth patterns in the absence of a green belt, a reliance upon analogy with cities in other parts of the world is not devoid of problems. These have been highlighted recently by Mann, who, in a discussion of the essential differences between urban and rural society, attempted to produce quantitative evidence to test a series of propositions culled largely from American works dealing with contrasts between urban and rural characteristics.[1] His statistics referred to England and Wales, and fell into four major classes: population structure, birth and death rates, health conditions, and social behaviour. Because of the nature of the population census and of the other sources available to him, the examination lacked the detail of similar studies undertaken in the United States,[2] but in a general way he was able to conclude that many of the propositions could be supported, while a number seemed to have no basis and a few were quite untenable, the relationships observed being found to be exactly the opposite of those proposed.

Two reasons were advanced for the variety of the results in the tests. First, some of the propositions rested upon studies which had been undertaken at some time in the past. The findings were consequently not strictly relevant to the present day differences which existed between towns and their hinterlands. Secondly, many of the propositions, because they were derived from American sources and therefore based upon a rather different geographical situation, could not reasonably be expected to represent conditions in this country. Mann pointed to differences between the United States and Britain in the scale of the country, in the density of the population, in the importance of coloured and immigrant groups, and in the nature of the transport system, particularly in respect of the importance attached to mobility by motor car. It is clear that analogies drawn with situations in other countries must be accepted only with some caution.

The study of purely urban and of purely rural situations led

[1] Mann, op. cit., 28–68.
[2] For example, O. D. Duncan and A. J. Reiss, *Social characteristics of urban and rural communities* (New York, 1956).

eventually to the recognition of the existence of an intermediate zone, the urban fringe, which possessed some of the attributes of each. On a sociological plane the urban fringe has drawn much recent attention from writers, such as Pahl,[1] who have been attracted by these areas because, though they are still apparently rural, they contain communities which, in terms of social structure and of mental attitudes, are often very urbanized. Pahl has already summarized the work undertaken in the United States on the social nature of urban fringes.[2] He describes the problems encountered in defining the urban fringe in sociological terms, examines some of the theories put forward to account for the development of new patterns on the peripheries of cities, and discusses in some detail a number of attempts to focus both upon the more general principles governing social change and upon the impact of change on particular communities. For example he considers the work of Martin on ecological change in satellite rural areas.[3] Martin, seeking the ecological aspects underlying population redistribution, propounds two principles. First, he argues that urban-influenced social change in rural areas varies according to the distance from, and the size of, the dominating city. Secondly, he concluded that those rural areas under strong urban influence are likely to show greater differentiation of function than those more isolated from cities. Pahl agrees that there is evidence to support the gradient hypothesis and also that a change from rural homogenity to heterogenity would appear to be an *a priori* characteristic of an urban fringe.

Pahl's main example of urban influenced change is derived from the unpublished work of Dobriner upon the village of Huntingdon, Long Island.[4] Huntingdon, once a self-contained village, has now become firmly part of the New York metropolitan region. It has developed two, almost distinct, communities; the one composed of long term dwellers who had close links with the village and with its institutions and organizations, the other composed of newcomers from New

[1] See, for example, R. E. Pahl, 'Education and social class in commuter villages', *Sociological Review*, 11 (1962), 241–6; 'Class and community in English commuter villages', *Sociologia Ruralis*, 5 (1965), 5–23.
[2] R. E. Pahl, *Urbs in rure*, London School of Economics and Political Science Geographical Papers No. 2 (London, 1965) 73–7.
[3] W. T. Martin, 'Ecological change in satellite rural areas', *American Sociological Review*, 22 (1957), 173–83.
[4] W. M. Dobriner, *The impact of metropolitan decentralization on a village social structure*, unpublished Ph.D. thesis (Columbia University, 1956).

York, well-educated, cosmopolitan, and in high income groups, who possessed no ties with the village. The two groups were separated socially and spatially rather in the same way that Pahl's own studies had revealed in his investigation of three villages in Hertfordshire, though here, of course, quite diverse social groups were involved and the relationships established between them were quite different.[1] The distinction between the two groups was not likely to disappear quickly, since the incoming population was highly mobile, almost all worked outside the area, nearly half of them in New York, and many looked upon the village as a temporary home before moving off elsewhere.

Johnson has entered some reservations on the validity of a socially defined fringe zone.[2] Modern methods of communication, and this includes radio and television as well as means of transit, are making the distinction between urban and rural social attitudes much less clear. Even occupations, upon which some authors have based their definitions of a fringe belt, provide an imperfect guide since with easier methods of travel both urban and rural jobs may be undertaken by members of the same family. Large parts of all densely developed countries in Western Europe feel the influence of urbanism upon social life, not only those areas in the immediate vicinity of cities. Johnson was therefore inclined to think that land-use, rather than social or employment factors, would provide a simpler, and more reliable guide to the character of the fringe zone and to the changes taking place there.

It was the obvious effects of suburban growth in the inter-war and post-war periods which stimulated geographers and others to pay particular attention to the land-use composition and function of urban fringe developments. As long ago as 1942, Wehrwein published an article on the rural-urban fringe which is now generally regarded as the early formative paper in this field of study.[3] In his investigation of American cities, and particularly of Indianapolis, the author recognized that railways were among the first decentralizers of urban population and urban land-uses, and that their effects were greatly enlarged when the automobile and hard-surfaced roads provided means of swift, unchanneled mass transportation which was added

[1] Pahl (1965), op. cit., 41–71.
[2] Johnson, op. cit., 142.
[3] G. S. Wehrwein, 'The rural-urban fringe', *Economic Geography*, 18 (1942), 217–28.

to the existing channeled mass transportation of the railways. The structure of simple agricultural zones about a city, such as those postulated by von Thünen, was transformed. Wherever a railway, inter-urban line, or highway entered a city, residences, commercial establishments, and industrial plants became strung out along their route. Since these means of transportation radiated in all directions whenever physical features allowed, the rural-urban fringe came to consist of rural territory pierced by finger-like projections of urbanized land-uses. Between the arms of the star shape thus produced, agriculture and other non-urban land-uses continued, but in more or less modified form.

A closer examination of the urbanized parts of the rural-urban fringe led Wehrwein to identify some of its important characteristics. The first lay in the nature of residential growth. Flexibility of transportation between city edge and city centre encouraged, in the America of the interwar years, a wild expansion of the main urban areas. Land agents and speculators rushed to lay out subdivisions for low density dwellings, often in excess of the building plots which were demanded. Therefore in addition to the great areas of built-up land which spread into the rural hinterlands of cities, the over-expansion of residential sites led to vacant, weed-covered land, expensively supplied with streets, water, sewers, gas, and electricity, and therefore, for all practical purposes, impossible to return to agriculture or any other rural use. Since such expansions took place in areas which had rural forms of government and lower densities than obtain in cities, the financial burden of unsold, unused, and unproductive lots was considerable.

The second characteristic feature of land-use stemmed from the recreational demands upon the urban fringe. Wehrwein describes with some gloom a situation on most urban fringes where land suitable for recreation had long been pre-empted for private use. Riparian land along lakes and streams was covered with summer cottages, resorts, taverns, dance halls, and fun-fairs. Roads leading to such resort areas were lined with established recreation areas and much pressure was exerted upon farm land by hunters in search of game. Nowhere, it seems, were the conflicts between farmers and the remainder of the population greater than in the areas close to cities.

The third characteristic of fringe land-uses recognized by Wehrwein was the result of institutional factors. For convenience, and because of their space requirements, many of the public utilities serving cities became located in the rural fringe areas. Recreation land, water supply and radio stations, sewage disposal plants, airports, and cemeteries were therefore among the urban necessities found beyond the outer edge of the city. But in addition to these uses, there were others, necessary but unwanted in the city, which it had been the practice of cities to force into rural territory by ordinances excluding them from the built-up area as such. Slaughter houses, wholesale oil storage, noxious industries of all sorts, junk yards, caravans and caravan parks, taverns and dance halls, sub-standard dwellings, carnivals, and the sale of fireworks had all been subject to restrictive city legislation at one place or another. Such activities escaped urban control by locating in the nearby countryside where rural authorities had neither the powers nor the resolve to take action. In his study of the Indianapolis metropolitan district Wehrwein discovered that within the unincorporated areas which lacked zoning ordinances of their own there were in all forty-three identifiable overspill uses of this kind. Nearly 50 per cent of these lay within a mile of the edge of Indianapolis, 66 per cent lay within two miles, and 85 per cent lay within four miles of the city limit.

Wehrwein's pioneering study has been followed by many others, focusing upon the land-use of the rural-urban fringe. A large number of authors, such as Balk in his work on Worcester, Massachusetts,[1] have provided detailed descriptions of the fringes of particular towns or cities while others like Andrews,[2] have attempted to identify the general land-use characteristics of rural-urban zones. Yet others have paid attention to more limited aspects of rural fringe areas. For example, Fellman has considered the alterations to the geography of areas close to a city which take place in advance of actual building,[3] Blizzard and Anderson have dealt with the problems of delimiting the rural-urban fringe,[4] Firey has studied the social and planning implications of rapidly developing zones around cities,[5] Masser and

[1] H. H. Balk, 'Urbanization of Worcester's environs', *Economic Geography*, 21 (1945), 104–16.
[2] R. B. Andrews, 'Elements of the urban fringe problem', *Journal of Land and Public Utility Economics*, 18 (1942), 169–83.
[3] J. D. Fellman, 'Pre-building growth patterns in Chicago', *Annals of the Association of American Geographers*, 47 (1957), 59–82.
[4] S. W. Blizzard and W. F. Anderson II, *Problems in rural-urban research: conceptualization and delineation* (Pennsylvania State College, 1952).
[5] W. I. Firey, 'Ecological considerations in planning for urban fringes', *American Sociological Review*, 11 (1946), 411–23.

Stroud have written about the influence of commuters upon rural areas,[1] Roterus and Hughes have described the problems for local government which arise on urban peripheries,[2] and Whitehand has attempted to recognize the fringe belts of earlier periods in the urban form of present day cities.[3] The literature on the rural-urban fringe is now copious and diverse, most of it dating from the period 1945–60. Attention here will be confined to two of the most recent contributions.

The first of these is a study of Sydney's fringe published in 1960 by Golledge.[4] It is of particular interest not only because it rests upon the extensive writing of the period up to 1960, but because the evidence on which it is based, unlike most of the earlier work, is not American. It therefore gives an insight into urban fringe conditions in a less familiar part of the world. The work is also of interest because the time-span of the investigation covers a period in which there were few land-use controls, followed by one in which a fairly strictly maintained green belt was in operation.

Golledge began by setting up a series of propositions describing the features which develop on the margins of big cities. The rural urban fringe, in his view, had seven major characteristics: it had a constantly changing pattern of land occupance, farms were small, crop production was intensive, the population was mobile and of low or moderate density, residential expansion was rapid, the provision of services and public utilities was incomplete, and speculative sub-division and speculative building were common. He then proceeded to examine each of these characteristics in respect of Sydney's fringe area.

The changing pattern of land was the least difficult feature to demonstrate. As the urban area of Sydney expanded, so increasing demands were made upon rural land by urban uses. As the edge of the city drew nearer the more rapid were the changes in land occupance and land-use. Farm sizes, he discovered, varied inversely with distance from the centre of Sydney. On the immediate urban fringe

[1] F. I. Masser and D. C. Stroud, 'The metropolitan village', *Town Planning Review*, 36 (1956), 111-24.
[2] V. Roterus and I. H. Hughes, 'Governmental problems of fringe areas', *Public Management*, 30 (1948), 94-7.
[3] J. W. R. Whitehand, 'Fringe belts: a neglected aspect of urban geography', *Institute of British Geographers, Transactions and Papers*, 41 (1967), 223-33.
[4] R. Golledge, 'Sydney's metropolitan fringe: a study in urban-rural relations', *Australian Geographer*, 7 (1960), 243-55.

237

holdings were small, often averaging as little as five to six acres in some local government areas; at greater distance from Sydney, for example at thirty to thirty-five miles from the city centre, the average holding was much more likely to exceed fifty acres, and in some local government areas the average was as high as 250 acres. The nature of farming also varied with distance from the city. The small fringe farms were highly specialized upon the production of perishable or semi-perishable market garden crops which gave a high return on invested capital and which helped cover the higher costs of production associated with proximity to the urban mass. Double cropping and interculture were common. In the outer country areas mixed farming predominated and a much greater emphasis was placed upon the single cropping of grain, hay, and fodder crops.

The population of Sydney's fringe area was highly characteristic. While population densities were low growth rates in the period 1947–54 sometimes exceeded 100 per cent. Most of these sharp increases were contributed by in-migrants, whose age structure was very heavily overloaded by persons in the age-groups 0–9 years and 20–34 years, that is, by young married couples and their children. Increases in the number of dwellings matched the growth in population on Sydney's fringe, but the provision of public utilities lagged badly. For example, within Sydney most local government areas recorded over 80 per cent of their dwellings fully connected with gas, water, and sewage facilities. In the fringe area sometimes as many as three-quarters of the dwellings were supplied with water only. In the better type of sub-division, builder-speculators provided all necessary services, including surfaced roads, and Golledge saw this as beneficial development.

Sydney's green belt seems to operate very much like that around London. Its purpose is to contain the city, to act as a buffer between the city and rural towns, to provide space for recreation and other pursuits which require a rural setting close to the city's edge, to reserve areas for government use, and to create a unified area around the city in which desirable standards of agriculture, dwellings, recreation, and amenity can be maintained. The belt was first proposed in 1947 and was fully implemented in 1951. Golledge's comments on its influence are of great interest. He sees its general effect as creating an artificial rural-urban fringe, less dynamic than that produced by natural growth processes. Dead land, resulting from over-development by speculators, had virtually disappeared, land tenure

238

had become more stable, and a clearer division had evolved between urban and rural land. Unsightly urban sprawl had been prevented, the residential character of settlements had been preserved by restricting industrial growth, and because settlements were more compact than hitherto, both government and private transport operators were able to provide a better and more economic service. In the long term, the green belt was bound to sever the urban-rural continuum, and would eventually destroy the fringe by removing many of the characteristics produced by the combination of urban and rural land-uses.

The second, recent contribution to the literature on urban fringes is the substantial text produced by Wissink in 1962.[1] As its title indicates, it is based largely upon American experience, and particularly on field data collected in 1955 and 1956 in Atlanta, Chicago, Los Angeles, Madison, Philadelphia, and San Francisco, but it includes also comparative assessments of French, English, and Dutch cities. It provides a thorough digest of the literature, as well as attempting, once more, to typify the urban fringe of American cities.[2] The difficulties which the author faces in doing this are readily apparent. There are wide variations from city to city and for few of them does he possess detailed quantitative data. Although in his description he is able to expand a great deal upon the work of Wehrwein, because of the variety of the detailed information at his disposal, he is unable, except in a very general way, to suggest a scheme of land-use typical of American fringe areas.

Wissink's generalized outline of land-use on American city fringes rests partly upon his own field work, and partly upon the work of Andrews.[3] He identifies, first, seven functions which involve substantial physical structures: residential, commercial, industrial, institutional, recreational, agricultural, and transportational. It seems rather strange to find agricultural land in this group, especially as truck farming is no longer a common phenomenon on city fringes in America. The forms in which these functions appear may be linear, at crossroads, interstitial, compact, or scattered, and they occur with open spaces intervening between them. The second group of functions, those not involving substantial physical structures, contains

---

[1] G. A. Wissink, *American cities in perspective: with special reference to the development of their fringe areas* (Assen, 1962).
[2] Ibid., 65–71.
[3] Andrews, op. cit.

only two items: recreational, and vacant or waste land. These are intermingled with the other uses.

The generalized picture of the urban fringe sketched by Wissink is unspecific. Almost all land-uses occur in almost all conceivable forms. It follows that the work is of low predictive value, particularly as the situations in which rural-urban fringes develop are themselves so varied. As Wissink himself admits, 'Conditions and patterns of transportation, governmental structure and system, local government regulations, degree and quality of planning, history of development (including rate of growth in different periods), economic and social structure, functions, size and existing overall shape, topography, cost of land and structures, social and historic values of the group, personal and group initiatives, all these and perhaps other factors will lead to an individual variation of the general scheme in every individual case.'

Wissink's book, more than any of the earlier works, points to the difficulties of argument by analogy in respect of London's green belt. Though he has collected together abundant material on the nature of city fringes, its applicability elsewhere must be open to doubt. As the above discussion has revealed, there are many characteristics which are common to most city fringes, but there are also differences. If Wissink was unable to arrive at more precise generalizations about the fringes of American cities then, given the different economic, social, and governmental conditions in Britain, it is unlikely that detailed conclusions can be drawn for London's fringe based upon American, or any other evidence from overseas. While descriptive comparisons throw some immediate light on the general nature of urban fringes, future progress in estimating the precise effects of London's green belt seem to lie more in the development of theoretical models of city expansion than in pursuing further the analogous situations, however detailed their documentation, in other parts of the world.

Index

241

243

Masser, F. I., 236–7
Meath, Lord, 47, 73–5, 76, 79
Medway towns, 69
Metropolitan Region:
  boundary, 65
  inner, 146, 159
  outer, 29, 32, 159
Middlesex, 81, 104, 106, 123, 140, 146, 149, 152, 218
Midlands, 67, 93, 162, 163
Mill Hill, 116–17
Milton Keynes, 70
Ministry of Agriculture, Fisheries and Food, 203
Ministry of Health, 50, 51–2, 56
Ministry of Health Act (1919), 50
Ministry of Housing and Local Government, 65, 66, 89–90, 92–3, 94, 100–101, 121, 137–8, 146, 152, 159, 169–70, 198, 205, 218
Ministry of Labour, 69, 158, 161–2
Ministry of Town and Country Planning, 62, 64–5, 86, 168
Ministry of Works, 110–11
Misbourne, 196
Models:
  concentric, 221–2, 224–5
  deterministic, 225–6
  gradient, 228–31
  multiple nuclei, 221, 223–5
  sector, 221, 222–3, 224–5
  stochastic, 225–8
Modern Architectural Research Society, 48, 61
Monte Carlo methods, 226–8
More, Sir Thomas, 72
Morgan, J. M., 42
Morrill, R. L., 226–8
Morrison, Herbert, 80
Motorway box, 36
Muth, R. F., 230

National Coal Board, 171
National Farm Survey, 208
National Grid lines, 100
National Parks, 90, 107–8, 204
National Parks and Access to the Countryside Act (1949), 107, 111
National Parks Commission, 90, 107–108, 112
National Playing Fields Association, 78
National Trust, 117, 118, 198, 199, 204

Nature Conservancy, 90, 111–12
Nature reserves, 90
New Lanark, 41–2
New towns, 33–4, 51, 55, 60, 62, 67, 69, 77, 100, 187
New Towns Act (1946), 62
New York, 233–4
Newbury, 67
Newland Park, 110
'Nibbling', 93
Niven, D. B., 76
Norfolk, 67
North Circular Road, 24, 29
North Downs, 106, 107, 109, 112, 117, 118, 166, 191, 193, 197, 214
North Mymms, 192
North Weald Bassett, 112
Northampton, 67, 70
Northfleet, 161
Northwood, 46, 112
Nyn Park, 196

Offices, 24, 27, 28–30, 35
Old Testament, 72
Ordnance Survey, 196
Orpington, 105, 110, 141
Osborne, J. G., 125
Owen, Robert, 41–2, 43, 72
Oxfordshire, 67
Oxhey, 148
Oxhey Wood, 218

Pahl, R. E., 145, 233–4
Paris plans, 49, 70
Park Royal, 24
Park Woods, 112
Parker, Barry, 44, 46, 85
Parkland, 75, 76, 79, 83, 85, 190, 192, 195–6
Parks and Open Spaces Committee, London County Council, 47, 73–5. See also London County Council
Parks Committee, London County Council, 80–1. See also London County Council
Parkways, 47, 73
Peak District National Park, 107
Pepler, G. L., 47, 50, 75–6
Peterborough, 67
Philadelphia, 239
Planned towns, 41–4
Pollards Park, 110

246

INDEX